THE LANGUAGE OF SPACE

Architectural Press

OXFORD   AUCKLAND   BOSTON   JOHANNESBURG   MELBOURNE   NEW DELHI

Architectural Press
An imprint of Butterworth-Heinemann
Linacre House, Jordan Hill, Oxford OX2 8DP
225 Wildwood Avenue, Woburn, MA 01801-2041
A division of Reed Educational and Professional Publishing Ltd

℞ A member of the Reed Elsevier plc group

First published 2001

British Library Cataloguing in Publication Data
Lawson, Bryan
  The language of space
  1. Space (Architecture)   2. Architectural design – Social aspects
  I. Title
  720.1'03

ISBN 0 7506 5246 2

Library of Congress Cataloguing in Publication Data
A catalogue record for this book is available from the Library of Congress

For information on all Butterworth-Heinemann publications
visit our website at www.bh.com

Composition by Scribe Design, Gillingham, Kent
Printed and bound in Great Britain

PLANT A
TREE

BTCV
British Trust for
Conservation Volunteers

FOR EVERY VOLUME THAT WE PUBLISH, BUTTERWORTH-HEINEMANN
WILL PAY FOR BTCV TO PLANT AND CARE FOR A TREE.

Contents

16030181 09

Acknowledgements

This book is the result of many years of study. I am grateful to all those who have funded or commissioned projects that have allowed us to add to our knowledge – in particular, grants from the Royal Institute of British Architects, The Architects' Registration Council of the United Kingdom, The Social Science Research Council, The Engineering and Physical Science Research Council, NHS Estates, Birmingham City Council, Allied Breweries, Bass Charrington, The Oxford Regional Hospital Board, and The Training Agency.

A considerable number of people have been involved. I am indebted to all these people for investigating and debating the ideas that appear here. Some have been colleagues with whom I have had many discussions, and others collaborators who have actually worked on projects. They include May Bassanino, Jane Darke, Ron Easterby, Angela Fisher, David Hale, Graham Harding, Lyndon Herbert, Margaret Newton, Edward Ng, Chengzhi Peng, Michael Phiri, Chris Spencer, David Walters, John Wells-Thorpe and John Worthington. There are simply too many students who have been involved to list them by name, but particular appreciation is due to a number of doctoral, masters and undergraduate students. They include Faisal Agabani, Abu Bakar, Ahmed Bakerman, Tami Belhadj, Barry Bowden, Andrea Cook, Adela Cotera, Jorge Cotera, Colin Darlington, Rashid Embi, Zoe Holland, Abu Hasan Ismail, Lee Shao Jun, Tang Hsiao Ling, Loke Shee Ming, Richard Painter, Alice Pereira, Marcia Pereira, Ruth Peternoster, Grant Pitches, Simon Pryce, Steven Roberts, Joongseuk Ryu, Prashant Solanky, Ben Stagg, Rodzyah Yunus and Mohammed Yusoff.

I am grateful to John Outram for permission to use the illustration of his work in Figure 4.9, and to Jeremy Till for his photograph of the Paris Opera in Figure 3.2.

1 Space as language

The physical environment that we construct is as much a social phenomenon as it is a physical one.

Harold Proshansky

Architecture is the art of how to waste space.

Philip Johnson, *New York Times*

Why a language?

It is well known that communicating by telephone is different to communicating 'face to face'. More recently we have had to learn to communicate by fax and by e-mail. It is now well recognized that all the new artificial and technologically supported media of communication have their strengths and weaknesses. All are useful when we are not co-located, and some are useful when we want to communicate asynchronously. I use e-mail extensively every day of my life, and could now hardly do my job without it. However, if we have to tell someone difficult, unpleasant or perhaps even tragic news, you and I know that e-mail is not ideal! What distinguishes all the other methods of communication from live conversation is that the latter takes place in space. The very phrase 'face to face' is implicitly makes reference to space. It tells us how people are arranged in space. They are not 'back to back', because they actually want to see each other's faces! This is very basic stuff. Unfortunately, it is so fundamental that we often forget about it when designing spaces. At the moment I am sitting in front of my computer writing this book. Well actually no, from your point of view, that was some time ago, because you are now sitting I know not where, reading it many months if not years later! I can assure you that although the text on your page looks continuous, the writing was not. I have re-ordered it, re-phrased it, and re-worked it many times. But more importantly I am forced to use a style of language I would never use 'face to face'. At times I also lecture about this subject to large groups. On such occasions I use yet another style and begin to interact with my audience a little, albeit in a rather formal way. I assure you I would far rather be able to sit down in space and talk to you 'face to face' about this subject than write this book, for then I could see your expression and know when I am either losing you or labouring my point.

Not all behaviour in space involves conversation, but much of our behaviour in space involves communication in some way or other. If truth were told, throughout our lives we probably communicate far more through space than we do with formal language. When we walk into a room, others are reading this spatial language long before we speak. What we wear, how we smell, the manner of our walk, our facial expression, where we choose to sit, the way other people look at us and acknowledge us.

We use the language of space, then, for many purposes. Through it we can express both our individuality and our solidarity with others. We can indicate our values and lifestyles, allegiances and dislikes. We can use it to help generate feelings of excitement or calm. We can communicate our willingness or otherwise to be approached, interrupted, greeted and engaged in social intercourse. We can control the proximity of others. We can demonstrate our dominance or submission and our status in society. We can use it to bring people together or keep them apart. We can use it to convey complex collections of rules of acceptable behaviour. We can also use it on occasion to signal our intention to break those rules!

So throughout this book I have likened our behaviour in space to a language. Of course, we often behave in space to some particular purpose, such as shopping, playing sport, moving from room to room. On other occasions we are less purposeful, as when strolling, relaxing in an armchair and even taking a nap! However directed and purposeful our behaviour it also communicates, whether we intend it to or not. Even when we are not there, spaces that belong to us or come under our control still communicate through the way we have laid them out and decorated them. This language of space is a global one, since many of its roots can be found in fundamental characteristics of the human race. Whilst Mandarin, English and Spanish are spoken by many millions of people in many countries, the language of space is truly international. And yet the advanced student of this language can often recognize where someone comes from by careful observation, since the language of space has regional dialects that comprise important features of local cultures.

The art of architecture

Wherever you find people gathered together collectively inhabiting some part of our world you will also find rules governing their use of space. Some of these rules may be purely a matter of local social convention, but many are a reflection of both the deep-seated needs of our psyche and of the characteristics of human beings. In our modern world most of the spaces we use have been designed for us professionally by architects, urban designers, interior designers and their ilk. It was of course not always so, nor is it so now in all societies. Before professionalism, the design and creation of space was a more social and vernacular process seamlessly integrated with all other aspects of a culture. However, if you are reading this book then it is highly unlikely that you now live in such a society. In our sort of world, space has also become a matter of economics, of technology and of art.

Many design theoreticians and critics write about architectural space as if it were some entirely abstract substance. They discuss such ideas as form, proportion, rhythm and colour as if they were parts of a private language used by designers and design critics. Through such criticism, architecture and the spaces it divides and encloses become seen as a refined art to be appreciated by the educated connoisseur. This is of course an entirely understandable and reasonable position. It is possible to argue that there is a distinction to be drawn between architecture and mere building. If we accept this position, then buildings can probably only become architecture once they exhibit characteristics that we might also use to identify art. This takes us into very difficult territory beyond the scope of this book, since commonly accepted definitions of art are rather difficult to come by. Somewhat cynically, Marshall McLuhan suggested that art is 'anything you can get away with', and some contemporary artists do seem to be trying pretty hard to live up to this challenge! However, a test of whether something is art as opposed simply to craft must surely demand some element of expression. The prolific architectural historian Nicolas Pevsner not only explicitly drew such a distinction, but he also took up a more extreme position by denying that architectural qualities could be attached to humble structures:

A bicycle shed is a building; Lincoln cathedral is architecture.

The philosopher Wittgenstein, who became very interested in architecture, was surely making a similar point:

Where there is nothing to glorify there can be no architecture.

An excellent and very concise discussion of this problem of architecture as art and its relation to meaning can be found in Nelson Goodman's discussion of philosophical positions on art (Goodman and Elgin 1988):

A building is a work of art only insofar as it signifies, means, refers, symbolizes in some way.

We could of course move from here into a debate about architecture as a system of signs and symbols. The post-modern period has produced much analysis of architecture on this basis, and such arguments are most often predicated on the fundamental notion that buildings can be read as texts. Often such analysis depends heavily on the supposed use of reference within the building to other architectural precedents or ideas. Although we shall deal later with the idea of buildings expressing ideas beyond their simple purpose, that is not the primary purpose of this particular book.

The social art

In this book we shall use a rather different interpretation, which is both more pragmatic and behavioural and social. Of course buildings can be seen in many different ways – they can, for example, be viewed as works of art, as technical achievements, as the wallpaper of urban space and as behavioural and cultural phenomena. Primarily this book will treat architectural and urban spaces as containers to accommodate, separate, structure and organize, facilitate, heighten and even celebrate human spatial behaviour. In so much as they do that, they will also be viewed as psychological, social and partly cultural phenomena. This does not mean that the author only regards them that way. One of the intriguing and endlessly fascinating things about the study of architecture is that one may come at it from so many different angles. Some authors, and regrettably very many architects, will try to have you believe that their perspective is somehow right and superior to all others. This is not new; Pugin claimed his 'gothic' architecture to be the only truly Christian one (Pugin, 1841). Gropius thought his new architecture to be ethically necessary (Gropius 1935), and James Stirling had a deep conviction of the 'moral rightness' of the path he followed (Stirling 1965). That path was at the time one of modernism, although by the time he died Stirling's work was viewed by critics as 'post-modern'!

Some commentators have argued that modernism inevitably led architects away from their consumers. Whilst there may be some truth in this argument, the curious paradox remains that along with its stylistic outcome in the International Style, modernism had its roots deeply interconnected with social intentions, if not even Socialism. However, Jenks in particular invented and defended post-modernism on the grounds that it was more readable by the general public (Jenks 1977). Whether this is really true has hardly been tested.

However, recent studies have shown empirically what many have thought intuitively. Architects as a group think about architecture in a distinctly different way to the rest of humanity. This is not surprising, since all professional groups begin to develop highly sensitized and specialized ways of both conceptualizing and evaluating the work in their field. They develop jargon as shorthand for some of these concepts, and communicate in ways that make it difficult for outsiders to penetrate. One study has shown, for example, that town planners quite clearly use different values about architecture to the public they serve (Hubbard 1996). The difficulty we have here is that planners are supposed to protect the public from wilful architects, who in turn present themselves as designing for society at large rather than just their clients! Architects have also defended their professional status on the grounds that they champion the quality of the environment on behalf of all of us. This seems to be the main justification for the Act of Parliament in the UK, recently revised, which legally protects the title of 'architect'. Wilson has, however, shown that, in spite of much rhetoric to the contrary, architects do indeed seem to use quite different evaluative systems to others (Wilson 1996). She has also shown that this tendency is significantly acquired during higher education, and that there is a strong correlation between the architectural preferences expressed by students within a school of architecture. Depressingly, her data also show these preferences to be strongly linked to stylistic attributes. This suggests that even now schools of architecture knowingly or otherwise still teach architectural style!

I have tried throughout this book not to take such a stance. Of course I too have my stylistic preferences and my weaknesses for some periods of history, particular architects and certain building materials. However, I have tried not to present any of these as somehow endowed with special value or having a fundamental rightness. This treatise then, like all others I have ever read about architecture, is extremely limited! It presents one way of looking at the forms and spaces that comprise architecture. It views them not as abstractions but as expressions of ourselves. It explores the deep needs and compulsions we feel, which frequently we are unable to express in more explicit and conventional language. Indeed, it views our behaviour in space and the architecture that contains it as part of a vital language that is central to human communication. Consequently, this book does not only look at our relationship with architecture but at the way architecture mediates our relationships with each other. Harold Proshansky, one of the pioneers of environmental psychology, is quoted at the top of this chapter expressing the view that buildings are as much a social as a physical phenomenon (Proshansky, Ittleson and Rivlin 1970). Tom Markus, in his fascinating treatise on 'buildings and power', takes an even firmer view of this (Markus 1993):

I take the stand that buildings are not primarily art, technical or investment objects, but social objects.

Of course, places are often very complex in terms of the opportunities they afford us for analysis. Two people visiting the same place at different times in their lives may be able to extract quite different character from it. In their study of how boys perceive places as they grow,

Malinowski and Thurber show a consistent developmental trend that may seem intuitively reasonable, but has been rather neglected by scientific investigation. This shows that very young boys probably appreciate places in terms of *who* they associate with them. As they grow older they come to value them for the *activities* located there, and eventually to see them *aesthetically* (Malinowski and Thurber 1996). Thus, as they summarize it, the lake may initially be a place to swim, but later a place to see a beautiful sunset. In recent years, my wife and I have been lucky enough to stay on a very small island in the South China Sea (Plate 1). To me these occasions offer good company, wonderful swimming and snorkelling, exotic wildlife, and a hot and sunny climate with stunning sunsets every night. Sadly our very presence there to some extent also encourages a tiny nascent industry that ultimately could threaten the coral reefs around the island and the rain forest on it, and thus the whole ecology of the place ultimately hangs in the balance. Therefore, what few native inhabitants there are, environmental scientists, economists and many other groups will no doubt 'see' this place differently to me. For them it may stand for quite different things. Indeed I might see it differently were I forced to live there indefinitely rather than visit occasionally. However for me, and for now, this is as near to paradise on earth as I have found!

The language of space
Space, and consequently that which encloses it, are much more central to all of us in our everyday lives than purely technical, aesthetic or even semiotic interpretation would suggest. Space is both that which brings us together and simultaneously that which separates us from each other. It is thus crucial to the way our relationships work. Space is the essential stuff of a very fundamental and universal form of communication. The human language of space, whilst it has its cultural variations, can be observed all over the world wherever and whenever people come together. In particular in this book we are interested in the space created in and around architecture. Architecture organizes and structures space for us, and its interiors and the objects enclosing and inhabiting its rooms can facilitate or inhibit our activities by the way they use this language. Because this language is not heard or seen directly, and certainly not written down, it gets little attention in a formal sense. However, we all make use of it throughout all of our lives as we move about in space and relate ourselves to others. Perhaps we tend only to notice this language when it is in some way abused.

When a person pushes in front of you in a queue, you feel offended not just because you are one place further back but also because they failed to respect the rules (Fig. 1.1). In most situations where we queue there are almost token signals from the physical environment that we should behave in this highly artificial way. The rope barriers

1.1 The queue is a most obvious form of conventionalized behaviour that is triggered by signals from the designed environment

sometimes used to form queues in public places are hardly able to contain a crowd physically, and yet without them the crowd would probably push and shove in a chaotic and possibly aggressive manner. Our civilization and culture enables us to be remarkably co-operative, even when we are actually competing for limited tickets at the theatre or sale bargains in the shop. However, remove all the queuing signals from the environment and our behaviour can rapidly regress!

When we talk to each other, the space between us is part of our communication. We probably all know a friend or colleague who habitually stands too close when conversing, touches you just too much for comfort, and generally seems rather more familiar than feels appropriate. The verbal language might well be at odds with the communication through the language of space, and we feel uncomfortable.

We can get remarkably irritated by strange, insensitive or just thoughtless failures of other people to use the language of space properly – the stranger who comes and sits at your table in a café even though other tables are empty; the newspaper boy who fails to shut the front gate after delivering the morning newspaper; the neighbour who habitually parks in front of your house rather than hers; the chairman of a meeting who arrives late and finds someone already sitting in the chair most suited to running the meeting.

Buildings can fail to speak the language of space properly just as much as people can. The American embassy in Singapore may have an interesting architectural form, but it seems consistently to send out the wrong signals. As you approach it, the building appears secretive and forbidding. It even seems to have a single eye from which you can imagine the occupants examining their visitors! The approach to the building offers no shade from the sun in a climate where all well-mannered buildings should (Fig 1.2). None of this is very welcoming, and I have lost count of the number of Singaporeans who have told me they feel offended by it.

Reading the language

We often need space to tell us how to behave, and the rather wry quotation from Philip Johnson at the start of this chapter nicely summarizes this for us. Of course good architecture does not actually *waste* space; it is just that often space is needed in order to prepare us for a change of mood, to establish relationships, to separate activities, and to suggest or invite appropriate behaviour. In fact it creates settings, which organize our lives, activities and relationships. In good architecture space does this for us without our noticing, hence the possibility of joking that such space is wasted! This book will explore just how that happens, and how we can learn to 'read' and work in this human language of space.

Really great architects seem to be fluent in this language – many probably without consciously studying it. It is as basic a tool of the

1.2 This building sends out rather unwelcoming signals probably quite at odds with the intentions of its owners. It is the American embassy in Singapore!

trade for an architect as body language may be to an actor. The great Dutch architect Herman Hertzberger has shown an extraordinarily high awareness of the language of space, not only in his buildings but also through his writing. He once told me of his fondness for the detective novel (Lawson 1994). He explained this by likening an architect to the famous detective who always solves the puzzle of which character committed the crime. In such novels the detective has no more information than the rest of us – he sees what we see and hears what we hear – but he has learnt to read the behaviour and motivation behind the actions and words. As Hertzberger says, the architect too must watch what people do. Yet sadly, all too often architects seem interested in buildings but not in their occupants. How often do the architectural journals even show people in the photographs? This was brought home to me when I was writing a critical review of a new building. I had visited the building extensively during the normal working day and solicited the opinions of as many of its users as I could find, but the photographer commissioned by the journal turned up very early one Sunday morning to 'get the best pictures possible'. I later challenged an editor of a highly regarded architectural journal about this, who assured me that the reason was that higher speed film had to be used if people were moving about in a scene and with this came increased granularity and therefore loss of picture quality. Clearly the editors of architectural journals think that picture quality is more important than picture content. This book questions this set of values and the attitude behind it that leads architects away from understanding their clients and users.

I find that undergraduate students of architecture come to university with a very wide range of expectations. Gradually during their studies many seem to learn to match their expectations about architecture with those of their tutors. As a young student myself I failed to do this. I found my education at Oxford focused entirely on buildings as physical objects. Mainly they were thought of as visual objects in a very abstract sort of way, with some occasional minor consideration of them as technical constructions. I continued to wish to see them as social objects, and gathered daily evidence of this as I looked at the many magnificent buildings in that wonderful city. I learned about architecture not through the glossy pictures in books, but by actually observing buildings being used. Consequently I grew impatient with my college studies, and some, though thankfully not all, of my tutors grew impatient with me!

It was this that drove me to study psychology for my masters and doctoral degrees. It has since taken many years of study in the field to put all this into some semblance of balance, and this book represents an attempt to help others who may wish to follow a similar path. However, I hope this does not read as a deeply theoretical book. After a lifetime of trying to understand architecture, I find it quite difficult enough without theories that seem only to obscure and overcomplicate. As a young research student I had been looking forward for some time to hearing a lecture by one of our leading and most influential ergonomists, who was due to visit the university where I was studying psychology. At the time I was deeply disappointed by his lecture, and was arrogant and impudent enough to express this in a question at the end of his talk. I said that it seemed to me that what he had taken over an hour to say boiled down to 'put dials where people can see them and controls where people can operate them'. He was surprisingly delighted with my impertinent question. 'Yes, you have it exactly', he said in a congratulatory sort of way, 'the trouble is though that we all know this and yet designers keep not doing it. That is why I have to keep telling them to!'. His answer of course makes another important point for us here. The vast majority of what I shall say in this book is known and understood by you already. You know it because you rely on an implicit understanding of the language of space for everyday life. Yet every year I find that young students of design, when they enter their studios, can detach themselves from this knowledge and quite innocently create the most unsuitable spaces. I hope this book helps readers to reconnect their everyday implicit knowledge with their more professional conceptual knowledge, and that as a result we get more spaces which help people and fewer that obstruct them!

Behavioural settings

Whilst in this book we shall certainly consider the purely physical characteristics of spaces, the objects they contain and the envelopes that define them, there is something far more important to us than that. Of course we are all different, but in general ultimately it is our relationship not directly with spaces or buildings that matters most to us, but our relationships with other people. What others think and expect of us is one of the most central of the influences that govern the way we lead our lives. It is our reputation and our association with others that we feel most strongly about. So it is the way space facilitates and inhibits these relationships with which we will be mostly concerned. Barker discussed psychology from what he called an ecological perspective (Barker 1968). He argued that places have synomorphy when there is congruence between people's actions and the physical and social setting. There are several great forces at work here, and perhaps the most important are those of privacy and community. It is how space enables these two appropriately that forms many of the basic components of the language we shall explore. These two appear in almost every building and space we inhabit in some form or other. Other great forces are those of ritual, display and surveillance. Some spaces exist almost solely to allow us to act out social rituals, as in a church. Others serve to display, not just objects as in an art gallery, but also ourselves in our society. Some spaces need to permit the supervision of some of us by others. This is most obviously so in a prison, but also more subtly in a hospital or a library. Space that facilitates display may not be good at providing for privacy. Space that is public domain may need to be recognizably different to space that is private domain. We rely upon space to create places appropriate to certain kinds of behaviour and to tell us what they are.

Look at the illustration of a simple house that belongs to a German artist and is on one of the smaller islands of the Spanish Atlantic archipelago (Fig. 1.3). The owner, who has a small studio and gallery next door, can somehow capture the spirit of this place with the very minimum of brushstrokes. We are standing in a narrow street of a small town looking over a low wall in which there is a small wrought-iron gate, which we cannot see in this picture. We could easily open the gate, and indeed it is so low it would take no more than a large stride to step over it! However, we are in the totally public domain of the street. The path beyond, which we can see, is clearly semi-public.

1.3   The entrance to this simple house shows a gradation of space from the fully public domain of the street and pavement (not visible) through the semi-public space in the foreground and the semi-private space behind the gate to the fully private space that lies beyond the closed door. Space has to communicate this 'right of ownership' clearly so that we can all behave in an ordered and orderly manner without constantly upsetting each other

We could open the gate and move forward without really invading any private domain. The postman or other delivery tradespeople will have to do this. We might get some strange looks if we simply dallied there, but no one is likely to question us if we are there briefly and appear to move purposefully. Beyond is a larger gate that we can see has no lock. Again we can proceed, but there is nowhere else to go but straight to the front door, and we feel it only appropriate to enter this semi-private domain if we intend to go even further. At the end of this short space is the front door, locked and with a bell to announce our arrival. If the occupant is there, she will open the door and we will then be able to see a solid wall about a metre and a half away blocking our view of the inside of the house. She can converse with us there quite privately, safe from prying eyes back on the street, or she may choose to invite us into the ultimate privacy of her home. It may at first seem as if all this space is wasted, as in Philip Johnson's words; however, of course he knew as we know that this space is far from useless. It symbolizes and controls the transition from public through semi-public and semi-private areas to the private domain. It signals changes of possession, of territory, of control and of behaviour. It speaks the language of space as fluently and eloquently as many grander and more celebrated pieces of architecture.

How this book works

This book is divided up for convenience and structure, but of course our experience is not. Above all else, the message here is that our experience of space is an integrative one; it is just that to understand it better we need to dissect it and observe and analyse the constituent parts. In doing this, however, the balance of importance can easily become distorted. I find that much architectural criticism does this by neglecting what we might call the human dimension of space.

Before we can discuss the rather more subtle elements of this language of space we need first to examine ourselves a little. We need to understand what drives us forward in life, and what our expectations and demands are from space. Then we shall explore how we see and understand space. The book will examine the mechanisms that such perception uses, and the ways in which it operates. Then we shall discuss the role of distance in space, our attitudes towards the space that we inhabit more permanently, and the space immediately surrounding us. After that we shall ask how well and in what circumstances we can indeed predict human spatial behaviour, and how we can measure both behaviour and spatial characteristics so their relationships can be investigated.

References

Barker, R. G. (1968). *Ecological Psychology: Concepts and Methods for Studying the Environment of Human Behaviour*. Oxford, Oxford University Press.

Goodman, N. and C. J. Elgin (1988). *Reconceptions in Philosophy and other Arts and Sciences*. London, Routledge.

Gropius, W. (1935). *The New Architecture and the Bauhaus*. London, Faber and Faber.

Hubbard, P. (1996). Conflicting interpretations of architecture: an empirical investigation. *Journal of Environmental Psychology* **16**: 75–92.

Jenks, C. (1977). *The Language of Post Modern Architecture*. London, Academy Editions.

Lawson, B. R. (1994). *Design in Mind*. Oxford, Butterworth Architecture.

Malinowski, J. C. and C. A. Thurber (1996). Developmental shifts in the place preferences of boys aged 8–16 years. *Journal of Environmental Psychology* **16**: 45–54.

Markus, T. (1993). *Buildings and Power: Freedom and Control in the Origin of Modern Building*. London, Routledge.

Proshansky, H. M., W. H. Ittleson, et al. (eds) (1970). *Environmental Psychology*. Holt, Rinehart Winston.

Pugin, A. W. N. (1841). *The True Principles of Pointed or Christian Architecture*. London, J. Weale.

Stirling, J. (1965). An architect's approach to architecture. *RIBA Journal* **72**(5).

Wilson, M. A. (1996). The socialization of architectural preference. *Journal of Environmental Psychology* **16**: 33–44.

2 Space and the human dimension

We treat space somewhat the way we treat sex. It is there but we don't talk about it.

Edward T. Hall, *The Silent Language*

The instinctive idiosyncrasies of the average person are of far greater importance than the deliberate originality of the individual.

N. J. Habraken, *Supports*

The human basis of the language

In the previous chapter we established the idea that there is a global human language of space. Our more conventional spoken and written languages come in many varieties and, although a great number of them use the alphabet with which this book is written, there are some that use quite different character systems. Arabic languages, for example, not only sound different to European ones, but also look entirely different when written down. In contrast, the Chinese languages such as Mandarin and Cantonese are based on largely the same character set, and yet sound different! Some people seem to have a facility with foreign languages, but for many of us learning another language is very hard work indeed. Perhaps then it may come as something of a surprise that underlying this huge variation in language there do seem to be some very fundamental common structures (Chomsky 1957). One school of thought in the study of psycholinguistics suggests that this underlying structure reveals some deeply embedded characteristics of the human brain. Whether or not this is true, in the human language of space we can certainly see reflections of our own makeup. At its most basic, we have our own ways of sensing space and of moving through space. At the more sophisticated level, we have our own ways of making meaning of space. All these and many more features of the human condition help to determine the way we communicate through space. In this chapter we shall explore some of these features in order to begin to understand the language more explicitly.

Whether we are inside buildings or outdoors, we are inseparable from space. The space that surrounds us and the objects enclosing that space may determine how far we can move, how warm or cold we are, how much we can see and hear, and with whom we can interact. It may heavily influence the mood we are in, and the way we feel towards tasks we might have to perform and people we might find in our company. So we demand a great deal from this space. At one very basic level we have specific needs for such things as adequate lighting and fresh air to breathe. We need to be able to reach furniture, equipment and other facilities to perform some tasks. At a rather higher level, we need space to help us to feel right about our current situation. Even this brief analysis suggests that to understand our interaction with space will involve us in a very wide range of psychological issues. We have already identified psychophysics, ergonomics and the psychology of emotions and feelings, for example. So just where should the focus of our attention be in this book?

The human psyche

We human beings have complex psyches that are undoubtedly a conjunction of inbuilt instinctive and acquired or learned behaviour. The history of human psychology is woven around the persisting thread of the 'nature versus nurture' debate. Put very simply, this explores the question of whether we are the way we are because of characteristics bred into us or because of the experiences which befall us in life. Only a fool would deny the obvious influence of both, but where the balance lies and how it can be changed remain intractable theoretical, philosophical and even political questions. Even as this book is being written the balance seems to be taking another shift, this time back towards nature with recent evidence from the study of genes.

When people learn that I am interested in the interface between psychology and architecture, they usually assume my concerns might be about things like colour and emotion. 'Ah,' they say, 'I suppose you can tell us what colour to paint the walls of a hospital!' Of course, to some extent this sort of problem is interesting, but this is an example of the relationship between us as individuals and the surrounding space. Rather more important in many cases is a less direct effect of space; the way it mediates our social life. We shall see in a later chapter that much of this can be traced back to our nature in terms of the senses we have and the way they in turn structure our perception of the space around us. For example, all colours are not equal in our eyes, or rather in our eye/brain system – we see some colours more clearly as a direct result of our physical mechanisms of sensation. On the other hand, we shall also see that attitudes even to the direct influence of colour vary culturally – for example, in some cultures black is the colour of mourning, whilst in others it is white. The colours of our national flags and even our local football teams have such an impact on our lives that it is impossible not to interpret colour both in terms of nurture and nature.

There are many ways of categorizing human behaviour, but to debate that would take us into the taxonomy of psychology, which is not really our purpose here. However, for the purposes of the subject in hand it is useful to recognize two important dimensions along which our behaviour can be plotted (Fig. 2.1) Sometimes we are very conscious of our own behaviour, whilst at other times we may be entirely unconscious of it. On some occasions we have virtually total control over our behaviour, but not always! Since these two dimensions of consciousness and control are independent, we can usefully think of human behaviour in four major sectors. Behaviour that is both unconscious and uncontrollable we might call instinct – the baby grasping when the palm of its hand is touched, the blink of the eyes or turn of the head when we see movement are all examples of instinctive behaviour. At the other extreme, behaviour that is both conscious and controllable we might call 'cognitive', and this clearly includes intellectual thought and the solving of problems. Conscious but uncontrollable behaviour we might call 'conative', which would include feelings and emotions. These can be either distressingly or joyously strong, but we can rarely will them in or out of our minds. Unconscious and yet controllable behaviour might seem at first an impossible paradox, but it is not. It includes the sophisticated skills on which we rely every day of our lives – simple walking or swimming involves such behaviour, and even, frighteningly, the driving of a motor car! Driving seems ridiculously difficult to do when you are learning, but once mastered you are also likely to listen to the radio, hold conversations and solve problems while driving to work every day. The advanced skills of playing musical instruments or sports only really work well once we specifically do not pay conscious attention to them, but instead concentrate on the interpretation of the music or the strategy of the game.

If then we are to consider how we relate to space and its role in our lives, we can see a wide range of types of behaviour comes into play. We drive and walk around in space; we are affected by the atmosphere of places which lift or depress our spirits; we need to find our way about in the world and solve problems of navigation using mental as well as physical maps. We cannot escape the surprise and instinctive reaction to sudden changes in the world around us. Since of all human life is lived in space, it inevitably forms one of the most vital and yet most neglected of the influences upon us.

Motivation and need

Motivation undoubtedly plays a central role in our behaviour, and any analysis of how we behave in relation to space must recognize this

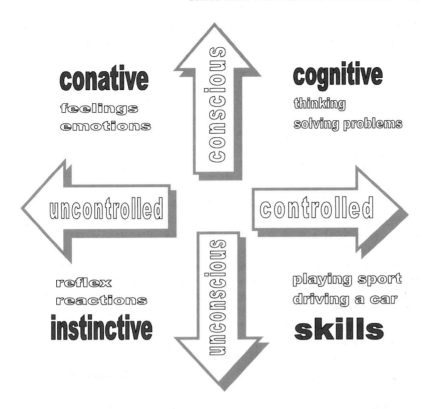

2.1   A very simple but useful model dividing up human behaviour. The two independent dimensions of control and consciousness give rise to four quite different forms of behaviour, each described by their own field of psychology

powerful force. Motivations are many and varied, and not only depend on personality and culture but also change with time and situation. However, we do seem to be driven by fundamental internal needs, or so a great deal of psychological theory would have it. Maslow and others since have described our behaviour in terms of the way we seek to satisfy a complex array of needs. In such theories, hunger, sex and avoidance of fear come pretty high on the list! However, there are many others that become important too. This view of the human condition has it that we first seek to satisfy high level needs, and only then turn to lower level ones. Certainly, those needs that architectural space can help to satisfy are not necessarily at the very top of the list. This becomes evident when we see disasters and human tragedies such as earthquakes and wars. Examples of each of these awful conditions were in evidence at the time of writing this book. Turkey had just suffered the worst earthquake in living memory, followed by another in Taiwan, and hurricanes were causing havoc in the USA and Hong Kong. We had just seen terrible atrocities committed by mankind on itself in Kosovo and in Indonesia. It seems almost trivial at such times to talk about our needs being satisfied by space in the way we shall here – although we must also recognize that many disasters, including wars, have direct links to spatial behaviour. However, for those of us lucky enough to live our lives free from violence, hunger, disease and natural disasters, space turns out to be very important indeed. The cultural anthropologist Edward T. Hall claims that: 'We treat space somewhat the way we treat sex. It is there but we don't talk about it!'. By the end of the twentieth century we seemed to talk about sex a great deal more than we did; perhaps then in the twenty-first century it is high time to talk more about space too!

Spatial needs

Let us begin then by thinking of the very high level emotional needs we expect space to help us to satisfy. Most of us hate being bored, and want some form of amusement or entertainment. We might see this as a need for stimulation, and we demand that the space around us should provide this. On the whole we also seek to avoid high levels of uncertainty and change, and we require a degree of stability and structure in our lives. We might see this as a need for security, and so we require spaces to keep us secure. Most of us seem to have a strong desire to belong somewhere. Many people I have known who have travelled widely in their lives describe an increasingly strong need to return to their roots in later life. We might see this as a need for identity and to belong somewhere, or in other words a need to be located in space. All these are examples of needs that the space we inhabit can help to satisfy (Fig. 2.2). Robert Ardrey was the first to suggest that not only do we seem to have these three important spatial needs of stimulation, security and identity, but also that this could help to explain the reasons for territorial behaviour. The debate about this notion of territoriality is something we must leave until a later chapter, but for now we shall explore the nature of the three needs.

Stimulation

This is perhaps the most obvious and simplest of the three to understand; however, it turns out to be rather more fundamental and less of a luxury than at first we might think. At its most extreme, boredom is not just dull, it is plain downright dangerous. Experiments in sensory deprivation go to extraordinary lengths to deprive their subjects of receiving any information from the outside world at all. A student once writing an answer to an examination paper I had set for a degree in psychology wrote:

Psychologists achieve sensory deprivation by hanging their subjects in tanks of warm water.

I could not resist writing on his paper, 'why bother about heating the water?' Thankfully such experiments usually do stop short of killing their subjects, and they do not intentionally inflict physical pain. However, most subjects find the experience very painful psychologically! Subjects may be placed in a darkened, silent and odourless space. In some cases they are loosely clothed, including soft gloves, to avoid any sensation of touch. In such cases subjects usually report vivid images flooding into their minds, soon turning into what we would recognize as hallucinations. Most subjects ask to be released from such awful environments in a remarkably short time, but characteristically they think they have been there for many hours! It seems we are quite simply not meant to exist in such a neutral space, and so we compensate by inventing our own internal mental stimulation, which can quickly get out of control.

By contrast, an environment in which we are bombarded with sensation seems equally disturbing, and sadly this is exploited in many forms of torture. Imagine such a world for a moment. You are in a cell and a blinding light comes on and off at totally unpredictable but generally rather short intervals. There is similarly an unpredictable but sometimes deafening noise, also over which you have no control. A series of quite dreadful smells wafts across the room. Ask yourself how long you would remain calm and at peace in such a place! Thankfully most of us need never endure either of these two extremes, but at times we have all felt bored or over-stimulated. Actually, of course, the level

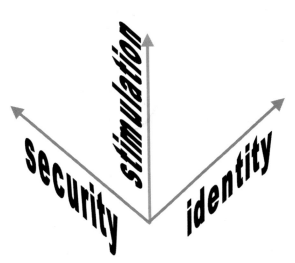

2.2   The three important needs of stimulation, security and identity can all be satisfied by the designed environment. Our balance of need at any time will depend on several factors, including personality, physical health and age, and social context

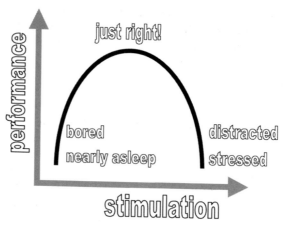

2.3 The stimulation performance curve, a sort of inverted 'U' shape that is characteristic of many psychological dimensions. If we are inadequately stimulated, we are bored and lose interest in our task. Over-stimulation means that we simply cannot concentrate. Our maximal performance comes somewhere in between

of stimulation we require varies – some people simply like the quiet life, while others prefer more action – but even then our needs change as our moods change and indeed as we age. It is of course impossible to produce an environment that all would feel ideal. However, there does seem to be a sort of inverted U-shaped curve of performance against arousal (Fig. 2.3). Take reading this book, for instance. If you are too sleepy, you really will not take much in; if you are too hyped up and distracted by other events, you are equally unlikely to get much out of it. Where we need to be on this curve depends upon our situation. Listening to a lecture requires a high level of attention and concentration, while relaxed chatting with a friend does not. There is clear evidence that over-stimulation from the environment can result in a form of stress that in turn disturbs the focus of attention and inhibits the carrying out of plans (Wohlwill 1974). One of the reasons that meeting new people is rather stressful is that you feel obliged to pay them polite attention, and because you do not know them well you need to concentrate hard on this. With an old friend not only do you know the sort of things they might say or be interested in, but also they will forgive you if your mind wanders away on the odd occasion!

There are certainly places we go to expecting them to provide large amounts of stimulation. The fairground, particularly at night, with its contrast of light and dark, the noise and hustle and bustle and the smells of food, is a prime example. We demand that such an environment should divert us – there is no need for internal mental activity here; that is just the point! Such a place is meant to drive away our cares and worries, to take us out of ourselves, as we say. There must be no half measures in such a place. A wonderful example of the genre can be found in the Tivoli Gardens in Copenhagen, which not only manages to provide a constant supply of stimulation but is also beautifully designed (Fig. 2.4). As the daylight fades the whole place needs revisiting, as the myriad of tungsten rather than fluorescent lights create what seems to be a completely new, magical and different world. The removal of long distance vision at night and the use of very localized tungsten lighting focus our attention much more selectively, so that as we move around we are constantly discovering surprising new places. This is wonderful, magical fun, but you can only take so much of it.

In general, people do not live and work in fairgrounds. In ordinary daily life people need more continuity and predictability in their surroundings, but, as Evans and McCoy suggest, they also need enough 'mystery' and 'complexity' to keep their interest in looking around them (Evans and McCoy 1998). Architecturally speaking, the problem is to find that point of balance on the top of the inverted 'U' curve that delivers a level of stimulation appropriate to the pattern of usage of the setting.

Security

We all have a very deep and fundamental need for a degree of stability, continuity and predictability in our lives. It might sound exciting not to have this, but just imagine how stressful it would be to lead a life of constant flux and unpredictability. We depend for our sanity upon knowing the rules, as it were. It is said that the two most stressful things in life are moving house and going on holiday! Remember how you felt on the first day at school, at university or in a new job. On the one hand this is exciting because it represents progress and a new phase in life. On the other hand we are not sure quite how to behave in this new context, uncertain about what is expected of us and apprehensive of how our new colleagues will see us. Every social group that has any degree of cohesion also has norms. These norms regulate behaviour, dress, and forms of language and even in some cases define entirely local aspects of spoken language.

I was a consultant some years ago to a brewery company that moved its headquarters into one larger open-plan office from a whole series of small buildings dotted around the town. The company had its own architects' department, which was initially placed in the middle of the scheme. However, the accountants located next to them soon complained, and it was felt sensible to move the architects to the end of the space. The architects had always worked together in a large drawing office. They worked in teams and had developed a strong set of social norms, which included community singing, rehearsing scenes from the previous night's television comedy programmes, and the

2.4 The Tivoli Gardens in Copenhagen in Denmark. A rare occurrence, a beautifully designed fairground calculated to 'take us out of ourselves' through massive doses of stimulation of all the senses

occasional bout of paper aeroplane making. No one had ever suggested that this distracted them from their work, and indeed it did not seem to since they could easily draw and sing at the same time! However, this distracted their neighbours more than the organization was comfortable with, since it conflicted with the more reserved nature of their social norms. It was not long before the architects were moved to the end of the office.

Social norms then are extremely powerful in that they give security to people in the group, allowing them to behave in a regulated way without fear of their behaviour being thought to be inappropriate by their neighbours, colleagues and friends. But are there spatial reflections of social norms? To some extent there are, and they form some of the most fundamental components of the language of space.

Behavioural settings

Spaces form important constituent parts of what we might call the 'settings' in which we behave. It was probably Barker who first elaborated the notion of 'behavioural settings', when he described how our behaviour is influenced and even constrained by these settings (Barker 1968). He pointed out that settings comprise both the physical and the social environment. The Dutch architect Aldo Van Eyck has described this nicely with his famous description of place:

Whatever space and time mean, place and occasion mean more. For space in the image of man is place, and time in the image of man is occasion.

This succinctly points out that a setting really consists of the space, its surroundings and contents, and the people and their activities. The impact of occasion on place is dramatically demonstrated by entering a football stadium that you know well when it is empty (Fig. 2.5). The whole place seems entirely different, not to say uncanny, because the occasion is so strange. This is the basis of the well-known football joke made at the expense of the fans of a neighbouring club – I might say to fans of Sheffield United that I would rather watch the grass grow at Hillsborough (where Sheffield Wednesday play) than go to see a game at Bramhall Lane (where Sheffield United play)! The dedication of the football fan to the concept of the club is thus demonstrated by the way that the home ground takes on the shrine-like qualities of sacred territory. Yet again, however, we are straying into the business of a later chapter.

Settings, whether they are parts of special territories or not, are important to us as ways of generating security. When we enter a library or an office, a theatre or a dance hall, a lecture room or a laboratory, the scene is set, as we say. Even though we may never have been in this particular library before, we recognize the setting as a library. Along with that setting come a series of social norms that are not so

2.5   A football stadium both full and empty. Is this really the same *place*? It is of course the same *space*

much attached to a particular group of people as to the setting itself. In plain simple terms, we know how to behave ourselves in a library. Without such properties of space and settings, life would be unbearably stressful. If every time we entered a room we simply had no idea at all what was expected of us, we should have to work very hard to identify and learn the local rules. By then it would be likely that we would have made many mistakes and upset large numbers of people, resulting in tricky situations and probably leading to social disasters with longstanding ramifications.

From time to time our situation approaches this chaos. When you take up a new job you enter a world in which the settings have been modified to local needs and norms. Because such a setting is used every day by more or less the same people, these norms can become very elaborate in their detail. So quite by accident you may find you are sitting in a seat in the rest room that is absolutely reserved for someone else. Of course no one warns you about this, because the language of space is essentially non-verbal. We do not express such things in words because they are based on implicit knowledge. Imagine now trying to explain in a full written description to a Martian how to behave in a particular setting. Of course you would miss all sorts of things out and describe other things so ambiguously that the poor creature would be sure to make a complete hash of pretending to be human. Several well-known films and television programmes are based on exactly this situation, from which they draw their comedy. Travelling abroad into other cultures can be equally stressful. I have been lucky enough to visit the Far East a great deal, but even now I still occasionally make mistakes on how certain settings are used in the local culture. For example, I remember for a long time being very confused in Malaysia as to exactly in which spaces you were supposed to take off your shoes and where it was considered acceptable to keep wearing them. It seemed important to get this right since all Malaysians naturally observed the rules and I thought not to would be seen as offensive. In truth Malaysians are generally far too polite and culturally generous to point this out, let alone complain about it.

In the late twentieth century, with the expansion of international travel, the world became physically smaller in terms of travelling time. Multinational corporations also started to make the world more legible and understandable in terms of settings. The international hotel with its foyer, reception desk, bars and restaurants provides an understood setting that offers the foreign traveller a haven of security within the otherwise illegible settings of the local culture. This was foreseen by the internationalist view of the modern movement in architecture. Le Corbusier, for example, envisaged buildings to be like ocean-going liners, maintaining an even temperature and constant environment wherever they went. I became suddenly aware of my reliance on such

2.6 McDonald's, an attempt to make a global place. A secure behavioural setting which as far as possible tries to present and trigger identical behaviour all over the world

security when in the southern city of Florianopolis in Brazil, where relatively little English is spoken in shops and restaurants. Being in a hurry one day I was passing a McDonald's and dashed in, intending to take some quick, trouble-free refreshment (Fig. 2.6). Foolishly, I tried to ask for something that they considered to be out of the ordinary, and the whole situation became dreadfully complicated with three staff and several other customers trying to understand my very poor English/Spanish attempt at Portuguese. Eventually a small crowd began to gather to see what the fuss was all about. I tried to change my order, but through politeness they refused to allow me to back down from my initial request. Eventually the manager of an adjacent electronics shop, who spoke excellent English, was called in to help. I got my culinary wish, but my hope of avoiding the insecurity of cultural diversity evaporated and, as I sat down, I felt a hundred pairs of eyes studying the way I consumed my food – presumably to see if that was as odd as the rest of my behaviour!

We use spaces and places to perform the important rituals of life that bring the security of constancy. Some spaces are designed almost for nothing else. The Christian church not only organizes space for ritual, but also uniquely locates each of the roles in the special society of worship. The choir, the congregation and the clergy each have their place, and a Christian visiting a strange church will have little difficulty in knowing where to go and how to behave. As Duncan Joiner has pointed out, the legal courtroom similarly places all the participants in space in such a way as to express their roles (Joiner 1971). The judge sits higher up; the accused is in a slightly lower and very exposed position for all to see; the jury is to one side, indicating their role as observers; and the two sets of legal representatives are on either side of an axis through the judge, demonstrating their opposition and his neutrality. The ritual of space, dress and procession is not only intended to aggrandize the legal process, but also to give us a sense of security in it. Imagine the effect on proceedings if the courtroom were simply a large square room with a few freestanding tables and chairs, all of which could be moved. The undignified scramble for a place and the difficulty of knowing who was who would totally disrupt the trial.

When at the end of every academic year my students graduate, they receive their degrees at an academic congregation. Not only is this whole ceremony highly artificial, it is not even legally necessary – it is quite possible to use your degree title without attending the ceremony! But the ceremony is there to celebrate an important event in a lifetime. It enables students and their parents, relatives and friends to feel some sense of occasion and climax. It also promotes a sense of moving on to the next phase, and the students may take leave of many of their close university peers for the last time at such an event. For all these reasons my university, like most others, conducts a grand and formal ceremony. I am not allowed simply to read out the students' names; I must also wear my academic robes and process slowly round the hall and onto the platform. I must doff my hat to the University Chancellor and await his permission to begin calling the students. As they are called forward one by one, the students walk across the platform, shake the Chancellor's hand and receive their certificates. More significantly, this setting is organized so that for these few moments each student in turn becomes the centre of attention of the whole arena. The space is laid out so that academic staff, graduands and relatives or friends are all separated in space, to emphasize the significance of the event and to heighten the ceremony (Fig. 2.7). In fact, in spite of all its medieval pomp, this ceremony is a largely modern invention. However, it is a reflection of initiation rites – passages of maturity to adulthood, birth celebrations, marriages and eventually funerals. All these share in common a way of explaining to a wider society just how certain individuals, groups and families are progressing through their lives. In turn, of course, this prepares other members of the society for these events in their own lives, and for the cultural norms that we attach to them.

However, this social structuring of society in space is not restricted to ceremonial and special occasions. Duncan Joiner has also studied a

2.7 A degree congregation. A social ritual to celebrate a special phase in life and recognize the changing status of the person. Note the highly symbolic arrangement in space of all the main groups. Parents at the back, newly graduated students to the front. Academic staff are higher and placed on view, with the senior university officials in front of them. The student passes through this special group of senior academics in order to graduate and to become accepted into their community. The wearing of gowns marks out these special people (in this one regard) from the rest

more everyday setting, that of the office. In this study he observes how the occupants position furniture in space in order to create the precise setting they require. The study of such matters has become known as 'proxemics', and we shall discuss it in detail in a later chapter.

Places also provide security and stability in our lives by effectively recording events for us. The accretion and decay of time through wear and tear gives visible evidence of continuing human activity, which we value. People often resent the demolition of old buildings, not just because they have particular architectural value but quite simply because this erases some treasured memories.

This brings us to the tension that seems to exist between the approach to contemporary architectural design and the needs of society. The modern view of architects is often very iconoclastic – that is to say, the unconventional interpretation of building typology is encouraged and valued. However, this can lead to the dismissal of modern architecture by a public who resent having the legibility of settings removed from them. A good example of this can be seen in the extraordinarily beautiful chapel at Pampulha just outside the city of Belo Horizonte in Brazil (Plate 2). This was built, early in his career, by Oscar Niemeyer, the architect who was to go on to become something of a national hero after constructing the new capital of Brasilia. This wooded lakeside site, together with Niemeyer's modernist views, provoked him to create a very unusual building. To our eyes today it may look rather unexceptional, but at that time and in that place it must have been very strange. In fact, on completion the clergy refused to use the building, claiming that the hyperparabolic form of the main space was a like a bell half buried in the ground. The inverted taper on the separate bell tower they said was a further concern. Of course they also knew that Niemeyer was a communist, and so they read all these signs to mean that the architect was trying to bury Christianity. This is actually a rather complex set of misunderstandings in the use of the language of space. Quite what the initial reason for the clergy's unhappiness was we cannot now know. Was it Niemeyer's communism, the symbolism they inferred from the forms, or simply their concern that the setting was not sufficiently legible to induce church-like behaviour in their congregation? In reality, it was probably a potent cocktail of all three!

A house must therefore not only provide shelter for people; we also expect that it will look like a house, and thus tell our visitors how to behave. Architects, however, will point out that society changes and so must buildings, and that we cannot always live in the past. Both points of view have validity, and designing spaces is often a tricky compromise of moving things forward but still signifying the setting clearly enough for people to be able to inhabit and behave with some degree of confidence. I remember standing for the first time in the foyer of the National Theatre, designed by the architect Sir Denys Lasdun, on London's South Bank. The building had only just opened, and I was fascinated to overhear the conversation between two old ladies also exploring this new national monument. One asked the other what she thought of it and, after a thoughtful pause, back came the reply: 'I suppose it will be alright when it's finished'. Her conditional approval obviously related to the deliberately exposed concrete finishes. Now we architects know that this board-marked finish is by no means cheap to produce, but it simply does not look expensive. Our architectural critic had therefore understandably assumed it would be covered up in such an important building.

The security of the passage of time

Places that have built into them some way of acknowledging or even measuring the passage of time often seem to have a reassuring effect on us. In particular, places that express the diurnal rhythm or the passage of the seasons are calming and reassuring. The need for windows is not purely a physical matter of providing light and ventilation, but of allowing the occupants of the space to remain in contact with the world outside. Being aware of the weather and of the time of day through the movement of the sun seems to bring a security which many people value very highly. Roger Ulrich showed that hospital patients who had a view of the outside world were likely to recover more quickly than those who did not (Ulrich 1984). Another study by Rickard Kuller and his colleague Lindsten compared the performance of children in classrooms with windows, in rooms with natural lighting but no view, and in rooms with no windows at all (Kuller and Lindstren 1992). This work suggested that the spectrum of daylight is actually necessary to maintain a good hormonal balance, and that children deprived of this may become less able to concentrate on their work. Perhaps our sense of discomfort when unable to see out of a window is one way in which our brain informs us of this need.

The substantial industry that trades on our wish to populate interior space with plants is another indication of the need we feel to remain in some contact with nature when architecture would otherwise separate us from it. Cities that have rivers flowing through them, trees growing and other similar natural signals of the progression of time often make popular tourist destinations. Herzog and Barnes showed that field/forest scenes and large waterscape scenes were rated as more tranquil than desert scenes (Herzog and Barnes 1999), although the desert might be thought to be subject to less change than those scenes with moving water and growing plants. Tranquillity then, it seems, is more than stillness, and also accommodates the idea of predictable and reassuring movement or change. Some parts of this book were written while sitting on a remote beach, which is sadly not a normal setting for the author! However, it is amazing how quickly one notices the falling and rising of the tide, its slight variations and the way high tide moves back to arrive later in the day as the week proceeds! Such ludicrous trivia become the central daily topic of conversation, and of course this minor obsession helps to restore the mind wearied by a less predictable and more stressful lifestyle.

The tourist industry, at which some may sneer, provides for the needs of both stimulation and security. The stimulation of new places, people, activities and cultures is undoubted, but effectively tourists are buying place. Some cities seem to have escaped relatively recent change and connect us very directly with the past. Bruges in Belgium was left undeveloped for many years after it ceased to be an active port due to silting (Plate 3), and now thousands of tourists flock to see an almost entirely unspoilt historic town through which run many slowly moving waterways. It is easy to see the attraction of not only the stimulation of somewhere new and interesting, but also the security of a slow-moving and highly stable place that contrasts with our bustling modern western lifestyle. Throughout history, space and time have often been linked in special ways. Places that mark time and express it are often regarded with special affection, if not even religious significance. Stonehenge is a huge testament to our need to build spaces that act as records of the passage of time as marked out by the movement of the sun and moon.

Identity

One of the most fundamental forces at work in our psychological make-up is the need to create and maintain our own identity. This was wonderfully explored by Erving Goffman in his study of the 'presentation of self in everyday life' (Goffman 1959). Goffman takes a somewhat dramaturgical approach to the subject, maintaining that to some extent we manufacture our persona. It is interesting that the derivation of the word 'person' goes right back to the masks that helped to define characters and roles in the early theatre. In real life we also play a variety of roles, and these are often associated with the situations or settings that have just been discussed. Goffman uses George Orwell's description of the behaviour of Parisian hotel waiters moving between kitchen and dining room to illustrate the facility we have to take on a persona in a setting (Orwell 1940):

It is an instructive sight to see a waiter going into a hotel dining-room. As he passes the door a sudden change comes over him. The set of his shoulder alters; all the dirt and hurry and irritation have dropped off in an instant. He glides over the carpet, with a solemn priest-like air. I remember our maitre d'hotel, a fiery Italian, pausing at the dining-room door to address his apprentice who had broken a bottle of wine. Shaking his fist above his head he yelled (luckily the door was more or less soundproof):

'Tu mais fas – Do you call yourself a waiter, you young bastard? You a waiter! You're not fit to scrub floors in the brothel your mother came from. Maquereau!'

Words failing him, he turned to the door, and as he opened it he delivered a final insult in the same manner as Squire Western in Tom Jones.

Then he entered the dining room and sailed across it dish in hand, graceful as a swan. Ten seconds later he was bowing reverently to a customer. And you could not help thinking as you saw him bow and smile, with that benign smile of the trained waiter, that the customer was put to shame by having such an aristocrat serve him.

Clearly, then, one of the roles of space is to create settings that facilitate the acting out of the range of identities we use in our lives. Much of this must be done not by architects but by the actors themselves, since the space is effectively an extension of their own behavioural mask. In turn, the challenge for architects is how to create space that invites and facilitates taking possession and personalization. In passing, it is worth noting that this is a rather different view of the task of architects to that which seems to dominate in many contemporary schools of architecture. Here it seems the task is to create space that is a monument to the originality of the architect.

Our need to belong and to identify places as either exclusively ours or at least associated with us is demonstrated everywhere by the things people do to personalize locations. Most of us abhor anonymity, and yet many spaces and places seem just that – especially, it seems, newly created places. A whole industry exists to provide items for people to use to individualize their houses and cars, and of course themselves through clothing and jewellery. As I move around, I continue to be amazed at the capacity people have to find new ways of expressing themselves in spite of the most banal architecture with which they are often provided on modern housing estates. Also astonishing is the amount of money and time people will lavish on this. The brick house that is covered in artificial plastic stone and fitted out with unmoveable wooden shutters says loud and clear 'this is where we live', but at considerable cost. Logically the money would have been much more productively spent improving the insulation, fitting low energy light bulbs or installing solar energy panels.

However, that completely misses the point and fails to recognize the strength of our need to individualize and to express our identity. Desmond Morris is quite outspoken on the importance of this need and the failure, as he sees it, of architects to appreciate it (Morris 1969):

One of the important features of the family territory is that it must be easily distinguished in some way from all the others. Its separate location gives it a uniqueness, of course, but this is not enough. Its shape and general appearance must make it stand out as an easily identifiable entity, so that it can become the 'personalized' property of the family that lives there. This is something which seems obvious enough, but which has frequently been overlooked or ignored, either as a result of economic pressures, or the lack of biological awareness of architects.

Of course 'personalizing' the family house does much more than this; it also signals to the outside world something about the values and priorities of the people who live there. Consider a house, the front garden of which is totally dominated by a ship's mast complete with naval flags (Fig. 2.8). The whole ensemble tells us not only that these people are house-proud, but also something about their lifestyles. When faced with this display we might guess at some involvement in the navy, a set of values about orderliness and possibly even their political leanings. We might even hazard a guess at the preferred dress of the inhabitants. Were a socialist political party campaigner about to knock on the front door to canvass, he or she would probably do so without much optimism!

Herman Hertzberger famously designed an office building in the Dutch town of Appledorn for Centraal Beheer, an insurance company, specifically to accommodate possession and personalization (Fig. 2.9).

2.8 This house signals a great deal to us about the lifestyle and values of the people who live there. If you are visiting for the first time, you may already feel you know quite a lot about them by the time they open the door!

The idea that people would express both their personal identity and that of the group in which they worked was a major generator of the design. Hertzberger reasoned that allowing people to fulfil this basic need at work was likely to make them more contented and therefore more productive. Sadly the experiment has since come to an end as the building is now under different ownership and these ideas are no longer in favour. We have no record of any evaluation of Hertzberger's scheme, and the idea does not seem to have been extensively followed up. Perhaps organizations find it hard to resist the corporate tendency to put the identity of the company above that of the individual

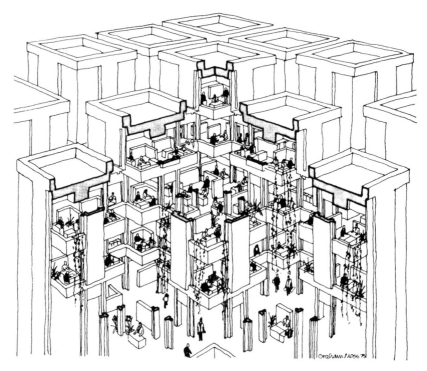

2.9 Herman Hertzberger's highly influential but now lost experiment at Appledorn for the insurance company Central Beheer. Here Hertzberger tried to design places for the occupants to take possession of and to express their individual and group identities. Such architecture looks very different to that which more conventionally seeks to express the identity of the organization, institution or corporation

employee. Hertzberger has over the years proved to be a remarkable thinker and a most humane architect. In his school in Amsterdam he provided display windows at the entrance to each classroom. This not only enables the visitor to see in and know whether they would be interrupting a class by entering, but it also allows the children to display their latest work and through this to express the class identity.

The expression of communal identity can be every bit as important as that of the individual. The village next to mine evidently recently raised a considerable amount of money in order to commission carved name stones at every road entrance to the village. We speak of 'putting somewhere on the map', and this almost literally seems to have happened in this case. I wonder how long it will be before the next village feels the need to follow suit?

The following of others in the expression of identity is a very subtle process (Fig. 2.10). A row of very boring, publicly built terrace houses

2.10 These houses are neighbours and all in a row. The architecture provides little in the way of concessions to individuality. By using a common material on the simple porch, the occupants have quite ingeniously and simultaneously managed to express their own individual family identity and their solidarity with their neighbours. On top of this there is also a little gentle competitiveness to provide the grandest display!

shows this at work. The only architectural concession to the expression even of the boundary of each dwelling is a projecting timber clad porch. Occupants of the first house have decorated this with a plastic-covered trellis material. Their neighbours have followed suit, using the same material but a different design. This expresses solidarity with the neighbours by using the same material and offers a sort of tribute to their idea. The fact that it is slightly more elaborate also suggests just a hint of competitiveness. However, the next set of neighbours has really gone to town, again with the same material but in a very florid design. They have also marked out all their territory in an otherwise open plan scheme by low fencing. The fact that even a small dog could easily jump over this fence illustrates its symbolic rather than practical value. We shall return to the marking of spatial territory in a later chapter.

Much of what we see here, then, is quite clearly display. It is behaviour that falls into a similar category to the way we dress, the car we drive, the badges we wear and the way we speak. Since it is display, it is entirely for the benefit of others. The house with the largest known population of garden gnomes in captivity (Plate 4) illustrates this beautifully! Every single gnome, whether in the garden or in the house sitting on the windowsill, is facing outward. The occupant of the house must go out and stand in the street in order to confront the gnomes face to face. The normal view from the living room is the back of a thousand gnome heads! Of course they are not for the benefit of the occupant but for those of us who pass by. This is illustrated more subtly by Williams's study of the sociology of an English village (Williams 1956):

The type of curtain material to be found on the windows of most village houses varied directly in proportion to the general visibility of each window. The 'best' curtains were to be found where they could be most clearly seen, and were far superior to those on windows which were hidden from the public. Furthermore, it was common for that kind of material which has a design printed on one side only to be used in such a way that the design faced outwards. This use of the most 'fashionable' and most expensive material so that it can be seen to the best advantage is a typical device for gaining prestige.

The balance of needs

As with many aspects of the human condition, one really best begins to understand this as a parent observing children growing up. I have marvelled over the years at the fascination shown by children in stories and drama. The traditional Punch and Judy show is an extraordinarily rich example of the way these needs can be provided for (Fig. 2.11). The characters are strongly portrayed. There is tension as evil and cruelty enters the scene, with of course the cruelty played out on the poor baby with which the children can identify. There is the dangerously exotic in the form of the crocodile. However, good prevails in the end, and even though part of the performance may be frightening

2.11   The traditional Punch and Judy show with its firmly established and restricted range of characters plays out battle between the forces of good and evil. It is at times amusing and at times frightening. However, it manages to combine stimulation and security into one package for the child, who can be momentarily terrified by the crocodile and yet know all will come right in the end

this can be tolerated in the certain knowledge that it will all work out fine. As a parent, I found that an excellent barometer of a child's state of mind was the choice of bedtime story. A request for a new exciting and different tale suggested that stimulation was top of the agenda. By contrast, yet another reading of an old familiar favourite tale suggested that security was the great need of the moment. If I had to read 'The Little Red Hen' once, I must have had to read it a thousand times! This experience also taught me to admire the freshness that only great actors can somehow bring into such an often repeated performance.

Spaces, as we shall see, can always contribute to all these three requirements of stimulation, security and identity. However, some by their very nature should provide more of one than of the others. The familiar fish tank in the dentist's waiting room is a simple device for providing an element of diversion with a great deal of soothing security. The patient is already anxious enough, so go easy on the excitement here! The waiting spaces at transport interchanges need not only to counter our boredom at the enforced wait, but also to consider our anxiety not to miss the train or boat or plane. A new railway station had a totally internal and relatively comfortable central waiting space. However, whenever I used it I noticed that most people waited on the platform in the cold (Fig. 2.12); they simply did not trust the announcements on the notice board and wanted to make sure they saw when the train came in and on which platform it arrived. Their need for security overcame their wish for comfort.

2.12 A railway station in which the architects assumed passengers would sit and wait in a central waiting space equipped with an announcement board. In fact they did not trust the technology and preferred to wait on the platform where they could actually see the trains come and go

Of course, this reminds us that people are not all the same. Just as circumstances vary, so do the personalities of the people involved. Some of the passengers at railway stations may simply be worriers, whereas others are more relaxed about their travelling. Such variation is even more noticeable if you take the time to observe your fellow passengers at an airport! The variation of need is frankly huge, so we must be careful about many of the generalizations that are inevitable in a book like this. I remember being astonished at the range of tolerance shown by people when I did work on the discomfort and annoyance caused by motorway noise in residential areas (Lawson and Walters 1974). In the most astounding cases I would have to repeat my questions when interviewing people in their home because I could not be heard clearly above the din, and yet these people showed almost no concern. Others raged about the awfulness of their condition, throwing open the window to allow me to hear the faintest background hum! However, on the whole most people are to be found away from such extreme positions. This and some further work on environmental insult led us to believe that the predisposition to complain is a significant factor in personality, and that people who complain about one thing are also quite likely to complain about others (Darke, Lawson and Spencer 1979).

The hospital ward needs to reassure the patient who may be anxious, in some pain and, later on, maybe a little bored too. Above all, hospital spaces need to do what in my experience they seldom do – they need to counteract the loss of independence and identity the patient feels. The last few weeks of my father's life were spent in the most

2.13 Two places for an evening out; a theatre in Dublin and a cinema in Brussels. Whatever the so-called 'architectural' merit of the Dublin theatre, it hardly gets the adrenaline flowing with the excitement of anticipation!

2.14   An English law court building. It speaks of the majesty of the law and the insignificance of the individual before it. This of course embodies a view of the legal process that was of its time, and may no longer be thought appropriate by all concerned

inhuman and anonymous hospital room. He was deprived of his own clothes, even though for some of the time this was not really necessary. He had to wear a numbered bracelet and was addressed by a name, which although it was his first he had never used it in over 80 years! Once this name was entered into the computer and his bed was labelled, it seemed there was no way of restoring his identity. When I questioned this, the staff said he had not complained. In fact he was grateful for his treatment and sympathetic to the difficult job done by the nurses, and so accepted this with an air of disappointed stoicism. The system lavished huge care on him medically, but the whole place provided an anonymous end to his life that denied the identity he had previously maintained. It all seemed so tragic and so unnecessary!

Not only can space counter the distortions of life, but it can also help us celebrate events and heighten experiences. An evening out at the theatre is something to look forward to; an event of excitement and entertainment. Which of the two buildings in Figure 2.13 helps to prepare us for that and 'gets us into the mood'?

Traditional and vernacular architecture often got things right simply by enough trial and error for us to find out what worked well. There was no need for theory. As we move into the modern, fast moving and changing world, we seem often to design spaces in a more abstract way, and so more frequently get them wrong. A common mistake is to concentrate too much on the central purpose of a space and thus to forget the rest of the human condition. Such a way of thinking leads us to the wonderfully efficient and clinically sterile hospital that treats the body and yet numbs the spirit! Another mistake is to copy the traditions of the past when they are no longer appropriate, but have become stereotypes. The great Victorian law courts built in so many British cities were designed to dwarf the individual and remind us of the power and majesty of the law (Fig. 2.14) – it was not our identity that was to be expressed, but that of the legal system. Today many new court buildings ape this intention when those involved in the legal system wish to see a more humane and sympathetic setting involving all the participants, including perhaps the victims who must also appear.

In the English language we have two words with overlapping but distinct meanings referring to our place of residence; 'house' and 'home'. The first seems to be a purely architectural concept, while the second includes overtones of humanity. One way of thinking about the purpose of this book is to see it as exploring the relationship between these two ideas of the physicality and humanity of space.

References

Barker, R. G. (1968). *Ecological Psychology: Concepts and Methods for Studying the Environment of Human Behaviour.* Oxford, Oxford University Press.

Chomsky, N. (1957). *Syntactic Structures.* The Hague, Mouton.

Darke, J., B. R. Lawson, et al. (1979). Grumblers and complainers about the environment. In Canter, D., T. Lee, et al. (eds), *Environmental Psychology Conference.* University of Surrey, John Wiley.

Evans, G. W. and J. M. McCoy (1998). When buildings don't work: the role of architecture in human health. *Journal of Environmental Psychology* 18: 85–94.

Goffman, E. (1959). *The Presentation of Self in Everyday Life.* London, Penguin.

Herzog, G. R. and G. J. Barnes (1999). Tranquillity and preference revisited. *Journal of Environmental Psychology* 19: 171–181.

Joiner, D. (1971). Social ritual and architectural space. In Honikman, B. (ed), *AP70: Proceedings of the Architectural Psychology Conference at Kingston Polytechnic,* pp. 7–11. London, RIBA.

Kuller, R. and C. Lindstren (1992). Health and behaviour of children in classrooms with and without windows. *Journal of Environmental Psychology* 12: 305–318.

Lawson, B. R. and D. Walters (1974). The effects of a new motorway on an established residential area. In Canter D. and T. Lee (eds), *Psychology and the Built Environment,* pp. 132–138. London, The Architectural Press.

Morris, D. (1969). *The Human Zoo.* London, Jonathan Cape.

Orwell, G. (1940). *Down and Out in Paris and London.* Harmondsworth, Penguin.

Ulrich, R. S. (1984). View through a window may influence recovery from surgery. *Science* 224: 420–421.

Williams, W. M. (1956). *The Sociology of an English Village.* London, Routledge and Kegan Paul.

Wohlwill, J. F. (1974). Human response to levels of environmental stimulation. *Human Ecology,* 2: 127–147.

3 Mechanisms of perceiving space

A great deal of what goes under the name of perception is, in the wide sense of the term, recall.

Sir Frederic Bartlett, *Remembering*

The brain responds only to certain selected visual features. No doubt in primitive brains these features were especially important, and so were highly selected while unimportant features were ignored.

Richard Gregory, *Perception*

Sensation and perception

In order to understand our relationship with space, we first need to explore how we become aware of it. Primarily of course we see it, since it is largely evident to us visually. The processing of visual sensations into perceptions of the world around us involves a complex interaction of the eye and brain. Our own characteristics are such that our visual sensations largely dominate our perceptions, since over two-thirds of the nerve fibres that enter our central nervous system are from the eyes! Because of this we have come to live in a very visually dominated culture, and it is easy to forget that space is also perceived through the sensations of sound, smell and even touch. Perception is actually more than just sensation. Perception is an active process through which we make sense of the world around us. To do this of course we rely upon sensation, but we normally integrate the experience of all our senses without conscious analysis. It is only when something is unusual or out of place that we notice the different sensations, our differential attention to them, and any incongruities.

I well remember going to the opening of St Catherine's College in Oxford, designed by the great Arne Jacobsen. As a young architect, I was naturally very interested in this building and the opportunity to experience Jacobsen's work at first hand in England. I had lapsed into self-conscious architectural analysis mode, and was walking around the dining hall when I dropped the pencil I was sketching with. Bending down to pick it up I was quite shocked to feel how warm the floor was. The material was of a type that one normally expects to feel cold, but it was warmed by the underfloor heating. Here the material and the sensation of touching it sent out signals that caused me to recall experiences of spaces that were on the whole smaller, warmer and more intimate than the great hall I was in. There was an incongruity between perception and expectation based on memory.

Not only does this illustrate the integrative nature of perception as opposed to sensation, it also demonstrates how active perception is. We are not passive observers of the world around us but active predictors of it. I had already expected what to feel, even though I was not aware of the expectation, and I was then surprised by the difference between unconscious expectation and experienced reality. In turn, this drew a conscious analysis of what until then had been unconscious.

The integrated nature of perception is further illustrated by the curious phenomenon of synaesthesia. A small but significant group of people, estimated to be up to one in 2000 of the population, experiences this condition. Synaesthesia literally means the coming together of the senses so that experience is reported across normal sensory boundaries. People with this condition reliably 'see' sounds and tastes. Of course they cannot genuinely detect such matters with their eyes, but their internal mental experience of the sensation is for them confused with experience actually seen. Although by no means fully understood, this phenomenon clearly indicates a neurological possibility of cross-communication between sensory organs such as eyes and ears and the parts of the brain responsible for our feeling of experience. What is remarkable about synaesthetes is the similarity of their reported experience. Particular sounds such as the letters of the alphabet are commonly associated with similar visual imagery. The vowels are particularly reliable in this way, with 'i' commonly thought to be pale grey, 'o' white, 'u' yellow and so on.

So we have seen that sensation and perception are by no means the same thing, and that to some extent our perception is an integrative experience. In normal life no one goes around in space looking, listening, touching and smelling, but rather we simply experience. It remains the case, however, that it is through sight that we get by far the most information about space, and it is on how we perceive space through vision that we shall concentrate here. We are also going to take apart the mechanisms through which this works. Again, perception does not in reality feel as if it is an analytical process but rather an integrative one. However, all the research we have accumulated on perception does suggest that this experience depends upon analysis by the eye–brain system. Perhaps one of the most accessible and stimulating discussions of this eye–brain system can be found in Richard Gregory's books (Gregory 1966; Gregory, Harris, Heard and Rose 1995).

Size and distance

How do we appreciate distances and size in space? Clearly this is a rather subtle and sometimes unreliable process. As a young architect I learned early on never to let the client visit the building site when only the foundations were dug. It always looks far too small at this stage, and several of my clients when shown the ground slab have panicked and questioned whether the builder has got it right or whether I have grossly underestimated the size of space they need!

In general we are not very good at any form of absolute perception, but we are much better when relying on relative comparisons. Few people have perfect pitch, for example, and most of us cannot, if asked, sing a specified note. However, once we hear that note we can generally make a pretty good stab at singing the major scale based on it. Similarly, we are notoriously bad at absolute perception of colour. How many of us can remember exactly the colour of our living room carpet when trying to choose some curtains to match in a shop? However, many of us do have quite a good sense of which colour curtains to choose if only we have a sample of the carpet with us.

So it is with distance. We estimate the distance of an object in space from several important clues: first, the size it appears to be, and secondly the way it seems to move in space as we move both our head and eyes. Finally our brain is able to perform some astonishingly clever analysis on the information coming from our two eyes, which give slightly different images. Those who have worked on machine recognition of objects have come to realize just how clever we are at this when they have to try to write computer programs to perform similar functions. However, almost all that follows in this book depends upon us performing this miraculous feat on a more or less continuous basis without conscious effort or even being aware that it happens!

Scale

This book will not discuss the detail of size and distance perception, but we introduce the subject in order to discover an even more subtle and important component of the language of space. Of course we know that objects do not actually change size as they move away from us – the people at the far end of a queue are not actually smaller than the people right next to us! (Fig. 3.1). So although the image changes, our perception does not. We hold the concept constant in our minds. Similarly, we learn that as something turns round in front of us it does not actually change shape. These are mental tricks we have had to learn and were unable to perform as very young children. The small child learns to recognize objects such as chairs, but initially may not be able to do so if they are placed in unusual orientations such as on their side or upside down. Even as adults we have all developed our own degree of sophistication at this skill. Matching complex and rotated or

3.1 The people at the far end of the queue have not really been waiting so long for a bus that they have shrunk! They are of course the same size, it is merely the effect of perspective that shrinks their image in this photograph. In normal live vision we hardly ever notice this phenomenon, since our eye/brain system operates a form of 'size constancy' that keeps things the same size in our minds even if their image has shrunk

mirrored shapes forms a common element of psychological tests to assess spatial ability. In general we might expect people like architects to be very good at this, whereas accountants, while better at other things, may find this particular part of perception difficult. So even at this very basic level of perception architects have their own way of viewing the world we all inhabit.

Like all sophisticated mechanisms, however, this trick can sometimes let us down. Most children are learning to perform shape constancy in its most advanced form when they start learning to read. For some this special world of words and letters can become confusing, and they may develop dyslexia and associated problems. The letters 'd' and 'b' and 'p' and 'q' are of course not the same objects at all; nor are 'm' and 'w' or 'n' and 'u'. They simply do not obey the normal laws of shape constancy that the child is cleverly but unconsciously mastering. This confusion caused at such a formative age may result in effects that last a lifetime. It is no surprise that we find a high degree of spelling diffi-culties amongst students who are sufficient spatially skilled to study courses in design! Some of these problems are believed to be connected with the way the two halves of our cortical brain operate. Whilst the brain is largely symmetrical in terms of how it controls bodily movement, it has been found that cognitive skills such as language reside rather more in one half of the brain than the other. The vast majority of us who are right handed are likely to use the left brain not only for steering our pen across the paper when we write, but also to decide what words to use. Left-handed people are quite likely to have quite different patterns of communication between the two halves of the cortex. It is interesting to note that when we look across a university as a whole, we find higher than average levels of both left-handedness and dyslexia in the faculty of architecture!

So there are many ways in which we maintain a constant perception in the face of changing visual sensation. The size, shape and colour of an object are all generally perceived by us to remain constant as it moves around in space, or as we move around it. Of course the visual sensations of shape, size and colour are continuously changing. Our size constancy mechanism is absolutely central to our appreciation of some of the most common of the tricks of the architectural trade. Architects talk quite specifically about the 'scale' of a building. They do not refer here to the scale at which they draw it, 1 : 100 or 1 : 50 and so on. Scale here means the effect the building has on us in terms of relative rather than absolute size. We can have buildings that are on a grand scale, or buildings that are on a more humble scale. As these adjectives suggest, the buildings seem to be trying to play a role in society with their grandness or humility. As a result, they speak through the language of space to us about the people who paid for, designed or occupy them. The famous Paris Opera was completed by Garnier in 1874 on an enormous scale (Fig. 3.2). Everything about this building is quite simply huge – the entrance, the foyer, the famous staircase and of course ultimately the auditorium itself all seem to be grand. So just how did Garnier achieve this effect of massive, almost monumental scale?

We read scale from those features of buildings that specifically relate to items in the world that we are most able to hold constant in our minds. That of course mostly means bits of the building that relate to us. There is nothing we are quite so attached to in this world as ourselves. There is nothing that we appreciate the geometry of more than the human form – quite simply, we are vitally interested in it! We see it, admire it and explore it every day. We have to relate to it when we interact with others. There is nothing more remarkable to us than a giant or a dwarf, and extraordinarily fat or thin people similarly inevitably attract our attention. The sight of the poor emaciated souls who suffered starvation in the prison camps of the Second World War strike a terrible pang of emotion in all but the most hardened heart. If someone we know well changes his or her appearance, we will (and indeed may be expected to) comment on this when next we meet. We are able to carry in our minds for many years an image of the size and

3.2   Garnier's Paris Opera is offers an excellent example of huge scale. Here all the features of space that relate directly to the human form are designed over-size. The floor to ceiling heights, doorways, windows and staircases are all lavish. Even the people using such a building had to dress to occupy more space than normal through the use of mountainous wigs and padded clothing! Such space is designed primarily not for moving through but for being seen in. It sets special people in special settings to establish their role and position in society. So effective was all this that opera as an art form still suffers today from the perception created here that it is only for the rich and famous!

shape of those we know well. This is odd, because most of us could not draw a recognizable picture of our closest friends and relatives, and we even find it hard to describe them sufficiently accurately for a total stranger to recognize them reliably. However, if we meet them after years of absence we might still suddenly notice all the changes that to them may have been gradual. 'My, haven't you grown!' is the most common greeting of an aunt or uncle to a nephew or niece! The growing in size signals the maturing of the child at the normal rate so important to us psychologically as well as physically, and thus the child is quite likely to be flattered and pleased with the remark.

So it is the features of buildings that appear to be provided specifically to accommodate our shape and size that also attract our attention. If these features seem rather too small or unnecessarily large, we notice it immediately. It is the door, then, above all else, that speaks to us of scale. The door is there exclusively for the purpose of allowing the standing human form to pass through – it is a sort of image of ourselves printed on the façade of architecture. Next as cues of scale come the apparent floor to ceiling heights of a building, being the most obvious indicators of the size of the people who might inhabit the spaces inside. The vertical rhythm of fenestration on the elevation of a building shows just how generous is the accommodation for its occupants. Windows, and specifically the heights of their sills, provide other important clues to scale.

Scale then is not some abstract architectural concept at all, but a meaningful and very human and social idea that even has commercial and political value. It is one of the most fundamental components of the language of space. Scale is in a way as much about people as it is about buildings. Of course Garnier and his clients wanted the Paris Opera to be grand – it was, after all, built to perform grand opera! But there was much more to it than that; it was a social idea. People were not simply going to arrive, sit down and watch the opera and then leave. They were going to be a part of the higher strata of Paris society. They were going there to see others and to be seen by others. The great staircase is not so much for getting up to the higher levels of the auditorium as it is an excuse to process grandly. Later it was to produce the dramatic central setting for the Phantom of the Opera.

Of course, to be effective within this huge scale environment the people needed to be large too! They needed to wear grand clothes, including high shoes, wide dresses and tall wigs, which enabled them to occupy more space. So everything about this works: it creates the excuse, if not even the need, for dressing up grandly; it parades its occupants before each other through clever changes of level in space; and it makes its occupants feel like actors themselves on some great stage. By the time the curtain finally goes up, the emotions have already been heightened to almost fever pitch. No wonder much opera of the time turned out to be so much larger than life!

However, scale is not just about size. It is quite possible to have small buildings that are large in scale, and indeed to have large buildings that are rather small in scale. To see how this works let us go to that most architectural of cities, Prague. First look at two particular and rather special houses in Prague, each occupied for a period by great artists, one by Mozart and the other by Kafka. Both were very carefully designed to place themselves appropriately in society and context through the clever use of scale.

Mozart stayed on several occasions at Bertramka (Fig. 3.3). It was not his own house – he was a guest – but he stayed long enough in 1787 to write *Don Giovanni* and to see it performed at the opera house in Prague itself. In fact, Bertramka is some way out of the centre of town. We can see that the owners were significant members of society, for the house presents itself fairly grandly. It is certainly not extravagant, and nor is it hugely formal. This not a stately home, but we might expect that its occupants would command some respect in their society. In fact it is actually quite a small house, and only has enough rooms for the basic needs of such a family.

3.3   This house known as Bertramka is where Mozart stayed while writing his opera *Don Giovanni*. It shows a scale larger than its relatively small size, intended to reflect the status of Mozart's hosts in Prague society. The columns, doorways and raised entrance level all contribute to the spatial effect of grandeur

How then does it achieve its effect? It employs a number of spatial tricks commonly used to aggrandize buildings. We can see that the house actually seems only to get going seriously some way up from the ground. The use of a lower floor or semi-basement, raising the apparent main floor off the ground, causes us to look up to the centre of attention. Immediately the effect has started to take hold. In fact the doorways in the basement level are so small an average person would have to bend down to enter, so this level really reads not as a floor level at all but as a base for the apparently extended floor above. The use of columns that rise vertically as high as possible is another common device.

By contrast, the houses in Golden Lane within the walls of Hradčany Castle, also in Prague, look as if they are trying to be even smaller than they already are (Fig. 3.4). These houses accommodated people who needed to be near to royalty but were mainly tradespeople such as goldsmiths and tailors. One of these houses is thought to have been used by Kafka when he was writing his most extraordinarily chilling work. The very sensible occupants of these houses recognized that it would be socially and politically inept for subjects who were allowed to live in such proximity to their king to then also compete by building large-scale houses, and all the dwellings in this lane appear to be emphasizing the humble positions of their occupants and performing the architectural equivalent of doffing their caps to the kingly palace just further up the hill! The smallness of scale here is achieved by the low level of the eaves of the roof, brought down to give a rather low floor to ceiling height impression on the façade, even though rather more of the space in the sloping roof is actually used.

So scale is often a vital part of the way a building communicates the role of its occupant in the world. The occupant of architecture is rarely an individual but more often a group or even an institution. Consider the magnificent façade of the Fidelity Bank on Walnut and Broad Street in downtown Philadelphia (Fig. 3.5). The message here is pretty clear: 'We are a big, permanent and prosperous organization, and your money will be safe in our hands. We will still be here tomorrow, next week, next year or whenever you want to get your money out again!' This message is communicated by the huge doorway revealed to us as massively beyond what could ever be needed by the size of the passing man. So large has this doorway become that it is now entirely symbolic and quite unusable under normal circumstances, and careful inspection shows another much smaller doorway cut into it for actual use. Of course the huge floor to ceiling heights needed to accommodate this doorway cannot be maintained all the way up the building, since this is already a huge building, so we see the scale reduces above what can be seen from street level. However, to see this from normal street level it is necessary to crane one's neck to quite a painful angle. Here of course, tucked well out of normal

3.4 By contrast to Figure 3.3, the house used by Kafka within Prague Castle was deliberately humble in its appearance. Here craftsmen who served the royalty of Prague were careful not to compete with their social superiors in terms of their occupation of space

sight, the much less important and entirely normally sized bank employees must work.

A more everyday example is the normal local suburban branch bank, as in the case of the Midland Bank illustrated in Figure 3.6. Although nowhere near as grand as the Fidelity Bank of Philadelphia, this building still dominates most of its high street neighbours. The whole of the height of the poor two-storey clothes shop and television rental shops

3.5 The Fidelity Bank on Walnut Street in Philadelphia. The floor to ceiling height and doorway appear made for a giant! The bank is clearly trying to impress its potential customers with its importance and dependability. However, it gives up the pretence on higher floors, where its employees work in much more practical accommodation

3.6 An everyday branch bank in an English suburb. We see all the same messages of scale and importance as with the Fidelity Bank, but merely carried out at a smaller size

on either side only manage to reach up to the top of the ground floor of the bank. Note too how this building puffs itself up by using a huge doorway. Such grandiosity, however, comes at a price, for in this normal working branch bank the doorway must have become too cumbersome to use and a normal-sized door has been fitted inside rather giving the game away! Note too how the building further puffs itself up by sitting on a base that actually rises three-quarters of the way up this normal door!

The use of columns that rise through several stories in front of the façade is a common device for increasing scale. The doubling up of columns, emphasizing the vertical, will also be found. A further trick is the combination of several floors into one architectural element disguising the window openings. This leads the eye to assume it sees a very tall floor to ceiling height. The example in Figure 3.7 is the Halifax Building Society Headquarters (BDP Architects). This produces a curious conflict of symbolism. The large scale is obviously intended, as with any bank, to indicate power, permanence and confidence about the security of money the customers will entrust to their accounts. In this case the building stands right next to some charming but humble little Yorkshire stone houses – the very sort of houses its customers might buy! The insulting arrogance with which this building appears to shrug them off was very

3.7   The Halifax Building Society Headquarters in its home town of Halifax in Yorkshire, England. A curious confusion of messages is sent out by this building, designed by BDP Architects. The grand scale appears to emphasize the importance of the institution. Unfortunately it also appears to signal an arrogant disregard for the more humble adjacent houses. Of course the society exists to enable ordinary people to buy just such houses!

clearly brought home to me when I was taking this photograph. It was not long after the building had been completed, and a little old lady dressed from head to toe in black and looking remarkably like the Grandma character from Giles' cartoons approached me as I framed the picture in my camera viewfinder. 'I suppose you're an architect', she said with an air of indignation, and as I reluctantly admitted to this failing she hit me with her handbag and stormed off, muttering 'It'd be alright in the middle of the desert'. This piece of perfectly judged architectural criticism absolutely captures the building's stunning lack of contextual and social sensitivity!

We have seen in our study of the two houses in Prague that scale and size are by no means the same thing. We have also seen that scale may vary considerably as we move around in urban space, and even within a single building. Handling this, though, often gives architects difficulties in maintaining a consistent language.

Many buildings through their internal functions suggest a scale they naturally want to be. However some building types make this particularly difficult by combining a natural scale that is out of step with the size of the building. This is true, for example, for very large office blocks, hotels or major residential schemes. Here in each case the function of the building suggests what we might call 'domestic scale'.

The activities inside are all divided up into small cells. This is exacerbated on downtown sites where land values are high and development is forced upwards to achieve the density of occupation that is affordable. Perhaps the large city centre hotel is the most difficult of all for this reason. Here a double message must be expressed about function and prestige. So many twentieth century buildings have struggled with this visual linguistic conundrum that we are used to the monstrosity that blights many of our urban spaces.

There seem to be a number of ways of handing the conflict. In the hands of the clever architect, both scales can be expressed. See how Louis Kahn cleverly manages to express both the scale of the individual laboratory and the scale of the university institution in his Richards Medical Laboratory at Pennsylvania State University in Philadelphia (Fig. 3.8).

This is not the case in this hotel situated just outside the centre of an English city on a main arterial road (Fig. 3.9). The building offers three quite different scales. At ground level the building seems to try hard to puff itself up into something grander than it really is for the entrance, but it largely fails and looks a little ridiculous in the attempt! Above this comes the largest scale of all, with floor levels disguised by the open concrete screen. In fact this is a continuous ramped car park, and draws attention to what should be a secondary service element of the building. Finally, the actual rooms above simply express their natural domestic scale. The whole effect is confusing and inconsistent, with inappropriate relative emphasis on the various components of the whole.

Another technique is simply to avoid expressing the smaller scale by removing the clues to internal functions. The huge glazed walls of a whole generation of curtain-walled buildings in the twentieth century have adopted this device.

Scale of movement

Our discussion of scale so far has tended to imply that the human viewer is static. Another form of scale is that which relates not so directly to ourselves, but to our pattern of movement. As pedestrians we not only have an approximately constant size but we also maintain a more or less constant speed of movement. The way buildings appear and move across our field of vision is largely dependent on this pace of life. As pedestrians we may walk directly past buildings, perhaps on the pavement of a street. In such circumstances we may not only be able to reach out and touch them, but also to feel their effects in a wide variety of ways. We might sense the change in temperature as they create shade or perhaps shield us from the wind; we may hear the sounds of the city reflected back off the walls; we may even smell the materials of the building or the preparation of food or other processes

3.8 The laboratory at Penn State University by Louis Kahn. This is a sophisticated piece of architectural manipulation of scale. Elements simultaneously manage to communicate both the scales of the institute and of the individual laboratory. The community of scholars who make up a university like this are thus beautifully symbolized

3.9 A dreadful jumble of scales! This suburban hotel seems totally confused about its message. The huge scale of the lower part of the tower actually conceals the least important space of the car park, and the small scale of the rooms above makes for an uncomfortable contrast. The functionally more important entrance tries hard to appear grander than it really is, but fails to convince us

inside. However, the modern technology of travel has changed this once constant speed of movement and removed this multi-modal sensory perception. When travelling at speed we are likely to be further away from buildings, to pass them more quickly, and to be inside a closed environment such as a motorcar, which insulates us from all the senses but sight. This fundamentally changes our experience of buildings through time. What works in terms of reading a building at walking pace does not necessarily work at the pace of a fast-moving road vehicle.

Great cities are approached in many different ways, but most frequently we now enter them by road. As a child I remember being taken to Birmingham for Christmas more than once. The old Great Western Railway line was forced to approach Birmingham at a steady gradient to accommodate its steam engines. As it did so from the south, the centre of Birmingham rose on what in vehicular terms today we would hardly think to be a hill at all. Yet as the train swept in, the city increasingly loomed above like some great citadel. Eventually even this gentle hill became too much for the early railway engineers and they gave up trying to keep the tracks above ground, and progressively they disappear into a cutting and finally a tunnel. So the city towered above and eventually disappeared from view and, after what seemed an eternity but in reality was barely two or three minutes, the train would burst out of the darkness of the tunnel into the great train shed that was Snow Hill Station. Soon we would emerge from the station into the very centre of the city itself. All this offered an experience of scale related to the sweeping movement of the train. As Birmingham built higher and higher more buildings came to break the skyline, and as the train sweeps around a great curve these tall buildings appear to move in relation to each other like dancers in some stately urban ballet.

Approaching many cities in North America by road offers a similar experience of scale. The intensity of the central business district creates a single experience from a distance able to live both with the scale of the open landscape and of the speed of motorway travel. It is surely the economics of territorial behaviour, which we shall discuss later, that drive us to build so high in these cities. The result in terms of scale is, however, wonderfully harmonious with long distance methods of transportation and the nature of perception from them. The approach to New York by sea with the huge twin towers of the Trade Centre slowly moving across the sky offers a similar experience. The final approach to Hong Kong when the old airport at Kai Tak was open offered yet another example of the city living with the scale demanded by the speed of travel. Nothing could ever quite compete as an urban scale experience with the dramatic late turn that aircraft needed to take and the final plunge down into the harbour. I will always remember the majestic and yet terrifying way the city used to revolve below you. It really seemed as if you owned the place. Then, in the very nature of air travel you landed and for a while could see very little as the aircraft docked into the terminal. You moved as if in another, this time pedestrian, world, through entirely internal spaces towards the taxi that would take you to your final destination. The shock as the taxi emerged from under the old airport to find now that all the buildings dominated you and towered above you produced a quite extraordinary contrast to the perception from the plane. Finally, to step out into the streets of Hong Kong from your air-conditioned taxi and feel the heat, noise and smell of the place was yet another kind of experience. It has always seemed to me to be a city able to make an impact on many different scales. One has a great sense of arrival at a special place.

The approach to Capetown when flying west along the southern coast of Africa is in its own way even more remarkable. It is necessary to begin the descent before clearing the mountains, so the plane banks first this way then that as it avoids the peaks, finally breaking out across the plains and revealing that most fantastic of sights, Table Mountain. This mountain towers above you and dominates the skyline when at the pedestrian scale in the town, but seems just the right size to live with the spread of the plain and the rate of movement when approached by air. Similarly the approach to Rio de Janeiro from inland enables Corcovada to reveal its 'scale from the air' topped off by the massive statue of Christ. When you stand below this statue, its scale is neck-breakingly huge. From the air it seems exactly the right size, as it appears to revolve in space with all the other hills surrounding the city. From the ground when walking along the great curving sweep of Copacabana it is merely a minor feature of the enormously rich scene that also assaults the ears and nose.

This idea, however, has been taken even further in those cities that are actually built around transportation. Though not necessarily central, this is one of the many interesting lessons to be found in Robert Venturi's remarkable book *Learning from Las Vegas* (Venturi, Scott Brown and Izenour 1977). Here, unusually, we find an architect examining the human and social language of space rather than the formal one. Such ideas have however continued to fall on many deaf ears in the architectural profession, which continues to develop its own remote and specialized perception of architecture.

Scale and the social order

Let us now return to Prague in order to make our most important point about scale. On my first ever visit to this wonderful city I found that quite early on I had taken a photograph of a scene I was to be drawn to time and again (Plate 5). We are standing on the famous Charles Bridge looking across the River Vltava towards Prague Castle, and on the skyline is the cathedral of St Vitus. Later on during my visit I noticed that this particular scene was represented in probably the most frequently sold postcard. In fact this image is everywhere! So why is this scene so popular? Of course, it has everything in purely physical terms with all the elements of land, water and sky, and there is always something about a bridge! But look again and I think you can see there is also a tremendous range of scale in the scene – look at the little boathouse down on the river, and contrast this with the hugeness of the Cathedral on the skyline. However, these variations in scale are by no means disorganized; the scale in fact rises with the eye from the river up to the skyline. At the bottom are the boathouses and the humble citizens' dwellings. As we move up the hill towards the castle the houses become larger grander and were obviously built by those with more noble blood, who might have more need to have access to the king. Next of course comes the castle, representing the ruler of all the people. Finally, right on the skyline and reaching up into the very sky itself is the house of the God of this society. So we can see that the scene is an architectural representation of the very order of society. It reminds us all of our place in the pattern of things, and spatially reinforced respect for this order amongst those who lived there. Today Prague is a very different place and some of the patterns of society have changed, but this scene more than any other I know encapsulates what tourists to Prague have come to experience. Yes, of course we want to see individual buildings and sail on the river, but more than anything we hanker after some contact with the lives of those long gone. It is people and society that ultimately matter to us. A history of architecture that dwells only on architectural style misses the most vital part of the experience. Scale is one of the most important elements of the social language of space, and a study of history shows us that it has always been so.

Foreground and background

The scene in Plate 6 is a street in that most multicultural of cities, Singapore. On either side of the street and nearest to us are rows of a building type known as shophouses. They come essentially from the Chinese tradition as adapted by the 'Straits Chinese' or 'Peranekans', a culture resulting from the intermarrying of Chinese sea traders and indigenous Malay women. These workplaces and dwellings were introduced in an early form of urban design guidance by the British occupier of Singapore, Sir Stamford Raffles, and they can be found at various points along the Straits of Melacca, most notably in Singapore, Johor Bahru, Melacca itself and Penang. In front of each dwelling on the ground floor is a thoroughfare, known as the 'five-foot way', for obvious reasons. This allows passers-by to progress down such streets in the shade afforded by the overhanging upper storeys. Not until you have tried to walk around Singapore with its hot, humid, tropical climate can you begin to appreciate how considerate and well mannered these buildings are! However, the visual effect is of a colonnade of many regularly repeated elements. At the far end of the street, by comparison, we find a building coming from a completely different cultural tradition, that of Islam. It is of course a mosque, using many of the architectural forms not of the Far East, but of the Middle East. The traditional Malay mosque in fact more normally uses a hipped roof rather than a dome. In this case, though, the dome is dominant in the scene. Its almost totally spherical symmetry together with its gleaming golden colour gives it strong foreground qualities. Note too that elements in the façade are generally repeated three times to add to the symmetry, but without any danger of exceeding the 'magical number seven', which we will discuss soon. This offers a clear example of the distant object framed by nearer objects, which in spite of their proximity to us nonetheless remain in the background of our perception.

This idea of foreground and background is fundamental to our perceptual systems. Just stop for a moment and count all the sources of information that are available to you. In addition to the tremendously rich and complex visual field that modern urban life provides, there are all the sounds that it generates. Just like vision, our hearing has foreground and background. There is much background noise to which we hardly pay attention at all, while other noises, like speech in our own language, are much more likely to be noticed. What is known as the 'cocktail party' phenomenon demonstrates the foreground and background of sound. When standing in a crowded room you can relatively easily have a conversation with your near neighbours whilst the rest of the people in the room busily chat to each other, but listen to a tape recording afterwards and it is hard to make sense of the cacophonous babble!

Of course we can also smell, touch and even taste the world around us. We even get information from inside our own bodies, through pain, thought and our proprioceptive awareness of our body in space. Quite simply, there is too much going on for our brains to take in and process, and we must be selective. The words of Sir Frederic Bartlett that head this chapter resulted from his now classic experiments that first gave us some insight into this process (Bartlett 1932):

Some scene is presented for observation, and a little of it is actually perceived. But the observer reports much more than this. He fills up the gaps of his perception by the aid of what he has experienced before in similar situations, or, though this comes to much the same thing in the end, by describing what he takes to be 'fit', or suitable, to such a situation. He may do this without being in the least aware that he is either supplementing or falsifying the data of perception. Yet, in almost all cases, he is certainly doing the first, and in many instances he is demonstrably doing the second.

Bartlett makes several important points for us here. First, he distinguishes between what we see and what we perceive. Clearly we see the whole of a scene, but may only perceive parts of it; we then use other methods, all relying on memory in some way, to recreate the rest of the scene in 'our mind's eye' if later we need to recall it. So just how do we decide which elements of what we see we shall go on to perceive? We decide on this normally without conscious effort, and indeed are not even aware that such a process is operating in our heads. Here we shall describe what it is that we shall actually perceive as 'foreground', leaving the rest as 'background'. In fact it turns out that in the visual field this process of selection follows some fairly well defined and reasonably predictable rules. These rules define the visual qualities of an object seen as having foreground characteristics and therefore being worthy of our attention, as opposed to the rest of the scene, which tends to become the setting.

Clearly in this sense 'foreground' does not mean to the front of a scene, and it is quite normal for items near to us in space to be ignored in favour of items in the middle or far distance. The Gestalt psychologists were particularly interested in this phenomenon and how we come to recognize a complete object, concept or situation. In spatial terms there are many features of objects that give them foreground quality, and any object can have one or more of these features and in many cases to a greater or lesser extent. The accumulation of these characteristics then will determine the likelihood of us paying attention to the object. Of course our own mood and motivation also affect this, as we shall see later.

Verticality

The psychologists Hubel and Weisel, using some rather unpleasant experiments on cats, were the first to show that the brain actually contains specific locations that respond to certain geometric stimuli. More recently we have been able to scan the human brain painlessly and have discovered many specialized areas. The brain can thus be seen to be a sort of bureaucracy with departments responsible for straight lines, curved lines, triangles, squares, the colours red and green and so on (Latto 1995). In fact the brain processes visual information through a kind of modular structure, which is at least partly hierarchical in organization (Rose 1995). We can understand our ability to recognize common objects, for example, as being when a particular combination of departments get excited by the scene in front of us. In England, a post box will certainly interest the departments responsible for the colour red and rectangles and squares. Of course we have to learn all this; our brains do not come pre-packaged like a computer with Microsoft Windows! The way we build our perceptual bureaucracy depends upon the way we need to and want to see the world, and in this regard we are all different. We now know that no two brains are absolutely identical, and that we each have our own particular layout of specialized departments within the brain.

As with all bureaucracies, not all departments are equally powerful. It has been found that the vertical and horizontal line departments are particularly influential. This is pretty important as so much of the world around us depends on these two common angles. It is not just architects who need to be able to tell if something is vertical. Of course the right angle is a special angle and the upright a unique orientation. I remember learning this the hard way when as a young architect I complained to my builder that the perpends in the wall he was constructing were not upright. 'Upright!', he retorted, with a knowing grin 'they're more than upright them!' His paradoxical oxymoron confounded me in my naivety, and I foolishly and sheepishly moved on to inspect something else and he got away with his sloppy workmanship. Thankfully experience has made me just a little wiser, and it would not be so easy for him to fool me now!

Symmetry

Symmetry is another foreground-giving geometrical characteristic. We are ourselves largely vertical symmetrical objects, so perhaps we take a particular interest in such things! Naturally the axis of symmetry itself tends to become the most foreground place, so it is hardly surprising that classically this is the location of formal main entrances in building façades. Ultimately of course the most symmetrical possible form is the sphere. Spheres and their subsections in the form of domes again feature in many traditional forms of architecture to create attention-seeking focal points in space.

Colour

In purely physical terms colours are merely changes of the wavelength of light, and so might be thought of a continuum as in the spectrum. However, the receptors in our eyes are not continuous, and so some colours appear more dominant than others; the yellow, orange and red parts of the spectrum claim more foreground attention than the blue, green and violet parts. In fact this works out rather well in the great scheme of things, as we habitually see blue skies and green fields in the background of the natural world. The great Bauhaus student of colour, Johannes Itten, experimented with colour combinations and produced compositions of complementary colours, such as red and green, showing the proportions of each needed to command equal attention (Itten 1970).

There is a very large literature on the effects of colours on our emotions, which taken together is fairly inconclusive. However, the general wisdom seems to be that colours are either 'warm' and 'advancing', or 'cool' and 'receding'. Many describe red and yellow as 'warm' colours that tend to advance and thus seem nearer, demanding more foreground attention. By contrast, blue and green are described as 'cool' and receding colours. A space painted in red will in normal circumstances seem smaller than one painted in blue, as the walls metaphorically advance in on the occupants. Empirical work has generated results that are more equivocal on these issues than conventional design wisdom, but it does still support the general conclusions. Kwallek and Lewis, for example, found subjects working in red offices to have higher levels of stress and anxiety, whereas those working in blue offices showed higher levels of depression (Kwallek and Lewis 1990). They also found fewer errors in a clerical task performed in the red office. This suggests that the warmer colours do indeed demand more attention, raise levels of arousal and alertness, and thus enhance performance.

Number

Simple and regular repetition of an object eventually makes the object itself disappear – quite simply, eventually we do not see trees but a forest. In architectural terms, the column eventually becomes part of a colonnade. But when does this happen? We know that our short-term memory system seems to work pretty reliably up to about seven items, but beyond that it tails off quite markedly. Look up a telephone number in the directory and you will be able to remember up to about seven digits quite well, at least long enough to dial. If the number were nine digits long you would be quite likely to make a mistake. Many years ago the British telephone system used letters rather than numbers for the part of the code that identified the town; three letters were used, and they were usually the first three letters of the name of the town itself. This meant they simply did not need to be remembered from short-term memory, but could be reconstructed from our long-term memory of the town name. The letters were reproduced on the old telephone dial in sequences corresponding to the numbers, but of course there were several letters for each number. For this reason, several different letter codes actually produced the same dialling sequence. Eventually, as telephone exchanges proliferated, there were no sensible remaining mnemonic codes, and the authorities decided to abandon the system in favour of the numerical codes in place today. I was part of a team who accurately predicted the increase in telephone traffic on the system due to the dialling of wrong numbers caused by the short-term memory problem.

As well as our memory system beginning to decay above seven items, so does our apprehension system. Look briefly at a random display of dots, and with up to about seven items you can tell pretty accurately how many are there (Fig. 3.10) – you simply recognize the number. Above seven, and you need to close your eyes and count from the image in your mind. Nine dots are hard to recognize. Arrange them in a square layout of three by three and they become easy to recognize again, but of course here we are cheating by recognizing not 'nineness' but 'threeness' and using our knowledge of the square of three to calculate the nine!

The answer to our question of when a repeated foreground object becomes background is therefore at about seven. Six columns form a portico that is the very centre stage of a classical façade. It uses symmetry and the point of the gable above to emphasize the line of the axis upon which the entrance is bound to be located. However, a row of ten columns tends to become a colonnade, and it might form a background in front of which we might expect to see a fountain or sculpture. There is a tension here when a building is trying to be grand. Surely a grand portico will have more columns than a rather humble one? Even the grandest of all, the Parthenon, only has eight. When it comes to repeated architectural elements, you can simply have too much of a good thing if you want to stay in the foreground and attract attention!

Meaning

We have seen that our short-term memory has a rather limited capacity. By contrast, our long-term memory thankfully seems to have an

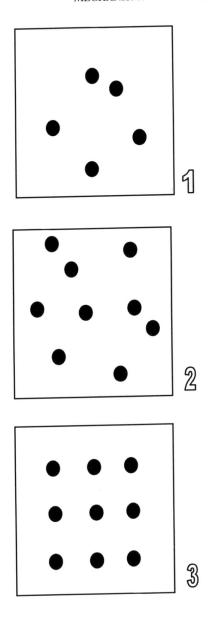

3.10 Look very quickly indeed at the first image and you are quite likely to be able to tell that there are five dots. Look at the second and you have real problems telling that there are nine dots, although of course you can count them slowly one by one. In the third image you know immediately that there are nine dots, since you can rely on your perception of three and use a simple calculation of 3 × 3 = 9. This demonstrates that beyond about seven our ability to recognize numbers rapidly diminishes

infinite capacity, and I have certainly never met anyone who has complained of running out of memory space! Students cramming for exams may not always feel this to be true, but it is. However, this memory seems to work on quite different principles to our very short-term memory. You may remember the seven-digit telephone number reliably for long enough to dial it, but by tomorrow it will have faded. We have already mentioned the work of the famous British psychologist, Sir Frederic Bartlett, who illustrated a very important feature of our long-term memory with an amusing experiment (Bartlett 1932). He played a kind of visual game of rumours with his subjects. As children we all played this game, although it is known by many different names. One child whispers a simple sentence to the next child, who in turn whispers it to the next, and so on along the row. The last child then tells what he or she has heard out loud, and of course it has changed and we all laugh. At least we did when young! Bartlett used adults rather than children, and he also used pictures, not sentences. He showed a simple drawing to his first subject and allowed the subject to look for a while and try to remember it. The subject returned to Bartlett's laboratory the next day, and was asked to reproduce the drawing from memory. This new image was then shown to the next subject and so on. Bartlett ran a number of sequences beginning with a conventionalized drawing of an Egyptian bird, the Mulak. To us it looks a little like an owl. In every sequence Bartlett finally ended up with a black cat. His subjects found it hard to remember the precise geometry, but were relying on descriptive techniques. The drawing looked a little like our conventional drawing of the cat and so that is what they remembered – a cat – and that is what it became. In some cases astonishing levels of detail were added to the drawing. Whiskers and even a ribbon tied around the neck with a bow appeared in some instances!

Our long-term memory therefore appears to work by using meaning and concepts rather than images. Since this is a much easier system to use, and because we are all basically rather lazy, we seek meaning in our surroundings. We love to imagine that we can see a face in the clouds, in the coals of the fire or in a rock formation. This inevitably drives our perception to seek out the meaningful and therefore memorable – we see what we want to see! The more ideas, concepts and words we have to describe the space around us, the more richly therefore we begin to perceive it. The Eskimos are known to have a huge number of words meaning 'white', since whiteness is so important to them. A paradox here is that an architect is educated with so many concepts about the built environment that he or she will be able to see far more meaning than most ordinary people. To many a brick wall is simply that, but to me it has many characteristics. Not all bricks are the same shape, and they can be made and finished in many ways.

The pattern of bonding or overlapping of the bricks is a source of enormous variety. The manner of shaping the joint can vary from round recessed, to struck at an angle, to flush and so on. Combine all of these and I hardly ever see two walls the same! Unfortunately this very sophistication about the physical form of architecture can lead architects to see and experience it quite differently. There really does seem to be such a thing as architects' architecture, and it can get pretty remote from the lives of ordinary people! So objects that have meaning for us, which we understand and for which we have concepts with names attached to them, are likely to have foreground quality.

Context

An important way in which meaning has an impact on attention is through the context of a situation. As I drive to work in the morning, I am doing many things. Obviously I control the car by steering and operating the pedals to regulate speed, and I watch the road and events around me to determine how this should happen. But I also listen to the radio and think through the day ahead, and maybe even compose some thoughts about the book I am currently writing. If you were to ask me later in the day which traffic lights were red this morning I would probably find it hard to remember, and yet thank goodness I have never once failed to stop at a red light. So I must be processing some information, almost in the background as it were, without paying much attention to it. All this goes on pretty well until something unusual happens. Perhaps a child steps out into the road suddenly in front of my car. At this point attention will change rapidly. No longer does the diary or the book feature; all mental faculties are brought to bear on the emergency action that needs to be taken. In fact we seem to have a number of loops of mental processing capabilities that facilitate this complex and sophisticated behaviour. We can think very deliberately and concentrate; we can 'daydream' while performing physical tasks; we can listen to music while watching for traffic lights to change and so on. Actually one of the signs of a highly developed skill is that we can perform it without paying attention to it. When you first started to drive a car your skill was so low that it took all your attention; in fact you may have even found it hard to steer and change gear at the same time! Listening to the radio and mentally writing a book were certainly not possible!

Not only does the development of skill change our attention; so does our whole learning process. George Rand delightfully illustrates this in his work on how children perceive houses and draw them (Rand 1980). He quotes work by Muchow, who showed how children develop in their perception of a department store. She pointed out that at the age of 6 years, such a place has quite different meaning. At that age you are not in possession of a budget and not responsible for furnishing and stocking the home, and the contents of a department store are thus almost inconsequential and become background objects. It is the stairs, escalators and lifts that attract the attention of the 6-year-old; they are novel and potentially a huge indoor adventure playground. I well remember my own son at that age causing us considerable difficulty and embarrassment. He would regularly press the red buttons on escalators and on the refrigerated counters in supermarkets. He was at the age of learning that he could act on the world, and knew that red buttons were usually quite effective in making something happen! Muchow points out that the 9-year-old will pay more attention to the contents of a shop, but this is for learning rather than acquisition. At that age the child may avidly collect advertising sheets, price sheets, packaging and other freely available mementoes of the visit. The 12-year-old is more likely to see the shop as a way of playing out adult roles, perhaps by trying on clothes with no intention of purchasing but revelling in the attention of shop assistants!

This whole question of how attention is directed by motivation, context and meaning is a much bigger issue than we can do justice to here. This is partly because we need to develop many other arguments before it can be fully explored. We shall, however, return to it again in a later chapter on how we measure place. The message here is, as in every chapter of this book, that what commands our attention and what we remember about places depends as much upon ourselves as on the physicality of the objects and places themselves. The language of space is not abstract at all, but is an essentially human one.

References

Bartlett, F. C. (1932). *Remembering*. Cambridge, Cambridge University Press.
Gregory, R., J. Harris, et al. (eds) (1995). *The Artful Eye*. Oxford, Oxford University Press.
Gregory, R. L. (1966). *Eye and Brain*. London, World University Library.
Itten, J. (1970). *The Elements of Colour*. New York, Van Nostrand.
Kwallek, N. and C. M. Lewis (1990). Effects of environmental colour on males and females: A red or white or green office. *Applied Ergonomics* 21: 275–278.
Latto, R. (1995). The brain of the beholder. In Gregory, R., J. Harris, et al. (eds), *The Artful Eye*, pp. 66–94. Oxford, Oxford University Press.
Rand, G. (1980). Children's images of houses: a polegomena to the study of why people want pitched roofs. In Broadbent, G., R. Bunt, et al. (eds), *Meaning and Behaviour in the Built Environment*. Chichester, John Wiley and Sons.
Rose, D. (1995). A portrait of the brain. In Gregory, R., J. Harris, et al. (eds), *The Artful Eye*, pp. 28–51. Oxford, Oxford University Press.
Venturi, R., C. Scott Brown, et al. (1977*). Learning from Las Vegas: The Forgotten Symbolism of Architectural Form*. Cambridge Mass., MIT Press.

4 Ways of perceiving space

It is a very inconvenient habit of kittens (Alice had once made the remark) that, whatever you say to them, they always purr. "If only they would purr for 'yes' and mew for 'no' or any rules of that sort" she had said, "so that one could keep up a conversation! But how can you talk with a person if they always say the same thing?"

Lewis Caroll, *Through the Looking Glass*

It is the common wonder of all men, how among so many millions of faces, there should be none alike.

Thomas Browne, *Religio Medici*

The classical rulebook

Look at the illustration of Blenheim Palace just outside Oxford, designed by Sir John Vanbrugh and constructed between the years 1705 and 1720 (Fig. 4.1). The building is just packed full of geometrical rules. In fact it is a very sophisticated visual essay in the making, respecting, twisting and even breaking of these rules. Of course a scholar of the Baroque period would know about these rules in a very formal way, and could explain how his style was influenced by other architecture of the time. We might discuss how Vanbrugh's use of this visual formal language developed at Blenheim compared with his earlier, equally well-known palace at Castle Howard in Yorkshire, and how his style changed further as he worked on other buildings. We could also study how the ideas behind this style depended on the precedents created by the Renaissance, which in turn depended on the classical language of Greece further developed by the Romans. Next we could examine how the Baroque deliberately twisted and distorted the visual grammar of classical architecture. So rich is this very formal material that there can be endless debate on it. I remember the great Nicolas Pevsner coming to Oxford when I was a student and giving a most erudite lecture in which he asked whether there really was an English Baroque, or whether such a style could only truly be said to exist in mainland European countries. The argument of course was

4.1 Blenheim Palace just outside Oxford, designed by Sir John Vanbrugh and constructed between the years 1705 and 1720. This whole building is dominated by ideas of formal rules. Whether in plan or elevation, the organization, arrangement and proportions of elements are governed by the rules of the style

entirely based on whether the rules of Baroque, as Pevsner defined them, were sufficiently accurately satisfied in England, so ultimately the debate, whilst entertaining, was almost entirely pointless!

What is absolutely clear, however, about Vanbrugh's magnificent pile is that it was the grammar of a formal visual language that drove the whole conception of the design. Symmetry is ruthlessly maintained about a dominating axis, which passes through a gate through the great court and then on towards the central block with its axial hall and saloon. We can now see from our study in the previous chapter of the foreground qualities of symmetry and the importance of the axis how cleverly this all works. Either side of the great court we find two other courts, which appear identical to maintain the symmetry, but in reality one was a stable and the other the kitchen. Convenience of layout and spatial organization are clearly sacrificed for the maintenance of the formal language. Inside the central block we find that the east and west wings are similarly compromised. What is a whole series of spaces on the east becomes one single enormous gallery over 50 metres long on the west; however, from the outside there is no hint of such a discrepancy. This is very sophisticated three-dimensional pattern making, and the pattern must be maintained at all costs.

Now if we listen to the music of Vanbrugh's period, the very early eighteenth century, we find a similar obsession with rule making and rule breaking. The talents of such composers as Telemann in Germany, the rather greater Handel in Britain and the towering genius of Bach were all applied to highly structured music. Here we find a great deal of auditory pattern making. Whilst much of Bach's work is extraordinarily complex, it remains highly mathematical. By comparison, Telemann and Handel wrote rather simpler but equally patterned scores. This is music to hum along to – it is music that we can appreciate the rules of and thus predict its future events well enough to sing along with. In fact it has become popular recently to stage huge productions of Handel's *Messiah* sung almost communally by the audience themselves! Although we may not be able to describe them unless we are scholars of architecture or music, we can still pick up the rules behind Vanbrugh's buildings or Handel's oratorios. We do not expect to be surprised when we move from the east to the west façades of Blenheim Palace, and we are not. We do not expect the reprise of the main theme in a Handel aria to be hugely different from its first appearance, and he does not disappoint us by breaking this rule.

Perception as an active process

This is an extremely important feature of the way we perceive the world around us. We have already recognized that perception is not a passive process but an active one, but just how does this work? Our eyes are not simply cameras recording the scene and playing it back on some mental screen of consciousness, and our heads do not contain some biological cinema playing to an audience of homunculi endlessly watching a projection of the world outside. Such a theoretical model of perception would of course actually get us nowhere. If in our head there really was a screen of consciousness it would have to be viewed by some other mental power, which in turn would have another screen of consciousness watched by another viewer and so on. So strong is our visual picture of the world and so televisual is our society that it is quite hard for us to understand that perception simply cannot work this way.

It is of course the direct connection of eye and brain that enables perception. It is the very analysis, decomposition and structuring of the scene that is at the heart of perception. We saw in the previous chapter that the brain has specific locations that respond to particular angles of lines and other geometric features in the visual field. Of course this process is largely an unconscious one since our actual experience of perception is not an analytical one at all, but quite to the contrary is integrative. We may not even be aware of the extent to which impressions we have of a place depend on the various sensory channels we use, such as sight, sound, touch and smell. So as we look at Vanbrugh's architecture or listen to Telemann's music we are continually but unconsciously taking apart its constituent elements and predicting how it will behave next. In fact, without such a process the world around us would simply generate too much information for us to deal with. In the last chapter we saw how the notions of attention and foreground and background help us with this problem. However we also rely upon structured and ordered rule-based events in order to survive this massive bombardment of information. To take it to the extreme, a totally random sequence of sounds does not seem to be music at all. Even the musical scale with its restricted range of notes organized in strict ratio of pitch is a huge structuring of the otherwise infinite range of possibilities. Whilst modern composers may experiment with atonal music and the removal of timbre, it is highly unlikely ever to become popular.

Order, pattern and redundancy

Armed with this view of human perception as active and predictive, we can now see that as an experience unfolds we can examine the extent to which we have prior knowledge about it based on our ability to predict it. Let us consider a very simple model in order to explore the way this works. We are watching a coin being tossed. We know from our previous experience of this kind of event that on about half the occasions this will come down heads and the other half will be tails. Both outcomes are equally likely, and no other result is possible. (Strictly speaking the coin could land on its edge and miraculously stay there, but this is so unlikely that we can discount it!) So we have some advanced knowledge about the outcome of this event, and if we guess we are likely to be correct about half the time. The actual taking place of the event therefore does not remove all the uncertainty it would if we had no prior knowledge. Similarly, if we are watching a dice being rolled and trying to guess the outcome, we also have some prior knowledge, but rather less. Here only about one in six of our guesses is likely to be correct. The event itself then removes more uncertainty than does the tossing of a coin.

Let us make the scenario a little more realistic and complex. We are waiting at a bus stop used by four bus routes. Again we might guess as to which route the next bus will be on, and we would be right on average one-quarter of the time. Perhaps, though, buses on these routes are not all equally frequent – the first route might have buses running every five minutes, with the second route running buses every fifteen minutes, and the other two running every half-an-hour. If we had no knowledge of this pattern of frequency we could not use it to help us guess. However, regular users of this bus stop would be aware of the timetable and could use this to raise their rate of correct guessing to well over half the time. The probability of each bus can of course be calculated precisely, and so can the extent of the prior knowledge we have as a result of understanding the route frequencies. This process of using implicitly held knowledge of the pattern of events offers a direct parallel with our ability to hum along to Telemann's music and to take in Vanbrugh's façades.

We can view this ordering of events as a kind of redundancy – in effect, we do not have to rely upon an event actually happening in order to remove all our uncertainty about it, so the event is partially unnecessary to our perception or, as we say, partly redundant. The English language as used in common conversation is massively redundant. Even a rather technical book such as you are reading now is still highly redundant; you simply do not need to read every word to understand the message, and you certainly do not need to analyse every letter. Everyday English is considered to be about 70 per cent redundant – that is to say, you need to hear about three words out of every ten to have a pretty reliable and accurate idea of the topic of the conversation. The study of such things was first developed mathematically by two brilliant scientists, Shannon and Weaver (Shannon and Weaver 1949), who were working for the Bell Telephone Corporation in the USA trying to decide how acceptable poor quality telephone lines were. What they found was that because English is so redundant, communication still survives the noise or interference of crackly telephone systems remarkably well – the listener is able to fill in the gaps from their implicit knowledge of the language. Shannon and Weaver went on to develop a complete mathematical theory of how this works, which forms the basis of all modern information theory.

In fact this capability of language to survive as useful communication even under poor conditions of reception can be further extended by introducing more redundancy. There is such a special version of English that is in use continuously all over the world today; the language of air traffic control. Here only a very limited range of words is allowed, which massively reduces uncertainty. Words are repeated, adding further redundancy, and they are even spelt out using another internationally agreed set of words representing the whole alphabet. 'Hotel, Echo, Lima, Papa' may be rather cumbersome, but when your life depends upon the listener understanding it is well worth the effort! Of course this international radio communications alphabet is particularly useful when spelling out codes or call signs which are not themselves words and therefore carry no redundancy of their own. Examples include flight numbers and aircraft call signs, which are combinations of letters and numbers that have no meaning other than their code.

These hidden rules of redundancy in language are of course very well known and understood by us. This knowledge is implicit rather than formal, but it is nonetheless important to us for all that, and we rely upon it all the time. Occasionally this knowledge forces itself into our more conscious actions. Playing the children's game of hangman, for example, brings this knowledge into play. We know that all letters are not equally frequently used in our language – in English, for example, it is sensible to try guessing the vowels first, with 'e' before the rest. The consonant letters 'r', 's' and 't' are very common, but 'z' is a relative rarity. This knowledge is made explicit through being encoded in the scores given to the letters in the more sophisticated game of Scrabble, with high scores given to infrequently used letters. What is often less well recognized is just how this is also reflected in the Morse code. Samuel Morse was an American scientist who had also studied art in London. In 1832 he came to devise a code for his electromagnetic telegraph, which simply had a binary state of on or off but could through this cause a pencil to make a mark on a moving strip of paper. He quickly decided to use a short 'dot' and a longer 'dash' as the only two characters in his code. Speaking English, Morse naturally chose to use the simplest and shortest codes for the more frequent letters. Perhaps his interest in painting had familiar-ized him with the printing trade, since he apparently arrived at his alloca-tion of codes by counting the numbers of each letter kept by printers in their trays of typefaces (Cherry 1957). This creates considerable incon-venience for speakers of languages such the Scandinavian ones, with their abundance of the letters 'j' and 'k' (Fig. 4.2).

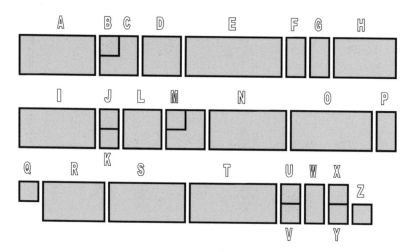

4.2   How Samuel Morse devised his famous code. He noticed that the trays in which a printer kept letters were not all the same size, so he counted the numbers of each letter in the tray and used the simplest codes for those letters most frequently found in English text. The diagram shows the approximate size of the trays he found for each letter in a printer's office

However, redundancy is a lot more complex than simply a variation in frequency of letter, which is known as 'first order redundancy'. In English, certain sequences of letter are also more frequent than others – for example, the pairings of 'th', 'sh' and 'ch' are common, as is the widespread word ending of 'ed'. The most obviously redundant sequence of all appears in this very sentence, with the letter 'u' that always follows the letter 'q'. This is 100 per cent redundant, and logically the 'u' is totally pointless! We can see these pairs of letters as 'second order redundancy', and of course the sequence continues with relatively common triplets such as 'ing', goes on up to quartets such as 'tion', and so on. Of course the whole thing starts again at the level of words (Fig. 4.3) – some words are more frequently used than others, and each individual has his or her own particular favourite words, phrases and sayings.

A language that was not in any way redundant would possibly be more efficient, but it would require huge concentration on our part to listen to it or read it. Such a language would also not be able to sustain poetry; without overlapping meanings and synonyms one could not imagine prose and poetry having any appeal! If there were only one way of saying something, prose would become entirely a matter of craft

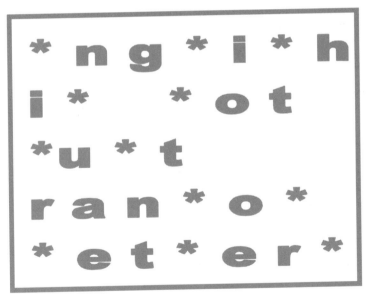

4.3 Try first to read the text above before you read the rest of this caption. You will have had to fill in the gaps using your implicit knowledge of the redundancy at many levels of the English language. If you know it well, you probably managed to discover the hidden text reads 'English is not just random letters'. The whole point, of course, is were there little redundancy you would stand very little chance indeed of filling in the gaps!

and could not be thought of as art. So it is with all art forms, not least music and architecture.

It is, however, much easier to understand redundancy in serial art forms such as literature and music than in the spatial experience of architecture. The poet and the composer decide the sequence of events for us, but the architect cannot do this. For this reason, much more work has been done to analyse music and literature than architecture in this way. These sorts of studies have generated ways of encoding artistic style. Each composer and writer has his or her own more popular words and phrases, and by such means it is possible to analyse a newly found sonata or sonnet to help decide if it really was by Bach or Shakespeare. The reduction of great art to such crude statistics seems rather an insult, but it does reveal the underlying structures that we experience and feel. How else can we recognize style ourselves other than through some form of analysis, albeit unselfconscious? In fact, research has shown that our response to a whole series of situations is closely correlated with these mathematical measures of structure and redundancy. Garner reports experiments showing that our short-term memory capacity depends quite directly on the level of information or redundancy in the objects being remembered (Garner 1962). Similarly, our ability to recognize a range of symbols and discriminate between them works in this way. Our ability to recognize patterns and understand their rules so we can predict their extensions offers yet another example, and our ability to learn languages and develop concepts can be seen to be heavily influenced by the levels of structure, order and predictability in the material under consideration.

Returning to Vanbrugh's architecture, we now see much redundancy. This of course comes from the basic underlying classical language upon which he bases his work. Certain features and shapes are common, whilst others may simply not be used at all – there are no pointed arches for Vanbrugh, whereas Pugin was later to extol their virtue and even claim they were somehow right and truly Christian! But again there is more to it than that. The classical language repeats not only shapes and forms and elements; it also repeats relationships. In particular it relies upon a sophisticated array of proportions, including the fundamental so-called 'golden section'. Centuries later Le Corbusier was to advance a whole theory of architecture based upon the use of a similar proportioning system, 'Le modulor'. Corbusier rather broke free of the repetition of elements and relied for his redundancy much more on proportion (Le Corbusier 1951; Fig. 4.4).

The good and the bad side of being redundant!
We have seen then that this kind of redundancy can be a virtue, in contrast to the expectation set up by the more common meaning of the word! In this context, redundancy simply means that every event

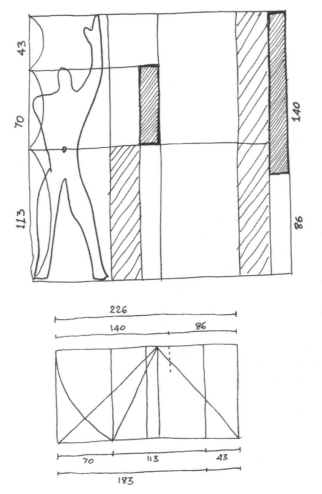

4.4 Le Corbusier devised a whole system of redundancy for use in architecture. Le Modulor depends not upon the repetition of elements themselves, but of the proportions of elements and their spacing. This allowed for a much more functionalist agenda to determine the rough location and shape of objects in the building than did the classical sets of rules

is not wholly unpredictable. Languages are characterized by having events that are not all equally likely, thus removing from us some degree of uncertainty about what is coming next. In turn this makes them redundant, since we can fairly accurately guess missing words or letters by reading those around them and using our knowledge of the pattern of redundancy. Without the introduction of some redundancy into material, whether it is prose, poetry, music, painting or architecture, we cannot have a discernible and identifiable 'style'.

Not only is redundancy necessary to produce architectural style; it also acts in a rather more fundamental way to make space readable and understandable. Just as a telephone line can be noisy, so the visual world around us is full of interruptions and discontinuities. The boundaries of an urban space may be entirely visible in theory, but are often not so in practice. A town square may reveal part of its surrounding buildings and yet conceal other parts through the canopies of trees. Street furniture such as lighting, phone boxes, umbrellas and so on also contribute to an obscuration of the complete elevations of surrounding buildings. However, the patterning of the individual façades together with a frequently-found locally shared architectural style ensure that we can fill in the gaps in the conversation. We can, as it were, hum along with the space, knowing where it is going next and where its important features will be (Fig. 4.5).

In turn, of course, architects can play with our perception of this. Redundancy sets up expectations about what will happen next or, perhaps in architectural terms, just around the corner. Architects may choose to confirm those expectations or occasionally to surprise us by breaking the rules. Sophisticated architecture can often be seen to have more than one simple set of rules and then to play games with the resolution of these separate systems of redundancy. In a way this is just what fascinated the architects of the Baroque period in which Vanbrugh was so expert. It took the well-understood classical rules of architecture, reinterpreted by the renaissance, and then began to break them. More recently, post-modernism has adopted a similar strategy. The Sainsbury Wing of the National Gallery in London's Trafalgar Square, by Robert Venturi, does this in an almost linguistically serial way (Fig. 4.6). Where the new building is closest to the original gallery by Wilkins, Venturi quotes the original architecture almost literally. As we move along the façade away from Trafalgar Square, however, he progressively reduces the accuracy of the quotation and introduces some entirely twentieth century forms and shapes.

Redundancy of itself should not be regarded as either intrinsically good or bad. Architecture is a much more complex form of human communication than the language of air traffic control! It does not try to convey a single simple meaning for a single and unambiguous purpose. The simple repetition of elements does not necessarily produce delightful architecture – just as a children's nursery rhyme is so full of redundancy it quickly palls to the adult mind, so over-structured architecture can appear dull and boring. The skill of the architect lies at least partly in getting this balance right and appropriate to the situation. We discussed our need for both stimulation and security in an earlier chapter.

4.5 This building façade has enough redundancy in it to be capable of surviving the obscuration caused by the landscape so that we are able to fill in the gaps

4.6 The Sainsbury Wing of the National Gallery in London, designed by Robert Venturi. Here a kind of architectural joke is played in which the rules of the original Wilkins Building are followed slavishly at first, and then progressively ignored as we move further away

The expression of romanticism

Compare now the architecture of Antonio Gaudi, approximately 200 years later than that of Vanbrugh with which we began this chapter. Here we see a much more fluid form, which is less dependent on conventional elements and altogether freer in its organization. Again, compare the music of Gaudi's time with that of Vanbrugh's and a consistent characteristic emerges (Fig. 4.7). At the time Gaudi was designing his famous and yet still incomplete masterwork, the cathedral of the Sagrada Familia in Barcelona, so Debussy was composing a fascinating little piano piece that he called *La Catedral Engloutie*. Literally this means the submerged cathedral, and it tells the story of a cathedral that rises from the water. We hear the bell sound as it rises to reveal its full glory before eventually disappearing again. Debussy's music is incredibly expressive. He was of course fond of 'programme' music. His great works, such as *La Mer* and *L'Apres Midi D'un Faune*, are described literally as 'tone-poems', and tell some sort of story and set a scene. Debussy is regarded as a musical 'impressionist', and his work could be seen to parallel the painting of artists such as Monet in its intentions. Gaudi and Debussy were inevitably part of a theme of their time. They were essentially romanticists, rather than classicists as were Vanbrugh and Telemann. The obsession in the early nineteenth century then was not of pattern making and the use of abstract rules; it was very much of expression and how art, music and architecture could express some idea, story or scene beyond its formal properties. Of course this greatly simplifies the artistic philosophies and motivations of these great minds, but the underlying differences are undoubtedly there.

We therefore find a quite different mode of perception in operation here. What we are responding to now is not just the internal structure of the notes in Debussy's music, but the way they can represent something entirely outside their own world or system. We can somehow hear that this music suggests some image, scene, situation or circumstance. When listening to *La Mer*, we may conjure up in our minds some images of the sea. Of course this music represents the sea very vaguely and imprecisely, and in a sense this is the whole point. The composer is asking us to do some work by imagining and relating our imagination to our perception of the sounds. Just how music can carry this sort of meaning is beyond the scope of this book. However, if we ask people to listen to Debussy while they look at Gaudi's architecture, and then play them Telemann and show them Vanbrugh, they invariably appreciate the connections and differences. They do not need to be architects or musicologists to do this. Our perception is integrative of sensory modality in a way that allows both pattern and structure and external meaning to be appreciated. We struggle to explain this to ourselves, often by using cross-sensory modal

4.7 The Cathedral of the Sacred Family (Sagrada Familia) in Barcelona, by Antonio Gaudi. Here we see work that has fewer obvious geometrical rules (although more recent analysis has shown they are still there), but rather a concentration on how form and space can evoke feelings and emotions. We think of this sort of work as 'romantic' rather than 'classical'

words to describe our experience. Goethe famously wrote in his notes: 'Ich nenne die Baukunst eine erstarrte Musik ('I call architecture a kind of petrified music'). In the opposite way we often hear musicians talking of the 'architecture' of a composition, referring to its structure and organization. Architects speak of the 'rhythm' of a façade, and musicians talk of the 'colour' of a note. One of the books I have struggled to use to help me improve my awful flute playing requires me to play a particular note as either 'yellow' or 'purple', and the author even paints a little word picture for the student, of 'an aquarium with deep, dark green water and silent fish swimming gracefully about', when describing how I should play a piece by Saint-Saens.

How buildings can signify

So how can three-dimensional objects and spaces such as buildings carry this external reference or meaning? In fact, it seems a number of mechanisms of perception can all contribute to this phenomenon. Our perceptual system allows for both what we might call 'iconic' and 'symbolic' representations, and we seem to handle these rather differently. As we walk along the street, we might see a cat cross the pavement. How do we represent this event in our minds and store the memory of it? There are at least three possibilities (Fig. 4.8). The first is that we have a totally accurate record of the image as it fell on our retina. If this happened we would be likely to be able to re-examine this image and recall detail, perhaps even beyond that which we noticed at the time. The police who try to get witnesses to recall events and people will testify that unfortunately we do not normally show evidence of having what we might call 'photographic memory'. Bartlett's experiments in perception and memory referred to in the previous chapter also suggest that this is not how we operate. The second possibility is that some iconic representation might be stored. Here some visual features or characteristics are recorded while others are not, but they are coded in terms of other well-known geometrical or visual elements. I remember as a young student of architecture that we had to be able to draw plans and elevations of famous historical buildings from memory in our examinations. Thankfully this pain is not normally inflicted on today's students of architecture! I can recall sitting with my fellow students as we helped each other to find iconic ways of doing this. These consisted not of single representations, but sets of rules for reliably reconstructing the images. The plan of Sancta Sophia in Istanbul could be generated by drawing a square, adding various rectangles, drawing a circle in the centre surrounded by another square, with various semicircles added on and finally making some minor adjustments. Similarly, our cat be can represented iconically by drawing a large circle with a smaller one above it and adding lines and a squiggle for the whiskers and tail. Such representations carry some

4.8   Three significantly different ways of representing a very familiar object. The photographic image of the cat seems to replicate the retinal experience of seeing the real thing. The drawing gives a formalized, almost cartoon-like representation, which reminds us of the basic geometrical properties of the major features, and we can think of this as 'iconic'. Finally, the word has no intrinsic relationship to the real thing at all save that the English-speaking peoples have agreed that it stands for it, and we might think of this as 'symbolic'. Which of these do we store in our memory when we see a cat?

of the characteristics of the real object, but not all. The third way we might represent the cat is by using symbolic means. We might for example use the symbol from common language, which in English is the word 'cat'. This word conveys the meaning quite precisely, but has itself got no qualities of the cat at all – it is a pure symbol, a kind of conspiracy amongst the English-speaking people of the world to attach this meaning to this collection of letters.

So buildings may carry meaning in similar ways. Goodman suggests that they can 'denote', 'exemplify', 'express', and offer 'mediated reference' (Goodman and Elgin 1988). They may actually look like something in some iconic way. Utzon's magnificent opera house in Sydney carries visual echoes of the sails of boats in the harbour, thus speaking to us of its context, and in this way it can be said to 'denote' sailing boats. In fact, in terms of our earlier discussion we can see it as being an iconic reference to sailing boats. Buildings may 'exemplify' certain architectural ideas. Such a concept is embedded in the British system of 'listing' buildings of architectural interest. Through this process buildings come to stand for a set of ideas, whether they be structural, constructional or aesthetic. The famous office building in Appledorn for Centraal Beheer, by Herman Hertzberger, exemplifies a particular approach to architecture in which the intention is to allow the users to take possession and occupy it in a very personal kind of way. This kind of meaning is one to which architects often refer in conversations and debates about architectural ideas, but which may nevertheless be 'meaningless' to ordinary people who have not studied those ideas.

Buildings may also 'express' ideas or feelings through properties that it possesses either literally or more often metaphorically. Goodman puts this with his characteristic lucidity:

A Gothic cathedral that soars and sings does not equally droop and grumble. Although both descriptions are literally false, the former but not the latter is metaphorically true.

Goodman therefore argues that the distinction here between the literal and metaphorical properties is a useful one, and prefers to see the former as 'exemplification' and the latter as 'expression'. This distinction seems particularly useful when we run across buildings that can both exemplify and express, but not necessarily the same things.

Goodman's final way of meaning is that of 'mediated reference'. In essence, this is where buildings refer through a chain of connections to something beyond their actual existence. We see particular attention to this kind of meaning in the post-modern movement. Here a building or feature of a building may be sufficiently similar to some features from an earlier style to indirectly refer to those buildings themselves. In a now famous and fascinating argument, Robert Venturi has advocated the development of such mediated references in such as way as to produce complex and even contradictory ideas (Venturi 1977). The argument here seems to be that such variety of meaning creates ambiguity and interest in buildings, which in turn provides a rich experience for the user who also becomes more engaged in the perceptual process. Whether this is really true does not seem to have been tested empirically, but has certainly become a tenet of some architectural theories. These sometimes complex chains of reference may be quite inscrutable to those who have not studied architectural theory in detail. Others, such as the English architect John Outram, well known for using such forms of symbolism as generators of architectural ideas, have argued that it does not matter whether people understand the chains of allusion (Lawson 1994). Outram claims that the use of these ideas in his work gives designs a form of internal consistency and coherence which is perceived whether understood or not (Plate 7).

However, Goodman's taxonomy of meaning does not include all the ways in which buildings can and do mean things. They may also represent organizations, people, events, ideas or values purely by association. In such a case the meaning has nothing to do with the architectural form and characteristics of the building, but rather comes from circumstance. By now in fact the Sydney Opera House has joined the harbour bridge as a symbol of Sydney and even of Australia as a whole. Note here that the initial iconic link between the sailing boat and the opera house has been connected to another, this time symbolic, link between the opera house and Sydney, thus forming a rather complex chain of connections. They can all be used to stand for or signify the place, the country and the nation in place of words. Of course such symbolic association can take place on a wide scale, as in this example, or more privately. For me certain buildings have meanings associated with significant events that have taken place in my life in or around these buildings. Sometimes those events may be shared by many other people too.

In reality, buildings can have meaning in none, one or many of these ways, and in sympathetic or contradictory ways. I found that my first visit to Berlin since the removal of the Wall gave rise to a particularly confusing set of meanings. The great Altes Museum built in the last century by Shinkel has always fascinated me. It represents an attempt to reinterpret Greek architecture, but is in some ways an extraordinarily modern building (Fig. 4.9), and yet it stands at one end of the open space that is the Lustgarten, famous for being the site of political rallies held by Hitler. The memories of this and a view of Shinkel's façade as the backdrop for these appalling events came powerfully and yet unbeckoned into my mind. Curiously, but perhaps understandably, at this point in German history there is no reference there to these events, and I found it distinctly odd to see tourists flocking around in the sun

4.9   The Altes Museum in Berlin, by Shinkel, contains references to ancient Greek architecture and yet was extraordinarily contemporary in other ways. It was later to become the backdrop for the hideous rallies of Nazi Germany. My only experience of it until the demolition of the Berlin Wall was from historic footage of these awful events. So strong were these images that the space continued to 'speak' of them to me on my first visit, and I could not help but feel uncomfortable with the way the tourists around me seemed oblivious to this! This place had perhaps one of the most complex and confusing layers of meaning of space I have ever experienced

at this place apparently oblivious to its terrible past. Then we go inside this extraordinary building and find it full of the art of the socialist democratic republic of East Germany. I cannot now think of this building without all these confusing and powerful associations; it is absolutely laden with meanings that sit uneasily together.

This at least suggests that buildings and features of buildings can acquire meanings for a particular group of people – perhaps because of some events actually unconnected with the spatial or material forms, but simply because they happened there. Other associations might be with the events for which the building was constructed and with the people and organizations behind those events, and consequently with their values and behaviour. Next, we might associate elements of buildings with other buildings either in the past or present. Architects of course are much more likely to make such associations than the rest of us, and the whole post-modern architectural movement is built on intellectual games played by architects with this kind of material. This can become a sort of secret language or a kind of visual jargon quite beyond those outside the circle of aficionados. Even when not playing such games, architects cannot avoid associating buildings and features with significant architectural developments, whether they are technical, social or aesthetic. Again the significance of this is usually lost on other people. I was recently taking photographs of the famous Owen Williams factory for Boots the Chemists in Nottingham. For me, this now restored building represents a breakthrough in the use of the reinforced concrete frame and curtain walling. Its plan is also a remarkably simple and direct diagram of the manufacturing process, from the arrival of raw materials through the chemical processes and packing to the dispatch of finished drugs to the shops. Many of the people who work there every day, however, seemed to have almost no appreciation of its significance, but to them it may well mean many other and quite different things. Clearly they find it hard to understand my particular interest in what for them is simply their place of work.

This book must avoid becoming a treatise on semiotics and how buildings mean and signify; there is already a huge body of literature on this field. That space and form can signify is introduced here to remind us that we operate on this level in parallel with the perception of order and structure. However, in this book we are more concerned with how space and form communicate in a more directly human and social way – in other words, how they speak both of and to the people who occupy that space. How space communicates such things is often much more a matter of its basic organization rather than simply its visual appearance. We shall be returning to this theme both later in this chapter and throughout the remaining chapters.

Internal and external meaning

Some analysts have suggested that only when artists free themselves of the constraint of redundancy can their work become truly expressive. This is a rather complex argument, both mathematically and philosophically, and is beyond our scope to fully explore here. However, Garner has articulated an important distinction between what he calls internal meaning and external meaning which helps to understand the concept in outline (Garner 1962). Imagine a picture that only consisted of dots. Clearly the dots could be entirely randomly placed, in which case in information theory terms the picture would have no pattern resulting from order or structure and therefore no redundancy (Fig. 4.10). However we can begin to introduce this order, or internal meaning as Garner calls it, by establishing rules about the relationships between the dots. Perhaps most simply we might introduce a minimum distance between any two dots. More elaborately we might allow them only to be positioned on the intersection points of some invisible regular square grid. Since now each dot has potentially four immediate neighbours on the four grid points next to it, we might say that each dot must always have two other neighbours. Even more structure might be introduced by

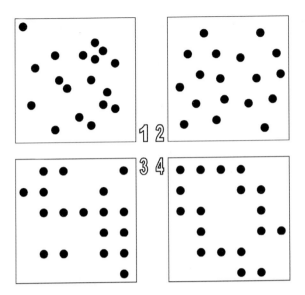

4.10   Various levels of rules governing how dots might be arranged in an abstract image. The first pattern is entirely random. In the second case, all dots are kept a minimum distance apart. In the third case, they may only appear on the intersection points of an invisible grid. In the fourth case, every dot must have two neighbours on this grid. In looking at such patterns we find it hard to make the rules explicit, but we may still perceive their existence and degree of constraint

introducing probabilities of occurrence by making points next to a dot more likely to have another dot than points in open space. We are now getting quite close to the famous 'game of life' computer program for generating such images. At this point we might expect the human viewer of these patterns to be able to detect their 'family likeness'. This is entirely due to our ability to recognize and appreciate the pattern rules without necessarily understanding them explicitly, and thus illustrates just how our perceptual system works in relation to redundancy. In fact, experiments have shown that our ability to recognize, discriminate and learn patterns of these kinds relates quite precisely to the mathematical theory describing their level of redundancy.

However, so far we have only considered what Garner would call internal structure or meaning. These dots could also have external reference. They might, for example, represent the location of aircraft on a radar screen. Here the order and structure is not between the dots themselves, but between them and some external reference. In order to be effective they now need to maintain relationships between themselves and the external reference as it moves, thus resulting in relationships between the dots, which are indications of the separation between aircraft. Now if we also introduce some element of the internal structure or order by, for example, maintaining minimum distance between the dots, the pattern begins to lose its ability to sustain external meaning. This might at first seem an absurd concept, but on consideration it is not. If for example we are using this screen for a human air traffic controller to manage the movement of the aircraft, we need to make sure that the significance of the pattern is maintained. Allowing two dots to come too close on the screen may cause the viewer simply not to notice that there are two, and to begin to perceive them as one. Paradoxically, this would happen just as we hope the human would see a problem – that of two aircraft in danger of collision.

Many years ago I worked on a whole range of such problems in helping to design the display systems used by people to control complex processes. We worked on air traffic control systems. The control of rather more slow-moving processes that had large time lags, such as nuclear power plants, posed similar problems. Finally, systems for manoeuvring indirectly controlled transport devices such as helicopters and hovercrafts were considered. In all these cases we needed to design display systems that had to balance the need for internal structure with external reference in order to enable the human operators to use them effectively.

This relationship between internal order and external reference can also be seen when looking at the problem of learning a foreign language. You obviously need to learn all the external references between the new language and your own, but these are rarely, if ever, perfectly correlated or translation could be entirely automated without difficulty. You also need to learn the internal structure of the foreign language in order to make grammatical sense within its own rules. These problems become more acute when the internal structure gets very high, as in the case of German, which seems to me to have enough grammar to go around all the European languages and still have some to spare! However the problem can also become more difficult when the external reference is to a language that uses fundamentally different structures. Here we might think of Arabic with its completely different symbol system or, even more problematically, the various Chinese languages such as Mandarin and Cantonese, which not only use a different symbol system but also different ways of referencing that to the vocalized version of the language. Of course translating simple instructions is one thing, but trying to translate poetry stretches our understanding to the very limits and beyond that of the ability of most people.

Once we take this argument further and try to apply it to complex situations such as architecture, the mathematics is no longer capable of working adequately for us. There are three reasons for this, and the first is that there are so many dimensions along which we could measure visual structure that the equations become too multivariate to resolve. The second is that we can never know what all these dimensions are. Philosophically, there is no way of being sure that we have detected them all. Finally, architecture is seen by so many people in so many contexts that the effects of varying attention and mental purpose further complicate the balance of importance of this multiplicity of dimensions. In spite of these difficulties, the distinction drawn here between our understanding of internal order and structure on the one hand and external reference and expression on the other remains useful even when the material reaches the sophisticated complexity of art and architecture. This is a rather contentious argument, but what really matters here is that the human mind most certainly works on both these two levels and is capable of operating them in parallel. In fact we might go further and say that we are rarely able, unless specifically trained, to 'turn off' either of these modes of perception.

We might call these two great modes of perception the 'formal' and the 'symbolic'. Most spaces and the objects in them and surrounding them can be and usually are viewed at both levels. Indeed, designers sometimes forget this at their peril. Consider the British Union Jack flag as an example (Plate 8). At one level it is purely an abstract pattern of red, white and blue colours. We can analyse it and find considerable structure. It is of course highly ordered and therefore very redundant – only vertical, horizontal and diagonal straight lines are used, together with the three basic colours. Symmetry is everywhere. But, like much art, just as we think we have understood it, it surprises us a little by breaking the mould. The offset arrangement of the red on the white diagonal just tweaks our perception a little, and catches out many infrequent fliers of the flag who are ignorant of exactly which way the asymmetry should be hung on the flagpole!

At another level, of course, this flag is a national symbol. It represents the country and all that this means to the perceiver. It might, for example, trigger emotions of pride in the patriotic Briton, or resentment in the republican Australian. Its potency may vary. For example, in Northern Ireland few will view it without a strong response, whereas probably most Dutchmen would regard it with relative indifference. As a young design student I was always taught to avoid using red, white and blue colour schemes because of the strength of their association with this flag. Suddenly in the 1960s along came Carnaby Street and the revolution that, amongst other things, brought the flag into popular culture. The mini car, beach towels, shorts and much else besides were suddenly adorned with the Union Jack. It has never been quite the same since!

In the 1970s, British Airways designed a new house style for their fleet (Plate 9). Many Britons will remember that in the 1990s BA tried

to get away from the flag, and were caused much public embarrassment by the famous incident when the Prime Minister, Margaret
Thatcher, covered the tail plane of a model of the new design with a
borrowed handkerchief to signify her disgust! Almost inevitably after
that they eventually had to return to the flag!

However, their 1970s version was a brilliant piece of design. It
worked both symbolically and formally. Just enough of the Union Jack
was used to be recognizable and for the planes to be seen as British at
any international airport. The geometrical redundancy of the flag was
also exploited in order to disguise the quite different shapes of the
many tails in the fleet. You would see the design on the tail of a Boeing
747 or a Tri-Star or a small domestic aircraft. In reality these are all
very different shapes and have quite different relationships with the
fuselage, and yet the design makes them all look the same. At yet
another level, the design used a portion of the flag, which is dart-like,
pointing forward and suggesting flight. This was brilliant design
exploiting our parallel use of both formal and symbolic perception.

Back to architecture!
Buildings are much more complex objects than aircraft tailplanes, but
we might expect the same principles still to apply. No building can ever
be entirely free of symbolic content. Some years ago my university
opened a new building for its psychology department (Fig. 4.11). It is
situated between a major arterial road and the sports fields, which are
at a lower level. The building commissioned by the university immediately prior to this was just a little way further down the same road and
had suffered badly from traffic noise problems, so this was emphasized
in the brief. The architects quite skilfully manipulated the accommodation so that nearly all the spaces facing the road had few if any
windows, which largely meant locating spaces such as lecture theatres,
laboratories and stores there. They also folded the building in plan to
offer the maximum façade towards the sports fields, which was then
heavily glazed in a fairly conventional manner. The resultant roadside
elevation by contrast had small windows occasionally punched into the
reconstructed stone walls. The architects were rather pleased with the
composition of this façade, assessing it purely as a formal abstract
composition. However, when we asked passers-by and visitors about
the building they revealed a very different perspective. Almost
uniformly they viewed it as 'fortress-like', 'secretive' and sometimes
'sinister'. Those who also knew the purpose of the building associated
the secretive appearance with a need to conceal its interior, and saw it
as 'malevolent' and 'threatening' (Lawson and Spencer 1978). This
contrast of perception illustrated a rather commonly found lack of
communication and understanding between architects of the late
twentieth century and their clients. While the architects tended to

4.11   The Psychology Department at Sheffield University by the architects Renton Howard Wood Levin. The street façade was carefully planned for functional reasons to have little glazing. The architects also worked hard to arrive at an interesting formal composition. However the results seem to be fortress-like, secretive and even sinister to passers-by

concentrate on formal abstract composition, the users often seemed more influenced by their symbolic perception!

Of course part of the problem for the contemporary architect here is of setting up visual rules or grammar afresh, since many architects no longer feel it appropriate to use styles from the past. This develops the internal structure and order which give the building enough redundancy to be readable and understandable in its own terms. This is necessary if the building is to look as if it is an entity rather than random collections of shapes, materials, proportions and colours. However, the architect cannot ignore the external reference side of the equation. This structure must remain capable of a number of external referential tasks. These vary from building to building but might include an attempt to express the nature of the person or organization that owns the building and the activities that it is built to accommodate. Most often we also expect a good piece of architecture to make external reference to its context in terms of neighbouring buildings, landscape and the history of its location.

An example of some of this in practice can be seen in the illustration of James Stirling's famous engineering building at Leicester University (Fig. 4.12). There is no doubt about the strong sense of internal structure and order, and this is achieved by using several dimensions. There is a fairly restricted use of shape and form, a limited palette of materials, and these two are also connected. The various key materials of brick tiles, *in situ* concrete and aluminium-framed glazing are all used in their own particular way. We soon read this structure and begin to understand the 'style', and thus are able to predict the building as we move around it. However, the use of these materials and the geometrical shapes, particularly those created by the roof glazing, seem to make reference to the engineering that will be taught and researched inside. Stirling used a similar 'language' on a number of other buildings at about this time, in particular the History Library in Cambridge and the Florey Building in Oxford, this repeated use presumably giving him a better understanding of how the architectural language worked in terms of its grammar. However, none of the others ever seemed to me to offer quite the same degree of appropriate external reference as that at Leicester.

This balance of intention and perception seems notoriously difficult to get right, partly because inevitably architects will always be influenced by their architectural education in their perception. A first step is to recognize that the problem exists and begin to address it explicitly. An amusing example of this happening concerns the design of the Roman Catholic Cathedral in Liverpool by Sir Frederic Gibberd (Fig. 4.13). The building is basically circular in plan, having been constructed on the substructure intended by Sir Edwin Lutyens for a massive basilica-like structure that was never finished. Gibberd was a modernist and used a simple slanted concrete structure, producing a wigwam-like appearance. Between each pair of concrete supports various different structures appear, sometimes using triangular or wedge shaped forms. There is thus great redundancy in the whole ensemble, and the viewer is easily able to predict how the major part

4.12 The Engineering Faculty Building at Leicester University by James Stirling. Both formal and symbolic language is clearly in evidence here. A form free of classical rules is nevertheless heavily redundant and rule-bound. The machine-like shapes also suggest the activities it contains and the professions to which its students aspire

4.13 The Roman Catholic Cathedral of Liverpool, by Sir Frederick Gibberd. Again we see high levels of formal redundancy structuring the forms, and symbolism in the crown of thorns and the centralized plan rejecting the conventional cruciform layout of the Christian Church

of the building will appear as one walks around it. However, there is also considerable symbolic intent. The circular form was a strong liturgical statement, and the whole was topped off by a dramatic glazed structure representing the crown of thorns. Some of the decorative work in the concrete was let out to a rather remarkable sculptor called Bill Mitchell. Mitchell showed me a wonderful model he had made for the bell tower representing the resurrection, but the actual built form is much less imaginative and very heavily redundant. Apparently Gibberd had quite clearly given instructions asking for the eventual sculpture to be 'less busy' than the initial model. The sculptor quite distinctly felt that it should be busy, as 'it was the resurrection and there was a lot going on'. Architect and sculptor had thus not been on the same wavelength in terms of the balance of formality and symbolism. Regrettably, but inevitably, the architect Gibberd won the argument.

The language of modern architecture

As an architect, I am all too frequently made aware that many people have not followed architects in the journeys they have made over the last century into the development of architectural form. Once one is able to get past the initial hostility, which can be very significant, one can often see some of the basis of complaint in terms of what we have been discussing in this chapter.

Of course all forms of art by their very nature move forward, and thus their contemporary manifestations may seem strange to those less involved in the movement. It is not new to find music, painting, sculpture, literature and architecture alienating and even scandalizing their contemporary societies. Architecture, however, plays so many other roles beyond that of an art form that this book suggests we must regard it differently. In the twentieth century architecture adopted a number of characteristics which, when combined together, seemed to lose touch with people. The modern movement abandoned the use of historical styles in the West. It had been preceded by periods in which earlier historical styles had been 'recycled' by architects even as they developed new building typologies – thus Scott was able to use largely gothic rules of architecture when building a great railway station like St Pancras in London. Although this in a way may seem strange now, it enabled people to continue to be able to read the architecture using their implicit knowledge of the redundancy or internal structure of the gothic style.

Just as the modern movement was abandoning historical rules, it gained enthusiasm for expressing the materiality and technology of the building. There were several problems here for ordinary people trying to understand this architecture, but two seem particularly important. First, this technology was itself also new and strange and developing at an increasingly rapid rate. It was, for example, possible to produce entirely new forms with reinforced concrete, which also gave little information on the outside regarding how it held up the building. Secondly, it did not relate to international or regional boundaries and thus disconnected people from their understanding of how buildings looked in their own particular territory (we will discuss the concept of territory later in the book). Building technology was now able to exploit modern materials and structures to achieve such a wide range of form that it further obscured and removed detail that had previously helped to explain buildings. In England, for example, the framed structures possible with reinforced concrete and steel made large flat spans possible purely through the strength of the material, without the need to resort to geometrical strength as had been achieved by roof trusses. The new materials could now cover these flat roofs and keep them watertight by providing an impervious membrane rather than relying on the geometrical method of throwing water down a slope achieved by overlapping tiles or slates. In total this resulted in an inscrutable building, in the same way that diesel railway engines failed to explain themselves as had steam engines – we could no longer see how the building worked. However, the traditional pitched roof form had done more than that; it had also given us information about the plan or layout of a building. When you look up at a pitched roof you immediately get a sense of what happens behind the visible façade resulting from the height and shape of the sloping roofs. The form thus indicates the plan and layout.

Architects should not be surprised if people were a little puzzled and even angry at these developments. It is a little like growing up learning a language and then having your country invaded by people who speak a foreign language and insist you learn it. Whilst you might willingly choose to learn another language for your own reasons, to go abroad on holiday or to work for example, it is quite another matter to find it becoming compulsory! While one can choose to go to a modern art gallery or whether to listen to modern music, one cannot always make such free choices about architecture. Unfortunately some populists can exploit the strong feelings of alienation that much of the public feels to campaign for a return to the past, and we have certainly seen influential figures in society do this in the United Kingdom! That return is neither possible nor real. Our reconstruction of the past is often unreliable and increasingly irrelevant to our contemporary society. Architecture, like all forms of human endeavour, must move forward, but architects must also find a way of doing this that enables people to read and use their buildings in their ordinary lives. People should not be seen as being conservative deliberately in order to obstruct architects, but rather as responding perfectly reasonably and sensibly given their implicit knowledge of the language of space and form.

We rely upon the clues given by architecture not only to read buildings as formal objects but also as behavioural settings. We have already introduced the notion of the behavioural setting and we shall soon return to it in more detail, but for now it is important to recognize that there are different social rules applying in different settings – what is acceptable behaviour in a nightclub is not so in a library, and so on. Unless architecture can communicate these settings, we simply cannot lead our lives in a reasonably secure way. To a certain extent, then, we find it necessary for a library to look like a library and not a nightclub! But what makes a library different from a nightclub is not purely its visual appearance. That appearance has a certain structure order and style which we can recognize and read, but it comes from the much deeper characteristics of architecture as a human and social phenomenon, which we shall begin to discuss in the next chapter. If architects understand and learn to speak this human language of space their work can become externally meaningful whatever visual style is applied to it in order to help make it internally readable. Of course our experience is generally integrative rather than analytical, and we are not normally conscious of identifying the extent to which formal and symbolic modes of perception comprise that experience. Only when we review architecture in a self-consciously critical light do the materials of internal structure and external reference reveal their individual contributions. Seamlessly integrating these two is perhaps one of the most sophisticated and advanced of the skills of the good architect.

References

Cherry, C. (1957). *On Human Communication: a Review, a Survey and a Criticism* (2nd edn). Cambridge, Mass., MIT Press.

Garner, W. R. (1962). *Uncertainty and Structure as Psychological Concepts*. New York, John Wiley.

Goodman, N. and C. J. Elgin (1988). *Reconceptions in Philosophy and other Arts and Sciences*. London, Routledge.

Lawson, B. R. (1994). *Design in Mind*. Oxford, Butterworth Architecture.

Lawson, B. R. and C. P. Spencer (1978). Architectural intentions and user responses: the psychology building at Sheffield. *The Architects' Journal* 167(18).

Le Corbusier (1951). *The Modulor*. London, Faber and Faber.

Shannon, C. E. and W. Weaver (1949). *The Mathematical Theory of Communication*. Urbana, The University of Illinois Press.

Venturi, R. (1977). *Complexity and Contradiction in Architecture*. New York, The Museum of Modern Art.

5 Space and distance

Some thirty inches from my nose the frontier of my person goes,
And the untilled air between is private, pagus or demesne.
Stranger, unless with bedroom eyes I beckon you to fraternise
Beware of rudely crossing it. I have no gun but I can spit.
                    W. H. Auden, *Prologue: The Birth of Architecture*

Clearly, then, the city is not a concrete jungle, it is a human zoo.
                    Desmond Morris, *The Human Zoo*

Abstract and meaningful distance
In the previous two chapters we have discussed both mechanisms and
ways of perceiving space and form. We have so far largely concentrated
on the visual appearance of architecture. We are now ready to move on,
and must recognize the more fundamental aspects of the language of
space and in particular the meaning of distance. Like space, distance is
not the abstract measure so often assumed in theories of architecture. As
with so much in this book, it is not the purely geometrical that is important but rather the way that geometry organizes our relationships. In any
situation or behavioural setting, the distances between people are seldom
accidental or arbitrary. We have a common understanding of those
distances that are appropriate and those that are not for all the normal
settings in which we find ourselves, at least within our own culture.
However, most interpersonal distance is not just a matter of social convention but is based on the essential characteristics of our ability to detect
fellow members of our species. The phrase 'personal space' has now
passed into everyday language, and become rather confusing since it can
be used in several different ways. We are all familiar with the basic idea
here, and understand it implicitly in our normal behaviour. It is as if we
are surrounded by a series of invisible bubbles of space nested like Russian
dolls. These have slightly indeterminate boundaries, and yet we defend
them and feel distinctly uncomfortable if they are inappropriately invaded.

Much of the research that gave rise to the more formal theories
about these distances was originally conducted not on humans but on

(a)

(b)

5.1 Some animals are described belonging to 'contact species' (a). They allow and even seem to ignore physical contact between members of their own species. Others, like humans, are considered 'non-contact', and do not normally touch other members of their species except under exceptional or accidental circumstances. However, the young are often allowed either to touch or come much closer than another adult (b).

animals. This 'ethological' work is valuable in that it gives us a way of looking at ourselves, but also dangerous in that we are clearly much more complex beings than most animal species. The study of the way animals use distance in their natural habitat reveals more directly some of the fundamental characteristics of spatial behaviour than does trying to watch us humans in our complex societies and highly technological habitats. We shall thus begin by considering some of these ideas from ethology whilst remaining sceptical about the extent to which they hold true in the modern human urban context.

Too close for comfort!

The phrase 'too close for comfort' reminds us that our well-being is partly related to distance. Some species of animals however behave totally differently to us (Fig. 5.1); they crowd together, allow regular bodily contact and appear not even to notice this or to discriminate between situations of contact and non-contact. Such animals, including bats, pigs and rhinoceroses, belong to what are described as contact species. We humans will usually apologize to each other if strangers bump into each other in public, but there is no rhinoceros equivalent of this etiquette. Other species like ourselves and including many that are domesticated, such as horses and dogs, are non-contact species. Non-contact species usually begin their lives with a temporary tolerance of contact in their youth, and even as this fades the distances maintained between the young and adult members of a species are often shorter than required between adults. A basset hound we kept was allowed very close to our friends' Rhodesian Ridgeback while she remained a puppy, and one of her harder lessons in growing up was that this was no longer tolerated. It happened quite suddenly one day, when he must have decided she was now an adult. It proved an irreversible decision that obviously puzzled her for quite some time!

Humans normally only allow bodily contact in a number of limited contexts: first, and most obviously, this is between sexual partners whether of the opposite or same gender; secondly, between close relatives, particularly parents and their young children; thirdly, between the very young before the social taboo of contact has been acquired; fourth, in greetings, when momentary contact is allowed as in handshakes, kisses or even nose rubs, depending on your culture; fifth, for the comforting of individuals in exceptional circumstances of distress; and finally, of course, in the highly specialized settings of professional treatment by doctors, dentists and so on. However, for the vast majority of the time in nearly all our relationships we feel uncomfortable if bodily contact is made and usually apologize if we accidentally bump into each other. As with all of human behaviour, we show many more variations and complexity than one sees in most animal studies. There is certainly considerable cultural variation in the use of distance. I find as an Englishman that as I move south-east, passing through the Mediterranean region and on towards the Middle East, that acceptable distances seem to be shrinking all the way. In general, though, we consider ourselves to be a non-contact species.

Flight and fight

Animal studies have also dealt with the distances creatures may keep between themselves and members of other species. Hediger was first responsible for identifying two important distances while studying animals in captivity (Hediger 1955; Fig. 5.2), and these distances

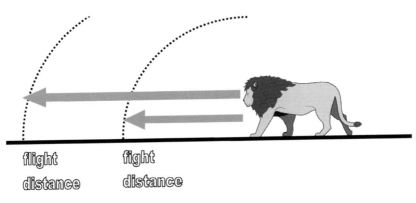

flight
distance

fight
distance

5.2 'Flight' and 'fight' distances (after Hediger). The animal will normally turn and run as we approach within its 'flight' distance. If trapped by its environment, however, it cannot do this, and as we continue to approach eventually we will penetrate the smaller 'fight' distance at which it will turn and use aggression to defend its space. These distances can be plotted quite accurately for each species and are generally correlated with the size of the animal itself

prescribe the functioning of the so-called 'flight or fight' mechanism. As an animal senses what it considers to be a predator approaching within its 'flight' distance, it will quite simply flee. The distance at which this happens is amazingly consistent, and Hediger claimed to have measured it remarkably precisely for some of the species that he studied. Naturally, it varies from species to species, and usually the larger the animal the longer its flight distance. I have had to use a long focus lens to take photographs of giraffes, which have very large flight distances. By contrast, I have several times nearly trodden on a squirrel in my garden before it drew attention to itself by suddenly escaping! We can only assume that this variation in distance matches the animal's own assessment of its ability to accelerate and run.

The 'fight' distance (often also referred to as 'critical' distance) is always smaller than the flight distance. The clue to this is that Hediger's work was on animals in captivity. If a perceived predator approaches within the flight distance but the animal is trapped by obstacles or other predators and cannot flee, it must stand its ground. Eventually, however, attack becomes the best form of defence, and so the trapped animal will turn and fight. This happens at the 'fight' or 'critical' distance. One of the major arguments against keeping wild animals in captivity is that this causes many of them to live more or less permanently with human beings passing inside their flight distance, and we can only assume that such an existence is highly stressful. Indeed we know that hormonal changes accompany the flight and fight mechanisms, putting the whole bodily system on alert and ready for action. Sadly the circus has exploited this phenomenon even more unkindly, where wild animals such as the big cats are manoeuvred around a cage by a so-called trainer who moves in and out of the flight and fight distances, critically causing the poor animals to advance and retreat. This, combined with the particularly close confinement that the mobile captivity of the travelling circus imposes upon its animals, must put wholly unnatural stress on such creatures.

Even the static zoo forces highly stressful and unnatural spatial behaviour on wild animals. Zoos were originally nothing more than the result of humans demonstrating our superiority over other species. To collect wild animals and put them in captivity was also a phenomenon born of an age when international travel was rare, expensive and restricted either to the very rich or to the professional adventurer. The Tower of London famously had such a zoo, which served publicly to demonstrate the power of the King of England over all creatures. By all accounts some terrible things were done to animals there by a society that did not have our contemporary sensitivity to animal rights. Even the great Victorian British collections of animals must be seen in the light of the society of the time. Little was then known of the essentially spatial nature of much behaviour in the way we are discussing it here. In the first half of the twentieth century we tended to stress the educational value of the modern zoo, but today we see popular movements to free whales and other great species. Of course captivity is not without some benefits to a species under certain circumstances; we may have so decimated the natural habitat of a species that there may be no alternative but to take some specimens into captivity to breed and release again into a restored and more suitable location. In general, however, the captive wild animal is far from its natural habitat. It may be fed, kept free from predators and disease, given shelter and even mates, but it is not free. That freedom is not some grand philosophical or political state of mind as it may be thought of in human society; it is the practical possibility of living according to the spatial rules that are innately set into the animal's way of behaving. A large animal in particular has large flight and fight distances, which are difficult to accommodate in the zoo. The sight of an animal pacing up and down in captivity as it tries to deal with such a stressful circumstance is sadly all too common. Desmond Morris in his controversial book *The Human Zoo* has pointed out that such animals exhibit forms of behaviour that are seldom if ever found in the wild (Morris 1969). Self-mutilation, attacks on offspring, over-eating to obesity and intra-species violence to the point of serious damage and death are all found in the zoo but not in the jungle. Morris draws parallels with such behaviour and the ills of modern human urban society. It is from such an analysis that he arrives at the conclusion quoted at the top of the chapter:

Clearly, then, the city is not a concrete jungle, it is a human zoo.

It is curious that we use this phrase 'concrete jungle' to describe the modern city. This implies that we find the jungle a frightening and dangerous place. In a way of course it is to us, since we have tamed nature very considerably in our cities, yet we fail to see that the jungle is also a complex set of highly structured overlapping societies, each of which depend on the existence and indeed prosperity of the others. The predator does not want to wipe out the species on which it preys, for its very life depends upon that species succeeding too. It is through organization in space that this ecological system is maintained. However these are issues that need to wait until we introduce the concept of territory before they can be more fully understood.

'I need my space'

In one of the scenes in Nick Park's delightful animations *Creature Comforts*, one of the characters talks repeatedly of the need to have its own space. We all understand this need to have our own space and not to be crowded in by other people, at least for some part of our life. So before we at last turn exclusively to the behaviour of humans, it is valuable to describe two more animal distances for which there seem to be obvious human parallels; the minimum and maximum distances maintained between animals of the same species under particular circumstances. The lesser of these distances is the minimum distance a species will maintain separating its members under normal circumstances. Confusingly Hediger first used the phrase 'personal distance' to apply to this, and hence the common use of 'personal space'. This use of the word 'personal' is understandable, since the distance is not one universally followed by a species but rather depends upon the social status of the individual animal in its society. Dominant animals are given greater personal distances by the other members of their family, group, tribe, pack or whatever social organization the species exhibits. We will discuss our own human variant of this distance in due course, but at this stage suffice it to say that we also tend to afford larger distances to individuals of high rank. The spaces in which this needs to be enforced, such as courtrooms or royal palaces, traditionally not only use divisions in plan to separate the judge or king from the commoners, but also changes in section to place them higher in space. The very phrase 'high rank' indicates a sophistication of the human language of space beyond that found in animal behaviour. Since we are able to construct spaces, we can also engineer changes in height. Higher locations are generally associated with prestige and seniority – we speak of 'looking up' to people we respect and admire, and we talk of the 'upper classes' in our society; we 'keep on top' of problems at work. The higher floors of hotels usually have the most expensive rooms, and the prestigious penthouse suite is always at the top of its building.

5.3 Some species use very sophisticated methods of communication in order to maintain their relative distance in space such that they can remain able to act as a group

'Keep in touch'

Like many common phrases, 'keep in touch' is now so fully embedded in everyday language that we hardly notice what it really means. Today the instruction is probably interpreted as 'write a letter', 'make a 'phone call' or perhaps 'send an e-mail'. Of course, literally it means do not move so far away we cannot continue to touch each other. This metaphorically rather than physically describes the larger of the two distances that are common to a species. Like personal distance, it varies between species. It represents the maximum distance over which a society can operate successfully, and is thus known as 'social distance'. It is of course largely determined by the species' methods of communication. Some animals have very sophisticated methods of communication using sound or even ultrasound, while others rely entirely on direct line of sight (Fig. 5.3). It is also noticeable that many species organize their societies in space in such a way as to maintain maximum communication within the group and maximum perception of danger or opportunity beyond it. A flock of flamingos will thus not only all feed together within their rather small social distance, but always ensure that various members of the group are facing in different directions (Fig. 5.4) Through this mechanism one member of the society may detect danger and communicate it apparently instantaneously to the whole group, who respond with movement apparently in unison as their flight distance is triggered.

5.4 Flamingos showing 'group perception of space'. The whole group is arranged so that they remain 'in touch' with each other, but so that they also survey the wider scene and any one animal can alert the whole group to spatial invasions

When my children were small, we frequently used to take them to see their grandparents who lived near Windsor. A special treat was to go to the castle in the morning and watch the changing of the guard. As the new guard marched through the streets of the town from their barracks they were normally accompanied by a military band, which played one or other of the simple well-known marches beloved of the ceremonial parts of the British army. The band appeared to need virtually no conducting, and kept time by marching to the beat. However, while the guard changed the band would assemble under the walls of the castle and noticeably abandon their clockwork-like military procedure, gathering round in a circle (Fig. 5.5). In this position they would play arrangements for brass and woodwind ensembles of a rather more sophisticated nature. Still they needed little conducting, but as a rather poor flautist myself I could tell they were communicating. Anyone who has played a musical instrument in a group knows what 'ensemble' means – the group somehow being as one and knowing how to keep together. It might appear to the uninitiated to be telepathic, but in fact it is rather more prosaic. There are nods and winks and intakes of breath and tapping of feet. There is an almost endless range of limited gestures that musicians learn to use and come to recognize that gives them this feeling of ensemble. True it is a little more tricky for us wind players than the strings, since we cannot use the full range of facial expressions without sacrificing our embouchures! For all this to work

5.5 Just like flamingos, humans need to be able to communicate in order to maintain 'ensemble'. Here, a military band gathers round in a circle to play more complex music than the simple march, which keeps them together through its rigid tempo whilst on the move. We can think of the diameter of the largest circle that works for this purpose as 'social' distance

the players must be able to see each other, and they must be close enough for these small signals to be recognizable. The distance at which this is possible is another important one in human relationships.

This 'social' distance is the limit beyond which we must rely on more formal means of communication such as spoken language. A colleague of mine who for many years trained long-distance runners described to me the need to keep together in a leading pack. This is strongly related to the notion of social distance. As a runner in a pack you sense the strengthening or weakening of the resolve of your competitors; their breathing, their stride and facial expression all indicate how comfortable they feel with the pace. When the going gets tough there is nothing so encouraging as knowing that your opponents are struggling too, and nothing so depressing as seeing them ahead and yet apparently comfortable. In the world of highly fit athletes, success or failure is a fine line often drawn not just by physical attributes but also by mental states.

This is an example of where the study of animals outlives its usefulness in understanding the human language of space. We have now extended our natural social distance though a series of human inventions. Once we have a formal language, not only can we speak, but we can also be recorded and our messages transmitted through the written and printed word. The invention of printing was actually one of the most profound developments in our whole history so far. It meant that one person could communicate with many others over long distances and times. More recently the telephone extended our ability to speak synchronously to each other at long distances, and video links have added the visual dimension to our contact. The Internet now connects millions of people every day, many of whom have never even physically met at all and probably never will. Each of these methods of communication has its own characteristics, and they have all changed our society. Through such devices we humans can now live in many kinds of societies, some of which are not defined spatially at all but are communities of interest held together by our technology. Although fascinating the development of our societies in response to such advances is beyond the scope of this book, but this has been interestingly explored by Nicholas Negroponte in his book *Being Digital* (Negroponte 1995) and by Bill Mitchell in *City of Bits* (Mitchell 1995) and *E-topia* (Mitchell 1999). In particular Mitchell points out how cities have been organized around features that brought people together, such as the water well. The distance we could carry water once largely determined the size of a settlement, but this was all to change when the mains pipe was installed. Mitchell intriguingly asks us what the new electronic world, where physical distance is largely irrelevant, means for the future structure and order of our cities. Ultimately the question must be asked as to whether the city as we know it will become an anachronism in the modern e-world.

Human distances
We are now ready to explore the meaning of distance within a specifically human language of space. Imagine yourself totally alone in a vast featureless landscape. It is silent and you can see to the horizon. Gradually on this horizon you see some movement, and soon recognize this to be an advancing fellow human being (Fig. 5.6). As time passes you begin to hear the footsteps of this stranger, and soon you can tell if this is an urgent stride or a casual stroll. Perhaps you begin to reflect on any intentions this person may have towards you. By now you would expect some recognition of each other, perhaps a nod, a smile, or eventually a verbal greeting. Soon you may hear the breathing and be able to tell how physically fit your visitor is. If the advance continues you are likely to be aware of any smells, whether intentional or not, natural or applied, which the intruder brings. By now you will be able to look directly into your visitor's eyes and may be able to discern from this any possible aggression or affection. Even closer still and you may feel bodily warmth or the movement of air caused by the advance. Eventually, of course, you will unavoidably or intentionally touch each other.

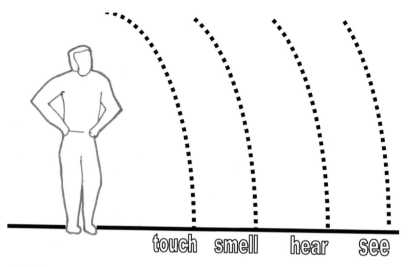

touch   smell   hear   see

5.6 Human distances. Distance is not abstract, since it quite strongly relates to the way we are aware of our fellow human beings. Under normal circumstances, the senses work in a series of nested spatial bubbles rather like 'Russian dolls'. We can see, hear, smell and touch people in that order

This absurd scenario is obviously entirely theoretical and is very unlikely to be reflected in any real experience. The point, however, is that we detect each other in a wide variety of ways. Each of these sensations has a range that is fairly rigidly fixed unless obscured by barriers of sight or sound or masked by other events, or alternatively is amplified by technology. Distance then is not a simple continuum, but has a series of perceptual thresholds. In that most important of all things in our lives, our relationships with others, distance is critical and crucial, for it determines how we will interact.

Let us persevere with some slightly more realistic scenarios to tease out the critical points in distance that cause relationships to change. Imagine now that you are waiting in a public place to meet somebody – perhaps you are at a railway station to collect a visitor (Fig. 5.7). This person knows you will be there, but you have never actually met previously so you do not know how to recognize your visitor. Naturally you will choose to make yourself very obvious so that it is clear you might be the host. You will stand out in the open and well away from other waiting people – literally, you will stand out from the crowd. Imagine now that another stranger also obviously waiting for someone to arrive comes onto the station. You will have expectations about where this person will stand. You would not normally be conscious of these expectations and therefore be highly unlikely to analyse them, but should the stranger fail to respect the language of space that you are

5.7   Waiting for a visitor at a railway station demands a certain kind of spatial behaviour. We need to arrange ourselves distinctly away from others in order to stand out and be obvious to the arriving stranger

relying on you may feel either uncomfortable or aggrieved or both. How close does the stranger need to come to you before you feel the behaviour is inappropriate? To some extent the answer to this question depends upon both individual personality and the conventions of culture.

Consider another scenario in the workplace. You are going to visit someone you do business with who works for another company. You have an appointment and arrive courteously early, but not embarrassingly too early! You enter the office building and find yourself in a foyer confronted by an obvious reception desk (Fig. 5.8). This is only a small business, and so the receptionist sitting behind the desk is doing some deskwork as you arrive. She (we shall decide on a female but of course it could be a male!) looks up and greets you, and you tell her of your appointment and that you are five minutes early. She picks up her telephone to call your host and indicates some nearby seats. These seats are at such a distance, perhaps a couple of metres, that although you are aware that she is talking on the phone you are unable to discern the detail of the conversation. She puts down the telephone, and raising her voice only slightly, informs you that your host is still busy with his previous appointment and asks if you would mind waiting for a few minutes. This you do, busying yourself with the papers for your meeting from your briefcase, as the receptionist returns to her other desk duties. You are far enough apart for these activities to continue without interfering with each other. For a while you may each ignore the other without embarrassment, insult or inconvenience on either side. However as time

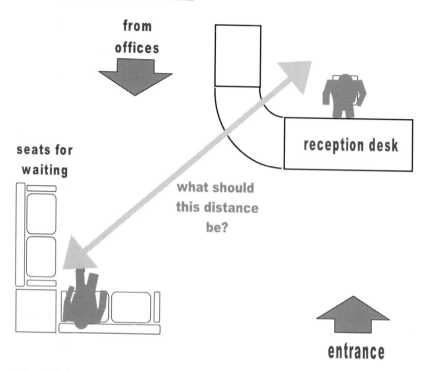

5.8   A delicate arrangement of human distances. The distance between the receptionist and seats for waiting must be large enough to allow the receptionist to continue to work without rudely ignoring the waiting visitors. However, it should not be so great that the occasional conversational interchange is not possible in order to 'keep in touch'

passes the well-trained receptionist lets you know that you are not forgotten by exchanging a few inconsequential words about the weather or the difficulty of parking or some such trivia. More time passes, and she lets you know that she can see your host is now on the telephone and she will buzz him as soon as he finishes. Minutes later your host appears from the interior of the office beyond and to the side of the reception desk. You stand, greet each other and exchange pleasantries as he apologizes for keeping you waiting. You dismiss this as of no consequence and, acknowledging the receptionist with a nod and a smile, you both move off to your meeting.

This all worked quite smoothly, and normally you would not notice any of this behaviour or the significance of the setting. However, now you might ask yourself exactly how far the reception desk, waiting chairs, entrance and office doors were apart. You might also ask how close together or far apart they might be before the relationships no longer work easily and naturally. You will almost certainly be able to tell this, and yet it is amazing how this ordinary implicit human knowledge of distance appears to be forgotten when we sit at a drawing board to design such a space! Believe me, I collect badly designed reception areas, and this is not a particularly challenging hobby!

In the next scenario, you have arrived at this office with a colleague and you are due to meet two hosts to whom you hope to sell some products. You have inevitably travelled some distance for a late morning appointment. On arrival your hosts will show you to a meeting room in which there will be a large rectangular meeting table. Your hosts will already have signalled where they will sit by arranging some papers on the table in front of them, and so they beckon you and your colleague to sit opposite. After some brief opening courtesies, you make a formal presentation about your products. They ask questions and you sense there is a real prospect of business. It is now very late in the morning, and your hosts ask if you have plans for lunch or need to get away. You and your colleague exchange looks, which without needing words tell you that indeed it would be a good idea to stay for lunch whatever other plans you might have. Your hosts then ask what you would like to eat, but before you have really had time to answer they tell of a restaurant a short drive away and also of a pub just around the corner which, they say enthusiastically, does quite nice lunchtime snacks. Again the looks are exchanged and you both agree that the pub would be fine, as you are not great lunch eaters. You all take the short walk to the pub and find a rather small round table set in a bay of fixed seating around which you sit (Fig. 5.9). The conversation turns to

5.9   Here the lunchtime break in the business meeting moves the participants to a different behavioural setting and allows them to engage in more social conversation and to develop more personal relationships. Business will be resumed later back in the office, and is likely to proceed quite differently as a result

families, football and other similar topics unconnected with business. You begin to use first names and to know the names of spouses and children; perhaps you learn or tell of the recent illness of children or their successes at school or in sport. The conversation continues in this manner quite informally. As the snack concludes, the senior host looks at his watch and reports that he has another appointment in half-an-hour. Now you all agree to return to the office and resume your seats around the large meeting table, and this time there is a quick period of negotiation concluding in an outline agreement to do business.

This apparently ordinary business meeting illustrates a number of vitally important but rather subtle effects of spatial distance. The original and final business meetings are conducted in a room with a sufficiently large table to keep the protagonists far enough apart to allow for negotiation. Negotiation depends upon taking up a position that is not necessarily your final one. The first price you quote may well not be the one you will ultimately accept. In effect, not to put too fine a point on it, business negotiation depends upon telling lies! Now it is extremely difficult to deceive someone who is very close to you, so business simply cannot be done at such close quarters. The meeting table is designed to hold people apart as much as to bring them together! In fact it is necessary to maintain a certain minimum distance.

After taking up their initial positions the actors in our scenario engineered a more social situation over lunch. Of course then the business stopped but the process of growing familiarity and sharing of experiences was designed to develop some trust. This increased level of familiarity was facilitated by the shorter interpersonal distances enforced by the fixed seating and rather small table in the pub. This in turn enabled the rapid completion of business back in the office, and by then the atmosphere was one of co-operation rather than confrontation. The entertaining of business customers does far more than simply give them a perk; it potentially changes the context of all subsequent social interactions. However, more importantly here, it crucially requires appropriate settings in order to weave its magic!

We have by now seen some crucial distances in human relationships. We have seen that these distances are not absolutely precise, but we have also learned that neither are they entirely arbitrary. In fact they are closely linked to how we sense and then perceive other people. How we choose to allow others to relate to us depends on a number of factors – these sensory factors, our own personality, and the occasion and our wider culture. The consequence of distance for us humans is far more complex than for all other species, largely due to our sophisticated culture. It is now time to define these distances more carefully. Different writers have tended to use a variety of terms for these distances, but by far the most authoritative exploration of them is that by Edward T. Hall. We shall therefore stick to his taxonomy here (Hall

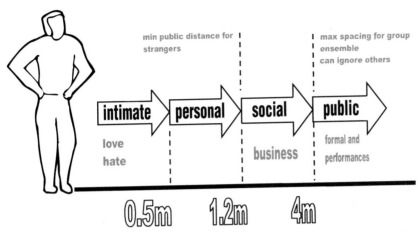

5.10   The most generally agreed taxonomy of human distances in space. 'Intimate', 'personal', 'social', and 'public' distances all have their uses and characteristics. The challenge of spatial design is to facilitate rather than inhibit the behavioural settings appropriate to the social purposes of behaviour in space

1966), and talk of 'intimate', 'personal', 'social' and 'public' distances (Fig. 5.10).

Intimate distance

Inside the distance of half a metre or so, we can touch another person. We may feel body heat and smell body odour, and we may smell breath and perfume. If facing one another, we can see the face in sufficient detail to appreciate emotion accurately unless very skilfully concealed. This then is a distance of trust and intimate activity. It is a distance that we enter normally only with permission. It is socially difficult to ignore someone within this distance, and some form of acknowledgement at the very least is expected. Indeed it may even be hard to ignore some else's presence simply because of the wealth of ways they can be sensed at this distance. Public display of the affection associated with such a distance is disapproved of in some cultures and many situations. Communication at this distance can be by whispering, and thus can remain private from all other people in the same space. Under normal circumstances, however, people are rarely this close for the purposes of extended philosophical debate!

In some settings we find ourselves compulsorily at such close quarters – for example, students sitting in a lecture theatre, or the audience at the cinema or theatre. For a large part of the time in the theatre the lighting level is low and events focus our attention on the stage or screen. In any event, the performance should so dominate attention that ignoring your immediate neighbour is clearly excusable! In such circumstances of course we strive hard not to establish eye contact, as this would suddenly bring into play an inappropriate level of intimacy for complete strangers. As you arrive in your seat at the cinema or theatre you are likely to feel obliged in most cultures to acknowledge your seat neighbour's presence at least with a smile or nod of the head if not a verbal greeting. The lift or elevator also often forces such intimacy. On these occasions most people try to stare absentmindedly into space, either at the floor or up at the floor level indicator, which offers an excellent apparent distraction. Generally in the lift you will notice that people often try to avoid spreading their limbs, with arms kept down by their sides to avoid the accidental touching of their temporarily intimately spaced companions. I once had a colleague who was rather tall and carried out conversations in an unusually loud voice, and to get into a full lift with him was always a slight embarrassment. Even though you might be on either side of it, because of his height he could see you and would continue to talk as if the other people in the lift were not present at all. You could invariably see slight puzzlement in their facial expressions at this behaviour. If they were alone this would tend towards discomfort or even annoyance, whereas if they were in a group they would tend to start looking at each other and showing some amusement. His behaviour clearly seemed to them to infringe their private space just too much, since they could not avoid overhearing the conversation!

Of course intimate distance is one of courtship and romance. Many of us may have relied at some point in our lives on a spatial setting that enforced close proximity to progress such matters! To engineer such a close distance artificially we might reduce the lighting and increase the background levels of noise, requiring conversation to take place by very close mouth to ear talking. The bar, the disco and other such places of social interaction use exactly these devices to normalize very close distances (Fig. 5.11) – you simply have to get up close in order to continue a conversation. The hard part has now been done, and both parties are clearly very much aware of each other. In such a situation the relationship will usually either quickly progress or demonstrate a lack of viability!

Finally, it is worth remembering that this distance is used not just for affection but also for the very opposite. Ultimately we physically need to get this close to fight, but it can also be used as a threat rather than an action. The two boxers who stare into each other's eyes from very close range while the referee is giving them their final instructions before the fight are doing exactly that. To be 'in someone's face', as we say, is to be threateningly close.

5.11 The pub setting uses sheer density of people to enforce 'intimate' distance. However, before it gets busy, background noise and careful orchestration by the host can simulate these conditions, as here

Personal distance

This distance runs out from intimate distance to about 1.2 metres. I rather dislike the name personal distance for this, since it becomes confused with other terms such as personal space and so on. Remember that Hediger first used this to refer to the minimum spacing between members of a particular species. The fact is that all four of the distances commonly exhibited by humans can, under certain circumstances, be minimum distances.

This, though, is the absolute minimal normally acceptable distance to separate individuals in most common settings. Although not so intimate as the closer distance, we are still likely to be very familiar with people with whom we use this distance in public. It is difficult to ignore someone at this distance, and again when forced into such close proximity strangers will normally acknowledge each other. When looking directly at each other the face is very clearly visible in the fovea. Once we are within personal distance of someone, the whole of his or her face fills our foveal field of vision. The fovea is that small central part of the retina that allows for the detection of fine detail, and has very high acuity. By contrast, our peripheral field of vision specializes in motion, which turns out to be pretty good survival kit in the wild! For this reason it is particularly hard to conceal emotion at this distance. Once at this crucial distance, for example, we can see the beads of sweat that might form on the face of a protagonist. We can clearly see those telltale little twitches of the corner of the mouth that are so hard to suppress when we try to deceive. Police and military interrogators know this and use it to considerable effect with perfectly practised timing when asking their most penetrating question. We saw in our business lunch scenario earlier in this chapter that for this reason negotiation is normally conducted at a further distance than this.

Social distance

This distance is generally considered to run from about 1.2 metres to 4 metres. The closer distance here is that which would be used in polite society under normal circumstances. At the minimum social distance we can still see each other's face clearly but not intimately. We can carry out conversation at normal voice levels under most conditions.

Imagine standing at a cocktail party chatting to two or three other people. You are most likely to be separated by minimum social distance. Of course as it gets noisier you may to come closer together to converse, as we have already seen. Working colleagues are likely to use this distance for conversations, but more formal business and negotiation would take place at the upper end of social distance. At the far end of social distance we can usually totally ignore others in public, and there would be no need to acknowledge their existence. The railway station scenario earlier in the chapter offers an example of the far end of social distance for exactly this reason. Also for this reason at the outer end of social distance we need to indicate more clearly that we are attending to another person who might be talking to us. Looking people straight in the eye and establishing a shared appreciation of eye contact is a necessity to maintain polite conversation. Larger gestures, such as smiling and nodding the head, are more frequently used to indicate continuing attention. It is certainly possible at such distances to know whether someone is listening to you and paying attention, and probably whether they understand or agree. It is the distance a seminar group might ideally sit around at to hold their discussions, and is also the distance our military band used to play their more tricky pieces. As we move beyond this distance the sense of contact with other people tends to get lost. For this reason, the far end of social distance is the point at which it becomes very bad news for the long-distance runner to trail behind the pack. Beyond this distance it is difficult to maintain ensemble in a musical group. In fact, beyond this distance we effectively relinquish our hold over or contact with other people in a space, and can ignore them without infringing etiquette. It is a most important distance to understand in making many behavioural settings work well.

Public distance
This is our final distance, and is generally considered to run outwards from the upper reaches of social distance. We will therefore call a distance of greater than 4 metres public distance. At very close public distance we probably find the nearest thing we can to the human version of the animal flight distance we considered earlier. If we go back to the very first and rather ridiculous scenario in this chapter, a person advancing towards you in a manner that was not overtly welcoming might seriously worry you as he or she reached about here! At the very near range of public distance one can carry on a conversation with only slightly raised voices. As we move out to a distance of 8 metres, the voice must be raised to what we might think of as a theatrical level. At this larger distance we can see little clear detail on faces; hence the extravagant makeup used in the theatre. Two people within close personal distance to each other and at far public distance from you could hold a quiet conversation without you being able to understand it.

For all these reasons, public distance is normally one at which we ignore other people in space. However, certain formal settings call for this distance to be used, and these are usually performances of some kind. Examples include a business presentation to a group of customers, a lecture to students, a concert, or indeed a theatrical event. The concert and the theatre offer very clearly defined roles for the performer. In early theatre the performers even wore masks to indicate their dramatic character, but of course also to conceal their normal identity. Such events, then, call for very special behaviour. The lecture or presentation is more difficult for some people to cope with since it involves the normal personality performing in a very public way. To be at public distance from a group is to be isolated and vulnerable. Some people can be completely terrified of such a situation, while others seem naturals at it. As an academic I see this demonstrated annually as another crop of students grapples with the situation in seminars, design crits and other such presentations of work to the group.

The personality that thrives on and relishes performing at public distance is probably one that we would associate with confidence, possibly even arrogance, and probably charisma. Such a performance requires a different speaking voice to that used in normal conversation. Not only must the voice be raised, but also the tempo and phrasing used are usually different. Particular groups of people who habitually speak in these situations seem to have acquired their own norms for doing this. The clergyman giving a sermon uses quite recognizable inflections and gestures and pauses. The policeman delivering a statement to a press conference after a serious crime, or giving evidence in court, tends to use a formal method of address, nothing like the way he might speak in normal circumstances. The holiday tour representative welcoming a party of tourists uses another quite different range of emphasis and gesture, as does the person demonstrating cooking or some new gadget at an exhibition. All these and many more can conjure up in our minds ways of holding an audience at a public distance and telling them quite clearly what sort of event this is.

Multiple distances in a space

Few spaces are designed exclusively for interaction at just one of the distances identified here. In most of the settings we might imagine, people move around, and in many cases different relationships might well exist between various people within the same space. In a hospital ward, for example, a patient may expect one set of behavioural distances with other patients, another with visitors such as family and friends, and yet another with the professional medical staff who attend them. The trick of good design in such situations is to facilitate all these kinds of relationships without putting any under stress. We cannot really examine that idea in any detail until the next chapter, since it is not just a matter of distance but also of spatial arrangement. However, the principle of multiple distances can still be illustrated by yet another of our scenarios.

A lecturer arrives to deliver a weekly lecture to her students at university. She finds the front row entirely empty and the back three rows completely full, with the intermediate rows each partly occupied (Fig. 5.12). The door to the theatre is at the front, and the theatre rakes up towards the rear so all can see the front clearly. So just why do the students climb more steps and give themselves less chance of seeing the slides she will project onto the screen at the front? There is a certain distance beyond which the lecturer will find it hard to establish recognizable eye contact with an individual student. This is public distance. Students in the back rows then achieve substantial public distance from the lecturer so they feel securely beyond personal contact. They reckon that they are unlikely to be asked questions by her, and in turn can make comments to each other without interrupting proceedings. I usually find this is the easiest scenario to describe in my lecture courses, since invariably the students have already demonstrated it! One year the students on my course sought to get their own back. As I entered the lecture theatre the following week I noticed that the front row was absolutely full and they were all wearing

Plate 1 This special place on a tropical island can be overlaid with many meanings. It could be an ideal place to enjoy active watersports, a place of quiet contemplation, an endangered natural environment.

Plate 2 The chapel at Pampulha by the Brazilian architect Oscar Niemeyer. It was just too iconoclastic for the clergy, who doubted its ability to offer the conventional behavioural setting required for Christian worship.

Plate 3 A popular tourist location in the town of Bruges in Belgium. Is there something reassuring about places that communicate the passage of natural time? The diurnal rhythm of the movement of the sun, the seasonal changing of the trees and plants and the incessant motion of flowing water leading eventually to the sea?

Plate 4 This house has the largest known collection of garden gnomes in captivity! Note that they have spread everywhere, blocking off access through the original front gate, and finally even inside the house itself onto the window ledge. However, also note that every gnome without fail faces the road. The occupant thus has a spectacular view of the back of a thousand gnome heads! Clearly display is the primary objective!

Plate 5 Prague, taken from the Charles Bridge looking up towards the Castle. Note the range of scales that cast all the members of society into their appropriate roles in a kind of symbolic spatial hierarchy. At the bottom are the humble boatmens' buildings, then the burgers' houses, the King's castle and finally, at the very top, God's Cathedral. Such well-structured cities serve as a sort of spatial index to the way society is organized.

Plate 6 Kampong Glam and the Sultan Mosque in Singapore. Here, foreground and background work in complex ways spatially. Those buildings actually near to us use spatial features which make them background, whilst the mosque at the end of the street uses a whole range of visual devices to attract attention and claim foreground.

Plate 7 John Outram's work, here at The Judge Institute in Cambridge, reveals that his design process draw heavily upon symbolic material to generate space and form. Whether other people understand these references is not important to Outram, and it is rather doubtful that buildings can communicate sufficiently directly and reliably for any very rich information to be accurately transmitted in this way. Nevertheless, Outram argues persuasively that people can and do perceive the coherence of the designed symbolism.

Plate 8 The Union Jack flag is an image that can be viewed entirely as an abstract formal pattern of colour and form. In such an analysis we could see that it is quite redundant, displaying repetition, symmetry and a restricted colour palette. However, it can also be viewed symbolically. In this analysis your reaction to it is quite likely to be significantly influenced by your relationship with Britain.

Plate 9 An earlier British Airways house style. This very clever design works at many levels. Formally, it disguises the many different plane shapes and outlines in the fleet and gives them a unity. Symbolically, it stands for all things British. Iconically, it has dart-like shapes suggesting flight. Whilst of course fashions changes and this style also communicates something of its era, nevertheless BA have probably never managed such a clever design again.

**Start your tan before you go on holiday.
And join in the fun straight away.**

Plate 10 Body language used to support the written message. The arrangement of the people in space sends strong messages, which we can all read, about the generally miserable condition of the couple on the right compared with those on the left. The happy ones demonstrate open-limbed postures and wide smiling mouths. Those on the right turn only their heads, leaving their bodies rigid and protected by the defensive arms. Get a sun lamp, get a life!

Plate 11 Look at the three different life situations that are conjured up by this advertisement. The dress is the same in each case save for the colour, which is described as 'delicious burgundy' (centre), 'after dusk pink' (left) and 'very late black' (right). But the body language is totally different. Buy the dress, win social success!

Plate 12 The Eiffel Tower and Hagia Sophia can be seen as icons for the capital cities. They as powerful enough to become symbolic 'heartlands' for their nations.

Plate 13 The new KLIA Airport, by Kisho Kurakawa, offers lavish space and accommodation far greater than the current needs of Malaysia. It thus helps to promote the territory of the relatively young nation of Malaysia and establish it on the international stage. The Petronas Towers designed by Caesar Pelli in Kuala Lumpur provide much more accommodation than Petronas actually needed. They have already started to become the symbol of the nation and to appear on tourist guides in the way the Eiffel Tower does for Paris.

Plate 14 Another deck access housing scheme in Sheffield. Here the decks pass the living rooms, which are fully glazed onto them. The emphasis is no longer on privacy, and the occupants 'own' the decks as a consequence. If you walk along these decks or stop to take a photograph, you must first engage in conversation with the occupants and feel obliged to ask their permission.

Complicated		simple
dark		light
private		public
happy		sad
feminine		masculine
warm		cool
informal		formal
soft		hard
heavy		light
small		large
closed		open
smooth		rough
full		empty

Plate 15 Two bars in a suburban English public house. The semantic differential shows that these two bars create very similar places with little 'psychological distance' between them.

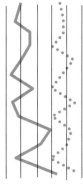

complicated		simple
dark		light
private		public
happy		sad
feminine		masculine
warm		cool
informal		formal
soft		hard
heavy		light
small		large
closed		open
smooth		rough
full		empty

Plate 16 Two more bars from another pub in the same town. This time the 'psychological distance' between them is much greater. The semantic differential can thus offer a tool for measuring and discussing the differences between places.

5.12 Students filling up a lecture theatre so as to maintain 'public' distance from their lecturer

formal evening dinner jackets complete with florid buttonholes! This caused great hilarity, but of course I was delighted because it meant they had paid attention the previous week.

At my university we built a new departmental building which had its own lecture theatre. In a survey conducted by one of my students, lecturers who used it thought it to be the best on the campus. Astonishingly, the students thought exactly the opposite and disliked it intensely. How can one space be seen so differently? Curiously, the likes and dislikes were for almost exactly the same reason. This lecture theatre is fan-shaped, with very long back rows and rather short front rows. For this reason, although it holds many students it feels to the lecturer like a theatre holding under half that number. No student is very far away, since it is fairly shallow front to back. As a lecturer you feel 'in touch' with your audience; you get feedback from them, can sense whether or not they are paying attention, and can probably even tell how well they understand your lecture. For those of you who have never lectured, please understand that this is very important to us teachers and extremely reassuring! Being modern and well equipped there are no windows in this theatre, so there are no blinds to operate, and all the other controls are centrally located at the lectern. It seems perfectly designed as an efficient and comfortable space.

However, look at it now through the students' eyes. We know many prefer to be in the back rows to achieve long public distance from the lecturer, but here they are not very far back and these rows are much longer than the front rows. Since it is usually the end seats that fill first (more of that in the next chapter), this causes much inconvenience as the latecomers arrive. The latecomers feel self-conscious about asking people to stand and let them into empty seats in the back rows when all can see that there are plenty of empty seats further forward to which they could get without inconveniencing others. Even after all this the students at the back feel uncomfortably under the stare of the lecturer, perhaps a little like animals caged in the zoo. Unlike the lecturer who comes to deliver a one-hour talk and then leaves, the students spend several hours at a stretch in this theatre. Even in the gaps between lectures there is no window to look out of, and they feel incarcerated. Now one argument might have it that the students are there to learn so they should not complain, but I doubt this really holds good. Most lecturers, this one included, overestimate the attention span of their students. Perhaps a moment or too spent looking out of the window might refresh the mind, which otherwise grows stale and then wanders off altogether in the darkened isolated space of this machine-like lecture theatre.

It is hard for the architect to get all this right. The well-known architect James Stirling, probably remembering his own student days, designed a large raked lecture theatre at Leicester University that had a rear entrance to allow the latecomers in at the back. The theatre was cantilevered out into outdoor space so this entrance was served by a stairway in a vertical glass tube. I am told by some who have used this theatre that on windy days, the tube acted rather like an organ pipe, and as the door opened a deep booming sound could be heard. Hardly the way to creep in late!

We have learned from this about another crucial characteristic of distance in human relationships. We have discovered that not all relationships are reciprocal and we have identified the need to see distance from both points of view. Curiously, human distances, unlike physical ones, are not equal when viewed from opposite ends! Again, a fuller discussion of that must wait for the next chapter.

Personality and context variation
Perhaps the most obvious example of the use of public distance is when a politician or public figure speaks at a political rally. You will notice that not only is the voice raised, with a greater range of dynamics, but also there is very clear emphasis and the use of repetition to create redundancy to ensure the simple message gets across even if there is a noisy background. The gestures are likely to have moved from hands and upper arms to using the complete arm. Film of Arthur Scargill, the leader of the miner's trade union in the United Kingdom, illustrates this behaviour perfectly. He had a habit of reinforcing his impor-

tant points with a downward movement of the arm from the elbow as if chopping some imaginary log. After several 'chops' with one arm he would usually change to the other one! Historic footage of Hitler speaking at his rallies shows someone highly skilled in using public distance. It is an irony of our public life that the people who can command attention and respect at public distance are not necessarily those who have a personality we might look for in colleagues or friends. They are often not burdened too much with doubt or uncertainty, which is particularly hard to communicate at long distance. For this reason I find that politicians tend to speak as if the world were much simpler than it ever can be. We go away from the great end-of-conference address by our political leader feeling charged up and optimistic. As real life kicks back in most of us begin to see its complexities and contradictions again, but we have already voted for the simplistic policies that can never succeed! Of course television has altered all this. The skill of speaking close up in an interview on television is much less one of using public distance and more one of near social distance with the interviewer. Alarmingly, when you have to do this, and then see the broadcast, you also realize too late that for the audience sitting at home you will be effectively even as close as personal distance. This has undoubtedly undone some politicians unable to adapt to the wide range of skills needed. The American president Richard Nixon was, for example, quite commanding at public distance, and yet somehow appeared insincere and untrustworthy at the personal distance of television close-up.

We find some people who really have never quite learned the rules of interpersonal distance. We probably all have a colleague or associate who is somehow just too familiar; the person who stands far too close when engaging you in conversation and seems insensitive to your backing away. I had a colleague who was notorious for this and on one occasion was astonished to find that I had backed all the way down a short corridor during our conversation, only to end up trapped against a doorway! (Fig. 5.13). By contrast, studies of patients with certain psychological disorders and of violent criminals all show larger than normal personal distance. In particular, studies in prisons have shown that inmates with a history of violent crime as compared with those whose crimes are entirely non-violent show personal distances of up to four times larger (Hildreth, Derogatis and McCusker 1971). This work suggests that such individuals feeling a greater insecurity as they are approached are also more likely to show aggression and to feel less empathy with their victims.

I once went to give a lecture at a conference at the huge International Conference Centre in Berlin. The Germans are generally more formal in their use of distance than the British, as we shall see later. I was given very specific instructions by post not to use the main

5.13 The conversation between the two people in the middle of this picture actually began much further up the street. The person on the right gradually retreated as the one on the left advanced. The folded arms signal a defensive posture, further indicating the feeling of an unwelcome invasion of personal space

entrance to the building but to come around the side where I would find a speaker's entrance marked, as in the manner of a stage door. The organizers clearly felt it important to maintain a distance between the speaker and the audience at least until after the event. As I result I was brought into the huge 2000-seat lecture hall through a door at the front, and after lecturing was taken away again by the same route. After a very short pause I was then very carefully taken by my hosts up an escalator along the building and then down another escalator. This last escalator descended through a large void into the space where the audience was now taking refreshment, so I felt rather as if I was appearing from some higher existence in a somewhat Wagnerian way! My host took me straight to a table and poured me a drink, but I noticed that the audience still maintained a degree of public distance. Quite soon, however, a brave soul, who turned out to be British, came and started to talk to me. It was not long into our conversation before I noticed that a more general crowd had now gathered around. The public nature of my duty was at last finally over, and I could interact with people like an ordinary human being! After the crowd had cleared and I went back to gather my slides I realized just how carefully this

5.14   The ICC in Berlin. This building is carefully organized to allow for great ritual in maintaining 'public' distance for speakers in a very formal way. Germans seem particularly fond of this way of dealing with space

whole building was designed to engineer exactly the effect I had experienced both through its plan and its section (Fig. 5.14).

My hosts at this event had to manufacture all this public distance carefully for me, although I would very much have preferred they did not. For really important people this seems to happen automatically. Just as we observe that dominant animals have larger personal distances, so very important people are often afforded public distance by others. Hall quotes a description from Theodore White's book *The Making of the President*. This describes the moment it became apparent that John F. Kennedy would win the nomination to run for President of the United States of America (Hall 1966). Even senior politicians of the day suddenly gave him a greater distance at a social gathering:

The others in the room surged forward on impulse to join him. Then they halted. A distance of perhaps 20 feet [7 metres] separated them from him, but it was impassable.

By contrast, interpersonal distances can also be reduced by context. Sommer amusingly quotes a newspaper excerpt in which the owner of a suburban cinema noted the differences in the densities of queues waiting to see a film. He calculated that when a film like *Tom Jones* was showing, the foyer would accommodate about three times as many people in the queue compared with a film like *Mary Poppins* (Sommer 1969).

Cultural variation

When in the Middle East and as far west as Turkey we find a much greater acceptance of bodily contact in public. Indeed the average European or American is likely to feel rudely jostled in cities like Istanbul. To be in public spaces in such cities is a much more socially intense experience than one is likely to find in most European cities. Not only do passers by frequently bump into you and move on without acknowledgement, but traders trying to sell you their wares come well inside our normally acceptable distances and may even lay hands on you to guide you further into their premises. Burgoon and Saine go so far as to describe some countries as having 'contact cultures', which appears to contradict the usual assumption that the whole human race is a non-contact species. They cite Central America, Arab states and India as examples of contact cultures (Burgoon and Saine 1978). Although most work on interpersonal distance has been conducted in the West, some studies of cultural variations have confirmed what the experience of travelling tells one more intuitively. Watson and Graves, for example, studied students at American colleges and found that ethnically Arab students would interact at closer distances than their American counterparts (Watson and Graves 1966). Similarly, Aiello and Jones have shown closer distances for black and Puerto Rican children compared with indigenous white children (Aiello and Jones 1971). Sadly, however, little quantitative work has taken place actually in non-western countries into the variation of interpersonal distance with culture.

Edward T. Hall learned about the human use of space partly through his experience of observing different cultures. For a while he had the unenviable job of training Americans how to behave overseas! We Europeans sometimes mock Americans for their cultural isolation. In truth of course the North American continent is as culturally rich as anywhere else, but so many Americans never leave this continent that they can often seem rather ignorant and rude when they do. Hall points out that much of what we have come to accept as a global theory of interpersonal distance actually enshrines many cultural norms. North America and north-west European cultures seem to share much in common in terms of the notions of public and private and how we relate to both acquaintances and strangers in public space. Hall argues rightly that the four distances of intimate, personal, social and public space are to some extent a reflection of those cultural norms. Such a taxonomy cannot, for example, accommodate behaviour subject to the caste system in India.

Spatial manners then are ultimately a cultural phenomenon, but underlying them all are some fundamental issues of the way we perceive space and sense the presence of others in it. However our story is not yet complete, since we have really only considered the distance component of the language of space in any detail. As we have seen, people will tolerate close proximity even of strangers in public under certain circumstances such as sitting in the theatre. The story is spatially and socially much more complex than a consideration solely of distance would suggest.

References

Aiello, J. R and T. D. C. Jones (1971). Field study of proxemic behaviour of young schoolchildren in three subcultural groups. *Journal of Personality and Social Psychology* **19**: 351–356.

Burgoon, J. K. and T. Saine (1978). *The Unspoken Dialogue*. Boston, Houghton Mifflin.

Hall, E. T. (1966). *The Hidden Dimension*. London, Bodley Head.

Hediger, H. (1955). *Studies of the Psychology and Behaviour of Captive Animals in Zoos and Circuses*. London, Butterworth.

Hildreth, A. M., L. R. Derogatis, et al. (1971). Body-buffer zones and violence: a reassessment and confirmation. *American Journal of Psychiatry* **127**: 1641–1645.

Mitchell, W. J. (1995). *City of Bits*. Cambridge, Mass., MIT Press.

Mitchell, W. J. (1999). *E-topia*. Cambridge, Mass., MIT Press.

Morris, D. (1969). *The Human Zoo*. London, Jonathan Cape.

Negroponte, N. (1995). *Being Digital*. London, Hodder and Stoughton.

Sommer, R. (1969). Personal Space: *The Behavioural Basis of Design*. Englewood Cliffs, Prentice Hall.

Watson, O. M. and T. D. Graves (1966). Quantitative research in proxemic behaviour. *American Anthropologist* **68**: 971–985.

6 Proxemics

Architecture is a gesture. Not every purposive movement of the human body is a gesture. And no more is every building designed for a purpose architecture.

Wittgenstein

Whatever space and time mean, place and occasion mean more. For space in the image of man is place, and time in the image of man is occasion.

Aldo Van Eyck

Non-verbal communication

We are fortunate that the great philosopher Wittgenstein developed an interest in architecture. As a result he left behind many interesting thoughts on the subject from a rather different perspective to that of the architect. Those of his words that head this chapter are particularly apposite in this context. Wittgenstein drew a clear distinction between architecture and the lesser concept, as he saw it, of mere building. In that distinction it is the expressive quality of architecture – one might say those aspects which might also make it art as opposed to craft – upon which Wittgenstein concentrates. Gesture can be raised to the very great heights of art in the form of dance, most particularly ballet; so building can also become high art in the form of architecture, seems to be the message. Wittgenstein also claimed that: 'where there is nothing to glorify there can be no architecture'. This argument might be taken to mean that the everyday building should not be considered architecture, which would seem to conflict with normal usage of the word. Wittgenstein's words are, however, doubly apposite here, since it is also interesting for us to distinguish between gesture and communication. Clearly when we use spoken or written language we intend to communicate, and when we use gesture we also intend communication without necessarily extending it to the high art of dance. However, whatever we do as we move around and position ourselves in space may result in communication even if we do not intend it. The fascination of non-verbal communication is that much of it is involuntary and even may reveal feelings or attitudes we would rather conceal. The distinguished film animator Rex Grignon, who worked on the trailblazing films *Toy Story* and *Antz*, summarizes this perfectly when talking to students. He tells them that: 'the real test of an animator is not whether he can move a character around on screen ... but whether, purely through its actions and gestures, he can make the audience believe that a character does not necessarily mean what it says'.

The way we use space is not a simple mechanical matter of distance. The language we use to communicate through bodily gesture in space and occupation of space is a powerful, subtle and complex one. The idea of body language became fairly familiar probably after it was popularized by Julius Fast (Fast 1971). Since then body language has become an everyday concept, and at least one national newspaper runs a regular feature in which photographs of some well-known personalities appearing in public are analysed. We are told how their postures and gestures actually reveal quite different relationships to those we have been given to believe by the publicity. Of course such assertions are never actually tested! Some observers have claimed that at least 75 per cent of all communication is non-verbal (Trompenaars and Hampden-Turner 1997), but this is rather difficult to quantify and so we must be rather cautious about such extravagant claims. However, those who try to do business, especially in foreign cultures, entirely by relying on the telephone or e-mail will soon realize that non-verbal communication is certainly not trivial!

Certainly body language is now far more than a diverting entertainment; it is used in highly professional ways to achieve quite serious objectives. Advertisers make extensive use of body language to communicate their message. A simple review of television and magazine advertisements shows many subliminal messages conveyed this way. An advertisement for a now rather old-fashioned sunlamp illustrates the point beautifully (Plate 10). There are two groups of people sitting at separate outdoor tables, chatting and drinking. They are all wearing beach clothes. One group is tanned and obviously has access to the advertised sunlamp, while the others are pale skinned and clearly do not. The unfortunate ones have tightly closed mouths while their tanned counterparts smile and show their teeth; the pale ones sit with hands clasped defensively in front of them whilst the lucky ones use open postures with limbs splayed out. The tanned ones turn their whole bodies to engage with their friends and clearly therefore benefit from social interaction, while the unfortunate pale skinned and thus miserable creatures turn only their heads and interact with no one, sitting instead isolated in their lonely worlds. Finally, in a totally non-behavioural finishing touch to the misery, the two glasses on the pale-skinned table are empty. On the tanned table not only are the glasses full of delicious orange juice, but they even have the jug too! Get a sunlamp, get a life!

As an amusing footnote to this, we might remind ourselves of the absurdity of the desirability of a tanned skin. Not only is this probably bad for your health, but it is also an entirely culturally determined fashion. This advertisement appeared in Britain, which has a temperate north-west European climate. In Singapore, which has a hot, wet, tropical climate, similar sorts of advertisements can be seen in the newspapers, although these are not selling sun lamps but chemical agents that it is claimed whiten the skin. Such is the nature of human vanity!

This enables us to see that advertisers often rely not on selling a product directly but instead try to attract us to their products by selling lifestyles or life situations. An ingenious advertisement for a dress shows it in three different colours (Plate 11). However, it goes much further than simply colour. The names of the colours and the body postures of the model change to evoke three quite distinct life situations. Buy all three and your life will be complete seems to be the message here! The model wearing 'delicious burgundy' is a working girl, and so she wears her sleeves tugged up ready for business. She wears a blouse under her dress and clutches a handbag modestly in front of her. She displays a pleasant but closed-mouth smile. She is business-like and confident but not overly assertive, and thus thoroughly likeable, dependable and unthreatening. She will get on easily with everybody as well as getting the job done. When the same model dons the 'after dusk pink' dress, she behaves quite differently. Here she pulls her sleeves down and looks much more assertive with one arm akimbo. Her smile is open-mouthed, and she is obviously having fun! Finally the scene changes yet again in 'very late black'. Now, added to the one arm akimbo, there is the touching of a minor erogenous zone, the earlobe. The hair is worn up, telling us that she has deliberately worked on her appearance and intends it to have an effect. The revealing of a leg through the split skirt daringly and suggestively shows more body. So we have a dress for three quite different occasions; you only have to put it on and magically the desired behavioural setting will materialize. The secure well paid job, the busy social life or the dashing elegant male companion will appear as if conjured by the genie from the body language bottle!

A foreign correspondent for a television company described to me how he interpreted the mood of the British Queen when she was travelling abroad by they way she carried her handbag. If it was down by her side, it revealed that she was comfortable and at ease, whereas if it was clutched across in front of her it suggested that she was less sure of her situation. Followers of the British political scene may recall that, as Prime Minister, Margaret Thatcher always seemed to carry her handbag at full arm's length as if ready to hit someone with it if needs be!

Jo-Ellan Dimitrius has made her living by selecting jurors for legal trials in the USA. Lawyers for the defence can challenge potential jurors and, through questioning, demonstrate that they are unsuitable for the trial. In reality of course the defence lawyers are seeking to find jurors who they most expect to be sympathetic to their client. To do this they need to find those with values and experiences that lead them to feel some empathy either with accused people in general or with the particular situation that their client is in. Perhaps most famously, if not notoriously, Jo-Ellan Dimitrius helped to select the jury that acquitted O. J. Simpson. She works by studying a whole series of factors of both verbal and non-verbal behaviour, which over the years she has associated with certain personality types, political sympathies and social attitudes. Her book *Reading People* shows just how advanced and reliable this science of non-verbal behaviour is, and how much we reveal about ourselves unwittingly simply by dressing and by moving about in and occupying space (Dimitrius and Marzzarella 1998).

Spatially defined roles

Our concern here is not so much with dress or the minor facial expression end of body language, but more to do with those aspects of non-verbal behaviour such as the way we arrange ourselves in space in relation to others. The populist student of human behaviour, Desmond Morris, suggests that we can change the result of conflicts by using the right spatial behavioural signals (Morris 1969). He advises the driver caught by the police for a minor motoring offence to behave submissively rather than aggressively. According to Morris, our response to appeasement behaviour is deep seated. He believes there is a strong biological predisposition to be appeased by submissive behaviour. Certainly this can be observed through the animal kingdom. On this basis Morris advises the motorist stopped by police not to respond by arguing his or her innocence, a natural intellectual approach but one that then forces the police into confrontation and counterattack, but rather to use the more biological strategy of submission:

If abject submission is adopted, it will become increasingly difficult for the police officer to avoid a sensation of appeasement. A total admission of guilt based on sheer stupidity and inferiority puts the policeman into a position of immediate dominance from which it is difficult for him to attack ... But words are not enough. The appropriate postures and gestures must be added. Fear and submission in both body posture and facial expression must be clearly demonstrated.

As we shall see in the next chapter on territorial behaviour, dominance and social hierarchy are not only extraordinarily widespread across species but are usually related to possession of locations in space. This leads Morris to his final advice to the would-be submissive motorist:

> Above all, it is essential to get quickly out of the car and move away from it towards the policeman ... by staying in the car you are remaining in your own territory. By moving away from it you are automatically weakening your territorial status.

Morris has clearly followed his own advice, since in a more recent book (Morris 2000) tells of how the trick stopped working after he revealed it during a television interview! However, he was still able to appease sailors who he cut up while sailing in Malta with that other great student of behaviour, David Attenborough. But beware! This advice should perhaps be modified by at least two caveats. First, the unnatural or forced use of body posture by the unskilled is rarely convincing in my experience. A colleague who told me he tried to use Morris's advice found himself in deeper trouble when the police were stopping people at a roadblock after a murder. His rather self-conscious and thus too rapid escape from the car and advance towards the policeman was interpreted as an attack, and so he was brought to the ground and searched for weapons! Secondly, the application of discretion in response to law breaking is itself overlaid with cultural complexities. Hall points out that in Europe or America the policeman may choose to listen to your apologies and pleas for indulgence and, recognizing your otherwise good behaviour, let you off with a warning (Hall 1959). However, in Africa or Asia this is unlikely to happen since policemen there do not culturally have such discretion, although they may, in some cases, be bribed. On the other hand, in these cultures the judge may take account of your good reputation or family background and dismiss the case against you, whereas in a European court the evidence would have to be heard, considered and the inevitable verdict reached.

The phenomenon of dominance and submission as methods of controlling aggression is commonplace in animal societies, but has progressively become disguised in human society. This is a complex issue, but is largely related to our increasingly technological way of waging war. The more removed we become from seeing signs of submission and from the consequences of continued aggression, the easier it is for us to persist with violence. The pilot in the military aircraft has no sense of the awful consequences of the missiles he releases. I remember when I was a young research student that my professor of the time was working on a number of military research contracts. He was advising on the ergonomics of the famous Chieftain tank, which had been modified to isolate the occupants in case of nuclear or chemical attack. He had noticed that since this happened the operators had become distinctly less responsive to commands from outside the vehicle in the theatre of war.

It has long been recognized that we need to use modified conversational techniques to replace the lost non-verbal communication when holding telephone conversations. Just watch any of your friends or colleagues talking on the telephone, and you frequently see them grimacing and gesturing pointlessly at the unoccupied space in front of them! However, I believe that e-mail has created yet another, possibly more dangerous, hazard. One of the best pieces of advice that can be offered in the business world is always to sleep on an angry letter – never respond in the heat of the moment, as it were. E-mail, though, removes the old delay of waiting to dictate or type a letter, and invites immediate reply. Moreover the now common accepted 'netiquette' promotes a terseness of style. I had several colleagues in a research team who were located many miles apart and used e-mail for basic communication. On several occasions I have had to call a face-to-face meeting simply to calm down the levels of aggression that were building up in the e-mails. On the first occasion I was quite apprehensive about how the meeting would go, since recent messages had been extremely hostile with several parties effectively claiming they could no longer work with other members of the team. I had no need for concern, however, since as they sat at the round table in my room they all behaved respectfully and politely and there was no hint of the previously expressed aggression and frustration! We have yet to see just how well video-conferencing can solve such problems, but for now at least the spatial co-location of people is still essential in allowing for the rich communication that lies beyond words. Both distance and actual arrangement in space come together in what is now known as 'proxemics'. The way we arrange ourselves in space has much to do with relationships, whether in the short term or over rather longer periods. In particular it reflects the roles we play in those relationships.

Spatial roles

Imagine two people playing chess, or negotiating a deal (Fig. 6.1). These are examples of what we might call 'reciprocal confrontational' roles; neither person is necessarily superior to the other, and yet each is seeing the world from a different perspective. In such situations people will naturally want this to be reflected in their arrangement in space. They will want to sit facing each other, and probably across a table. Imagine how awkward it would be if you were in tough negotiations with someone and yet had to sit alongside them on a sofa! Even in practical terms this would be problematic, as you could hardly make or consult notes without them being read by your opponent. We might call this role the 'confronting' role, for shortness. If one person changes the spatial organization it is quite possible to put the other at a disadvantage in the confrontation – perhaps, for example, sitting with your back to a window so that your opponent's face is well illuminated and

6.1 The 'confronting' role. When two people are in conflict, even if only in a game, they symbolically view the world from opposing angles, conceal any private information, and look searchingly into each other's eyes

yours is concealed by glare. Sitting higher up or on a more upright chair gives you a degree of concentration that comes from the bodily memory of the posture. A colleague of mine who was professor of economics once surprised me by delivering a formal lecture standing at the front of the platform with his toes over the edge of the stage. He talked for an hour without notes, simply standing with hands clasped behind his back. He later explained that he had found over the years that standing in this way kept him mentally alert and sharper in the development of his argument. It also seemed to me to have the added benefit of keeping the audience's concentration too. Though they would not admit it, many were really watching to see if he would fall off the platform!

Professional interviewers know these and many more tricks postural tricks, which they use to their advantage. They can be observed simply by watching rather than just listening to television interviews. Clive Anderson, who is trained as a barrister, hosts a television show in the UK in which he specializes in repartee that often gently mocks and denigrates his guests. He generally sits behind a desk while they sit exposed on a lone chair. David Frost when famously interviewing the then Prime Minister Margaret Thatcher seemed to catch her quite off guard at the end of a long interview. She was provided with a very easy reclining sofa, but had countered this by deliberately sitting bolt upright on the edge of the seat throughout. It was widely thought at the time that she had been receiving voice training to lower the tone of her voice to create a sense of gravitas, and it seems highly likely she was also advised about posture. Frost appeared to reach his peroration and effectively ended the encounter by announcing a break for a news summary and thanked her for agreeing to the interview. However, after the break he was still alert and suddenly asked the most penetrating question of the interview. By now she had relaxed back into the sofa and as a result probably said more than she had intended. This section of the interview made the evening news and was widely debated and quoted for some considerable time.

A quite different role relationship might be two people sitting at a table in a café for a morning coffee, travelling together on a train or waiting together to see the doctor. Again in such roles they are reciprocal, but this time there is no sense of confronting and rather more one of 'consorting' (Fig. 6.2). They might perhaps be colleagues who are early for a meeting with a potential customer. There may be no particularly focused task to perform, but they want to see the world from the same

6.2   The 'consorting' role. When two people are conversing or collaborating, they tend to arrange themselves to 'see the world from the same perspective'. In this case the table only has room for one seat on each side, so these two sit around the corner and then lean towards each other to look at documents and a computer

point of view. In most cases we find such a relationship more likely to be expressed by a sitting alongside or perhaps around the corner of a table. I have observed that a shorter-term romantic involvement is much more likely to lead to people sitting opposite as they signal their obsession with each other by looking into their partner's eyes. A longer-term relationship causes this need to wane and to be replaced by a wish to share the same view of other people who inevitably form a major topic of the conversation! This eliminates the need for that most awkward of prefaces to a remark, 'don't look round now but that woman opposite is ...'!

A more extreme form of this consorting is what we might call 'collaborating'. Here the two involved need to work on some project together. Perhaps we have a design student and her tutor looking at some drawings and sketching new ideas, or we might have some business colleagues looking over some financial figures. Here the need to view some specific features of the external world make an even stronger force to draw them to sit alongside each other.

Another particular form of consorting is the conversation. People 'conversing' are likely to want to see each other's faces to enhance the communication through all those important facial expressions. Sommer showed this through experiments that involved sofas facing each other in a lounge. People wishing to sit and talk together sat facing each other, one on each sofa. However, as the experimenters moved the sofas further apart the distance of normal conversation was stretched too far. Once the sofas were moved over a metre apart the heads of those relaxing in them would now be at least 2 metres apart, and at this distance more people began choosing to sit alongside each other on the same sofa. Distance and proxemics thus interact (Fig. 6.3).

Finally, let's think about a common role relationship that needs designing for and so often is not. Consider two strangers on a train sharing a seating bay, two students at university sharing a table in a library reading room, or two unrelated patients in a doctor's waiting room. All these situations involve people who have a relationship solely because they find themselves sharing a space. We might call this 'co-existing'. Such a relationship is best expressed by a reciprocal arrangement diagonally separated to minimize eye contact. This setting causes more trouble than all the others put together. Imagine the scenario I frequently experience as I board the train after a meeting in London to travel back to my home town in the evening. The coaches have a central corridor and bays of seats facing each other across tables on either side (Fig. 6.4). In second class there are bays of four seats on each side, and in first class four on one side and two on the other. The station, like all major ones in London, is a terminus, so passengers all approach from the back end of the train. Many start walking up a coach and begin their search for an empty seating bay. If successful they will sit down.

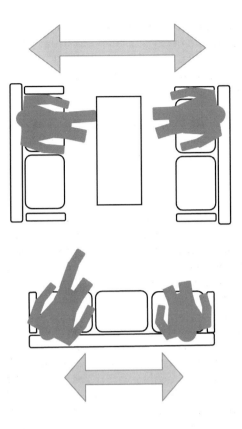

6.3 The 'conversational' role. Two opposing sofas allow for looking into each other's faces and thus reading all the non-verbal expression. However, when the two sofas get too far apart to see this clearly, people chose instead to sit on the same sofa and turn to face each other. In such a case a three-seater sofa allows for personal rather than intimate distance! (After Robert Sommer)

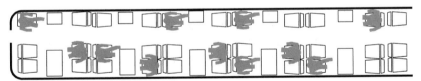

6.4 The 'co-existing' role. A typical railway train layout. Note how people generally adopt the 'co-acting' role if they are alone. This allows them to ignore each other without rudeness, and here even the empty seats actually perform an important spatial role

If not, they turn around to move back towards the rear of the train and begin looking for a bay with only one other person. When this is found they often ask the occupant the most ridiculous question – 'is anyone sitting here?' they say, pointing to the patently empty seat diagonally opposite. Although ludicrous if taken at face value, this British politeness has enabled them to invade what up to then was clearly regarded by the incumbent as their temporary territory. The enforced reply of 'no, I don't think so' acknowledges and accepts the invasion. Thus a modified behavioural setting is created in which both participants have acknowledged the enforced breaking of the conventional rules associated with the 'co-existing' role.

Let us continue with our railway train scenario for a short while. As the train begins to fill, we find that frequently territories are marked out by the apparently casual depositing of a briefcase or jacket on some of the unoccupied seats. Soon all the bays are fully occupied by 'co-existing' individuals sitting diagonally opposite one another, and the seat hunters start coming back down the train and reducing their standards of territorial independence. Those progressing up the train in search of a good seat get panicked by seeing them coming in the opposite direction, and are stealing the next free seats. This whole farcical comedy is played out nightly on dozens of trains departing the capital. If viewed from above by some all-seeing superior creature we would look like nothing so much as colonies of demented ants lugging briefcases and bags in an apparently pointless and doomed ritual of puzzling compulsion. In the end most seats get taken, as the train is very popular, so the ritual fails to create a result any different from a logical filling up from the back. Of course the idea that we might behave so logically is inconceivable!

This scenario of a train is rich in attempts to defend space from invasion. Observation shows that passengers vary greatly regarding the extent to which they might be seen as offensive rather than defensive in their behaviour. The most defensive will retire to a window seat, put their luggage on the rack overhead and place their immediate needs for the journey, such as books, neatly on the table directly in front of them. The more offensive characters will sit in an aisle seat, isolating an empty window seat beyond them. Their bags and coats will then be strewn on the window seat and sometimes even on the seat opposite too. Their papers and other belongings are spread out over the whole table. Typically I find two other forms of behaviour with a common aim of defence are often employed at least until the train leaves the station. The first pattern is characterized by spreading out the evening paper and poring over it in a very concentrated way, and the second involves making a series of telephone calls to colleagues or friends. The content of these conversations can frequently be overheard, and I have rarely noted that any of these conversations result in the receipt or transmission of important or useful knowledge; they are even less likely to result in an action being agreed. The main purpose it seems of both these actions is to avoid eye contact with another passenger who may try to invade the seating bay. It is much more difficult to ask the incumbent if a seat is free when he or she is engaged in a telephone conversation!

Sommer reports a series of more rigorous studies in which his researchers systematically collected empirical data of similar behaviour in university library reading rooms (Sommer 1969). Various personal belongings were used to spread around the tables to defend seats, and in some cases the experimenter would depart the table altogether, leaving behind a pile of books, a jacket or other such belongings. In general, it was found that the more valuable the defensive place marker, the longer it would defend the seat from invasion. In another experiment the researcher would ask a neighbour to save his chair while he was gone. Here less valuable markers would still enable the willing neighbour to defend the seat, although this tailed off with the length of absence. It is also interesting to note that the neighbour's willingness to defend the seat was increased if the researcher had first struck up some inconsequential conversation, such as asking the time.

All too often the provision in spaces such as library reading rooms is unimaginatively of four- or six-seater tables, which appear full to the co-existing readers when only one or two people are sitting at them. In such a reading room studied by one of my students, only just before the semester examinations did these tables actually get fully occupied – in spite of planning data books recommending such layouts to architects as yielding the highest density arrangement. This is another example of space considered in the abstract with no acknowledgement of spatial behaviour. If only people were machines, planning would be so much simpler!

Sommer's now famous study of all this also involved action research by Nancy Russo. To do this work, she must have spent many hours sitting either too close to people or in inappropriate spatial configurations to them. It is a very odd way to earn a living! The experiments took a standard form of observing individuals in a university library reading room. They had already observed the patterns of behaviour described above – that is to say, new occupants of the room would seek to space themselves out as evenly as possible, keeping maximum distances between themselves and other occupants. Typically readers would each occupy their own separate table, sitting at a chair at the end of one side. Avoiding any cross-gender behavioural implications, Nancy Russo would choose to occupy another chair at a table already occupied by a single female reader. Sometimes she sat alongside the victim, sometimes directly opposite, and so on. These invasions of space were then shown to drive the poor victim away more quickly than expected. Hardly surprisingly, sitting next to the victim and moving her chair even closer was the most effective invasion of all!

By comparison, the great Charles Rennie Mackintosh showed how it could be done in the library of the Glasgow School of Art. Mackintosh is sometimes mistakenly thought to be a decorator, whereas in fact he was a brilliant place maker. Study tables are always located in relation to other building elements. The great windows that rise so dramatically up the great west façade have heavily splayed and recessed reveals which naturally serve also to locate a table, and beyond them the columns that support the balconies above further help to create places. Where study tables are out in the centre of the space, Mackintosh gives them low screens to blank off the stare from those facing each other. A tiny obscured glass panel informs the occupant of a neighbour's presence without revealing more or causing distraction. None of Mackintosh's tables or reading positions are just anywhere; they are all places carefully located in space. You can go there and 'belong' for a little while in your own special and entirely appropriate place.

These three main roles of 'confronting', 'consorting', and 'co-existing', with the major variants of 'consorting' in the forms of 'conversing' and 'collaborating', help to map out many of the common spatial situations in which people have to relate to each other in close proximity. A study quoted by Sommer shows just how strongly these role settings influence spatial behaviour, and one of my students has found almost identical results (Fig. 6.5). Here we must imagine a six-seater rectangular table with two seats on each long side and one at each end, and one person already seated at one of the side seats. Sommer's statistics show the frequency with which people chose each of the available seats when coming into this situation. We can see that the role definitions used by Sommer are very similar to the ones used here. This is one of the features of the language of space that is extremely well understood and to which very strong conventions are attached.

Sociofugal and sociopetal space

We shall now move our enquiry on to consider situations where more than two people are involved. I am indebted to Herman Hertzberger's analysis of Gaudi's Parc Guell in Barcelona (Hertzberger 1991). The romantic curved parapets also provide sitting places (Fig. 6.6). Gaudi cleverly designed the balustrade itself to be the back support for continuous seating. However this whole assembly snakes backwards and forwards in a series of reversed 'U' bends. Gaudi's use of these alternating convex and concave curves naturally creates places for people to congregate and consort where the curve is concave, or to remain more private and co-exist where the curve is convex. As one moves along this arrangement one can see groups gathered in the concave parts talking animatedly and more solitary figures on the convex parts simply watching the world go by. Whether Gaudi consciously engineered this brilliant behavioural setting, implicitly understood it, or achieved the effect accidentally we shall probably never know.

In effect, what Gaudi has created here are alternating areas of what Osmond first called 'sociopetal' and 'sociofugal' space (Osmond 1959). These words are ingeniously woven together based upon the Latin *centripetus*, which literally means seeking the centre. So sociopetal space

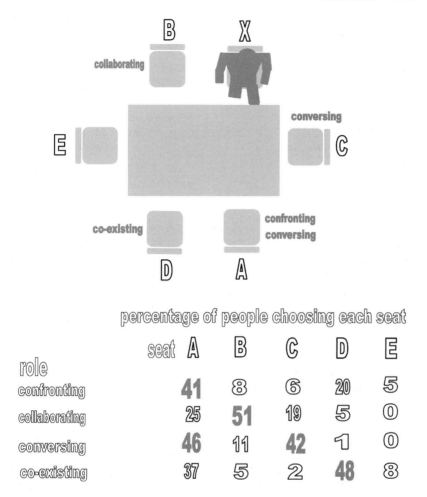

6.5 Statistics showing how the most popular choice of seat is related to spatial roles. This six-seater table has one person already sitting in seat 'X'. Which seat would you choose if you were (A) going to compete at a game, (B) share notes on some papers before a meeting, (C) have a cup of coffee and a chat, (D) work independently in a library? (an experiment replicating work by Sommer)

is that which tends to draw people together, and sociofugal space is that which tends to throw them apart just as centrifugal force throws objects away from the centre of a spinning axis. Actually Osmond could have a claim to be the father of this whole field. His concern about the extent to which patients in a geriatric ward were communicating started all these investigations and gave Robert Sommer the chance to begin the work that was to be reported in his seminal book, *Personal Space*.

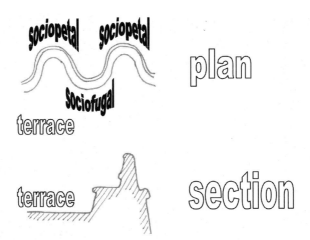

6.6 'Sociofugal' and 'sociopetal' space for sitting, brilliantly provided by Gaudi in his Barcelona Parc Guell. People can choose to sit in groups and converse in the concave segments (socipetal), or individuals can sit in relative isolation, perhaps reading or simply contemplating the scene in the convex segments (sociofugal)

Clearly some spaces are intended to create settings that are particularly sociopetal or sociofugal in their effect. Outdoor places that provide an opportunity for people to gather round and chat can become well known meeting places and greatly enrich urban life. An excellent and much frequented example is the tiers of curved spaces provided at the junction of Scotts and Orchard Roads in the centre of Singapore (Fig. 6.7). Also providing shade from the sun and shelter from the occasional tropical storm, these simple spaces adjacent to sources of food and drink are extremely popular. I have never once passed this spot and failed to see animated conversation. One sometimes thinks the whole of Singaporean youth culture must be run from here!

A more formal and obviously sociopetal setting might be a table for a dinner party. The whole purpose of the event is to bring the people together, and in fact the food is often in reality simply the excuse for this social communing. It seems a very human and particularly English failing not to be able to invite people simply to be close for the sheer sake of it. We need some sort of excuse for it, and to pretend that the food at the dinner table is the real reason. So this table, unlike the business meeting table, is one to bring people closer rather than to hold them apart. It should focus on its centre, and perhaps the round table is the most sociopetal of all! We might surround our table with those wonderful high-backed chairs designed by Charles Rennie Mackintosh originally for Miss Cranston's tearooms in Glasgow. They would

6.7   A whole series of 'sociopetal' spaces that provide ideal opportunities for impromptu outdoor gatherings. In the tropical climate of Singapore, these also provide the basic need of shelter and shade from the sun

beautifully emphasize the purpose of the setting by creating an implied wall around the seated group. We might choose to turn down the main room lights and just illuminate the table. Perhaps this is why candles are still so popular on the dining table long after the advent of electricity – they provide a very localized light that further draws attention to the centre through its delightful and capricious unsteadiness.

Dining rooms in restaurants often fail in this duty to be appropriately sociopetal due to the closeness of adjacent tables. I have hardly ever been in a restaurant in which the arrangement could not be improved in this regard, and usually without requiring more space. It is very much a matter of ensuring that seats from different tables only find relationships that are suitable for co-existing. If this cannot be achieved by pure plan arrangement, then screens are always at the disposal of the designer. Again Mackintosh, who seemed to understand all this so well, used screens in his famous tearooms and thus achieved a remarkably high density of occupation in an entirely satisfactory setting.

Much more recently Sommer has argued that whether a space is designed to be sociofugal or sociopetal may not just be simply a function of the broad building typology, but might be seen as a matter of style. In particular he argues that this aspect of space may be seen to reflect the social values and lifestyles of those controlling it. In an amusing study of retail environments he compares the American Co-op with the now ubiquitous supermarket (Sommer 1998). These shops are truly co-operative ventures with volunteer staff and are significantly different to their more institutionalized British counterparts. Sommer had already shown that those who choose to use such shops are identifiably different in lifestyle and social and ethnic background. In his study of the spatial organization of these shops he showed a much less clear demarcation between staff work areas and the public space than is found in normal supermarkets. However, he also observed how the layout seemed to encourage meeting and chatting between customers and staff. He showed how in the Co-op the aisles are narrower and are interrupted by bins containing unpacked bulk food. He noticed how customers having to bag their own purchases dally much longer in one place and may thus have much more contact with other shoppers. By comparison the supermarket aisles seem like 'motorways' for shopping trolleys, emphasizing speed and independence and thus enabling a 'grab and run' behavioural pattern. By contrast, then, Sommer has noticed how the Co-op enables and encourages a community spirit in which like-minded people share space in a more co-operative manner. This is a highly sophisticated and yet deep-seated example of the language of space in operation.

Non-reciprocal relationships

We do not all always want a community spirit. Many people frequently find themselves co-existing in a space with others who they do not particularly wish to engage with socially. The most disturbing arrangement in such a situation is that which is non-reciprocal – that is to say, the two people do not have the same view of each other. There is nothing more disturbing than knowing that someone is looking in your direction and yet, because you are not facing them, you cannot tell if they are looking at you. One of Robert Sommer's students found that by using such a seating pattern in a library reading room she could drive away the earlier occupant of a table more quickly than by adopting the more normal 'co-existing' position. An example of this would be the familiar six-seater rectangular table with two seats on each side and one at each end. The first occupant of an empty table is quite likely to sit on one of the side seats, and then probably spreads books and papers out to defend the seat next to him. He would expect the next occupant to choose the seat diagonally opposite so that both can look into space and ignore each other in the classic 'co-existing' relationship. If, however, that second occupant sits at the other end of the table, as the experimenter did, then she has the unpleasant and socially unfair advantage of overlooking but not being overlooked (Fig. 6.8).

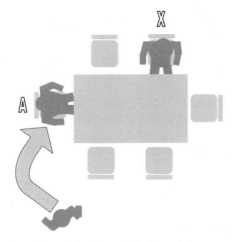

6.8 A deliberate breaking of the 'co-existing' spatial convention that is likely to drive away the original occupant of the table sitting at 'X'. The newcomer choosing to sit at 'A' obtains an unfair advantage of non-reciprocal vision, which often makes us feel uncomfortable

The importance of facing or not facing people has been studied in meetings and discussion group settings (Steinzor 1950). It was shown that when people are seated in a circular arrangement they tend to use non-verbal behaviour to indicate their interaction more with people sitting directly opposite to them than with other members of the groups, unless there is strong leadership in the form of chairing. Where this strong leadership exists, interaction is increased between adjacent individuals.

Waiting spaces
The obvious example of a sociofugal setting is the waiting space in all its various manifestations. Yusoff Abbas, a research student of mine, has completed a very detailed study indeed of how people choose their seat in doctors' waiting rooms (Abbas 2000). Whilst some people will know each other, most will either not do so or do not wish to talk anyway. In spite of this the vast majority of such spaces are laid out as if there was going to be a meeting of some kind, or in some cases even a performance! Unfortunately in our study we were not able to move the seats around in order to show how they could create a more sympathetic setting (Fig. 6.9). It is extraordinary that doctors who should be concerned about the whole of their patient's welfare seem so blind to the simple and totally cost-free actions they could take to make the all too frequently long wait more pleasant. A while ago I had to visit the outpatients' department of one of the leading teaching hospitals, which is related to my university. During a long and tedious

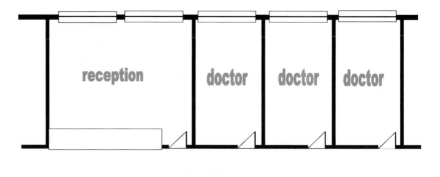

6.9 Why ever do doctors, who should have a better appreciation of our feelings, allow their waiting rooms to be laid out as if for some congregational religious event? Sadly, although this is a particularly bad example it is quite representative of the way the language of space is ignored in such situations

day I found myself in no less than five different waiting spaces, and I whiled away some of the time by trying to redesign them. It was hardly difficult, since all were simply appallingly badly arranged! Part of Yusoff's study was to look at the differences between Malaysian and British behaviour in such waiting spaces. Almost all the waiting spaces in Malaysia were arranged with rows of seats facing the reception desk. One could imagine that the doctor was about to deliver a public lecture with glowing Bunsen burners and bubbling flasks brought in to stand on the counter as if in some Victorian medical society meeting!

British Airways has started to recognize the complexity of settings required in the waiting space of an airport lounge. Most open public waiting spaces in airports seem designed to make waiting even more boring and tedious than it already is in such situations. The seats themselves are often one of the generally available linked seat proprietary products, which, whilst they allow the odd table to be interspersed in the row, otherwise offer a military and entirely sociofugal arrangement. Many people waiting for an aircraft, however, are not alone but are in the company of others, whether they are close family relations going on holiday or business colleagues going to a meeting. Only in the business class lounges do the airlines themselves have some say over the design. Here the need to improve business generates a higher level of customer focus than one usually finds in those areas dominated by the airport authority itself. British Airways has begun to fashion its business class lounges as a series of settings rather than a single waiting space. Different kinds of seating arrangements are used with tables and chairs. It is possible to find a café-like area where a group may sit at a table and eat some snacks. In another area, there are meetings tables for business discussions. Quite separate individual spaces are provided with computer links for lone laptop users. Heavily upholstered and relaxed chairs are located near windows, where there are good views of aircraft movements. Some spaces have children's toys and facilities mixed with nearby seating for accompanying parents. My observation of such lounges is that they generally seem to work well. There are enough clues to ensure that most of the time the behavioural settings are observed, and people do indeed seem to choose the area that suits their circumstance and temporal needs. Waiting spaces do not have to be designed always to remind their occupants that waiting is what they must do!

Furniture

For the receptionist in our scenario from the previous chapter we accept that the telephone and the computer and the filing cabinet are tools of her trade. We may also think that the desk is, but we need to see that the waiting chairs and, most importantly of all, the space between are vital tools.

To understand this more fully we shall develop yet another very simple scenario, and it is developed from a straightforward idea first described by the renowned social psychologist Michael Argyle (Argyle 1994). The setting is an office. It is occupied by one individual and is a space of the kind we might find in businesses and public authorities in cities all over the world. The occupant of this office works at a desk, which he or she sits behind more or less facing the door, but across the room from the door. In front of the desk is another chair for visitors who come to discuss matters. Also by the door there is another chair, and yet another alongside the desk. In the scenario a visitor arrives. We shall explore several alternatives (Fig 6.10).

In the first one, the occupant remains seated and continues working at papers on the desk but perhaps without even looking up asks the visitor to state the business in hand. The visitor is more or less left standing just inside the door. This clearly implies an assumed or real dominance on the part of the office occupant. The seated position is a curious social exception to the general rule that to be higher is to be superior. This is evidenced by the way we stand when a judge enters the courtroom. No one is allowed to be seated when the king is standing, so when the king rises, we all rise.

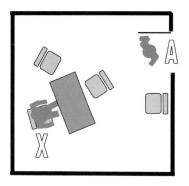

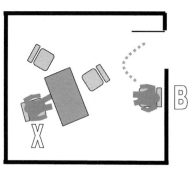

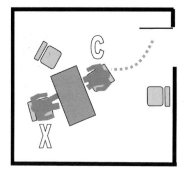

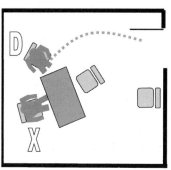

6.10 A simple office with its occupant seated behind the desk in chair 'X'. A visitor arrives. There are four scenarios: in A the visitor is left standing just inside the door; in B the visitor is beckoned to a seat by the door; in C the visitor is beckoned to sit in front of the desk; and in D the visitor is welcomed and invited to sit alongside the desk. Imagine how you would feel as the visitor in each of these cases (after Michael Argyle)

In a second version of this scenario, the office occupant may indicate that the visitor should use the seat near the door. This removes one element of the dominance in the previous version, but still leaves the visitor fully exposed to the stare of the occupant, who is partly concealed by the desk.

In the third alternative, the occupant beckons the visitor to sit on the chair in front of the desk. Here a clear welcome is extended and a sense of equality implied, which could be further embellished by standing or a token momentary rising out of the seat until the visitor is seated. The positions established then represent ones in which competition, confrontation or conversations are all possible. This is thus a neutral rather than dominating scenario.

In the final scenario, the office occupant gets up from behind the desk to meet the visitor half way across the room, who is greeted with a handshake and then brought round to sit on the chair at the side of the desk. This not only implies a degree of deference in the rising from the seat and the leaving behind of the personal territory, but also then results in an arrangement which suggests a common viewpoint and collaboration as the intended mode of interaction.

We can all imagine being the visitor and feeling the range of welcomes we have been given. The atmosphere of the meeting has already been set, and we may hazard a pretty good guess that it will continue as it has started and that this will have a significant effect on its outcome and productivity.

Amos Rapoport describes how an architect who had also studied social science used the principles behind this scenario in his own office as a way of assessing visitors (Rapoport 1982). His desk was located on the opposite side of a rather large room from the two doors that connected it to both his partner's office and a waiting room (Fig. 6.11). Behind him he had his drawing board against the wall, so he sat behind his desk more or less facing a visitor entering. Against the wall near the door and opposite his desk were placed several chairs. He thus waited to see which of three common alternative behaviour patterns a visitor would adopt. They could sit on a chair where it was, or draw one up to his desk, or simply lean against his desk. His view was that these three alternatives showed increasing levels of status and self-confidence!

Duncan Joiner illustrated this rather more empirically in an interesting piece of research into how people use their offices (Joiner 1971). He prepared a sort of compass template drawing, with the office occupant at the centre and the desk in front. He divided the rest of the office into segments, with one to the front, one to each side and forward, one to each side, and one to the rear of the occupant. While asking a series of questions in a more normal questionnaire, he in fact plotted the location of major features of the office on this template –

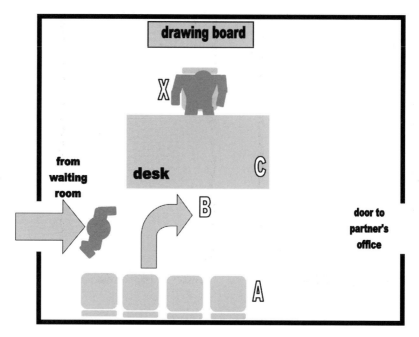

6.11   What does the visitor do here when not given any clues by the office occupant (sitting at 'X')? Sit in isolation against the wall at A, move a chair up to the desk at B? Or perhaps even perch on the corner of the occupant's desk at C? Does this offer a useful spatial version of a personality test, as the original occupant argued? (after Amos Rapoport)

for example, was the door to the front, to the side or behind? Where was the window? Where was the visitor's chair? And so on. He analysed his results into a number of basic arrangements, and found that these were correlated with job occupations. He found that in all the government offices and virtually all the commercial offices he studied the door was visible from the chair behind the desk. However, only a quarter of academics used this arrangement. In a study I did of tax inspectors' offices I found the most common arrangement used the desk to block off space, which clearly became the occupant's exclusive territory into which the visitor was not invited. The desk was a veritable barrier. The tax inspectors would typically sit with the window behind them or at least over their shoulder. Of course this affords good light on the desk surface, but it also puts any visitor seated opposite at a distinct disadvantage (Fig. 6.12).

One of my students did a study of the way in which university lecturers arranged their offices, using similar techniques. In simple terms, the seniority of the lecturer was clearly reflected in the room arrangements. The more junior lecturers, perhaps only recent graduates themselves,

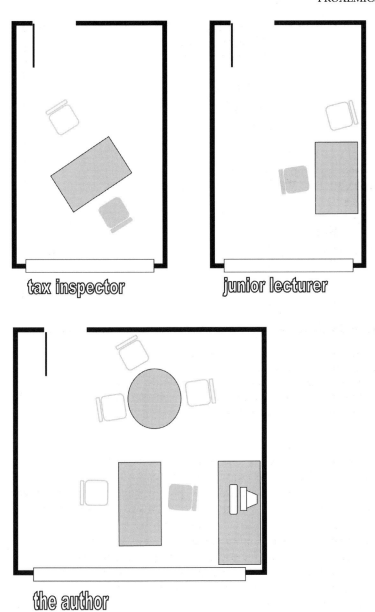

6.12   Duncan Joiner and this author have found that the way people arrange
the furniture in their office is not just formal, but helps to organize and structure the behavioural setting. Joiner showed a correlation between spatial layout
and job description that relates to spatial roles we have already discussed. Note
the 'confrontational' arrangement of the tax inspector, the 'collaborative'
arrangement of the junior university lecturer, and this author's privileged space,
enabling 'collaboration', 'confrontation', and 'sociopetal' meeting arrangements

would typically arrange their desks against the wall so that any incoming student would automatically be on the same side of the desk as them. Through this they expressed their wish to remain on the student's side, as it were – a sentiment that many students no doubt appreciate, at least until the first set of examination results demonstrates the uncrossable divide that ultimately separates them whatever they may wish! At the other end of the scale, the more senior professors and heads of department tended to make barriers of their desks. Of course they more often bear the responsibility of conducting discussions that include some element of reprimand, whether it be to the poorly attending student, the outright plagiaristic student or even the member of staff not performing as well as might be expected! Readers may well be wondering how the author organizes his office, and so it is only fair to tell. In fact I am lucky enough to have the space for two desks and a table. One desk is against the wall and has my computer on it, and this is where I might work with a research student. Another desk is a barrier, and here I might perform less pleasant, perhaps even disciplinary, duties occasionally. Finally, the table is circular and here I can sit to discuss with one or more colleagues. Our building does however have standard rooms for more junior lecturers, which although quite large enough for the occupant alone are just too narrow to allow a desk to be placed so that the visitor can come into a collaborating or confronting position. This inevitably irritates many members of staff, and quite rightly, although many of them find this hard to articulate. As a basic tool of trade to set the scene for professional interactions, these offices are very poorly designed indeed. Furniture in the form of fixed or semi-fixed and freely movable items offers essential features of the language of space. What we have seen here then is that the arrangement of such items in space is not a matter of formal composition for most people; rather it structures the behavioural settings they wish to engineer so that they can play out the roles chosen for them in relation to others. We have also seen that sometimes both the amount and shape of space can either enable or restrict the occupant's ability to create the behavioural settings needed for the job.

'Front of house', 'back of house'

Joiner's work provides an example of an important architectural embellishment of normal interpersonal distance. All the government officers and most of the commercial managers in his sample used their desks to defend what we might refer to here as a 'back of house' zone. The area in front of their desks into which a visitor might be invited we might think of as the 'front of house' zone. In many occupations people find themselves sharing part of their accommodation with visitors. These visitors may often be complete strangers (as is probably the case with tax inspectors), they may be remotely known (as when a patient visits a doctor), or they may be frequent visitors (as in the case of colleagues). It seems that control over both zones and the ability in particular to make clear the distinction between them is important to people. The notion of these zones is perfectly summarized by Erving Goffman in his study of the 'presentation of self in everyday life' to which we have already made reference (Goffman 1959):

Two kinds of regions have been considered: front regions where a particular performance is or may be in progress, and back regions where action occurs that is related to the performance but inconsistent with the appearance fostered by the performance.

I have chosen to use rather theatrical titles in order to emphasize the presentational quality of the distinction. The areas behind the stage in the theatre are necessarily hidden from view in order to maintain the magic of the performance. If we could actually see the make-up rooms, the scenery waiting to come on, the changing areas, the green room and the wings, the whole effect would be lost. Moreover, the performers would be under the stress of constant overlooking. Similarly, in a restaurant the kitchen and its associated areas need to hidden from view in order that work can proceed and the effect of calm and order maintained in the dining room. The illustration in Chapter 2 of the waiter moving from one setting to another and changing behaviour as he did so makes this point precisely. In the traditional grand house there was always a back stair, and access to it was marked by a green baize door. This enabled the servants to move around the house without being seen by the main residents and their guests. The messy business of the servants' job was thus concealed, and they would appear is if by magic in the right place, at the right time and with the right objects. Jean Anouill has written a number of plays about the problems that ensue when those on the civilized side of the green baize door fail to respect the division, and fail as it were to play the game. A relationship across this divide was thus always problematic. Other settings make this separation of front and back of house even more sensitive. The architect Richard Burton ingeniously designed a building cross-section enabling this in his innovative and highly regarded St Mary's Hospital (Davey 1991). Here, men in boiler suits carrying tools coming to fix the plumbing will never pass in front of the patients' eyes, and I am sure that if only they knew it those patients would be most grateful for such a sensitive piece of spatial organization.

In offices and many other spaces, however, the problem is made more difficult because the 'back of house' areas may not be physically divided off. There is no green baize door, and the message must be sent out through the arrangement of furniture and other objects.

In other cases the division between front and back may be physical but not secure. Normal social rules require that even in such cases the visitor should refrain from invasion. Goffman reports an incident, which was reflected in my own experience, although thankfully with a different outcome. A customer arriving at a garage to purchase a spare part for his car rather overstepped the mark. He went into the store-room himself and correctly found the required part and emerged with it to complete the purchase. The proprietor, offended by the invasion of back of house, refused the sale by pretending the part was in fact not suitable for his car. I once had to wait for a very long time in front of an open counter at a DIY shop in a similar circumstance while the store attendant dealt with a particularly troublesome customer. We had actually already discussed the part I needed the previous day, but I had gone home to check that it was correct. I could even see the item on the open shelving behind him that I needed to take to the checkout. I expected him to acknowledge me and perhaps nod an acceptance that I might go and collect the item. He did not, so I stood waiting, proba-bly showing increasing signs of frustration but still respecting his 'back of house' zone.

Recently we have moved a whole wall in my university department simply to achieve a 'back of house' zone for our secretarial staff. My secretary and one other share a room off which my office opens (Fig. 6.13). Inevitably they have many 'visitors' into this space. They range from myself, through colleagues to students and outside visitors. The two secretaries have 'L'-shaped desks that were arranged so they left the space between them open to these visitors. This meant that the secretaries were constantly concerned that some of the many papers and documents on the desks, or even their computer screens, might be overlooked by these visitors. Some documents might be entirely appro-priate to some visitors and yet not to others. A draft examination paper, for example, may be seen by colleagues but must not be revealed to students. So serious was this problem that the secretaries wanted to turn their desks around to face a leg of the 'L' to make a barrier between 'front of house' and 'back of house'. Unfortunately the room was simply not large enough for this, so we had to move the wall to increase space. What is important here is that the additional space was not really required, only the division between front and back of house. Tight spatial planning as we had here, as it so often does, actually forces a wasting of space in order to get relationships right for the setting.

In my study of the English public house I was reminded on many occasions of how bar staff dislike central or island bars where they are surrounded by their customers. This is not of course because of any physical invasion by the customer into the area behind the bar, but bar staff feel that these areas are overlooked. They feel that customers can see the dirty water in the washing up bowl and the other parapherna-lia of the job that they prefer to keep hidden from view. In other words,

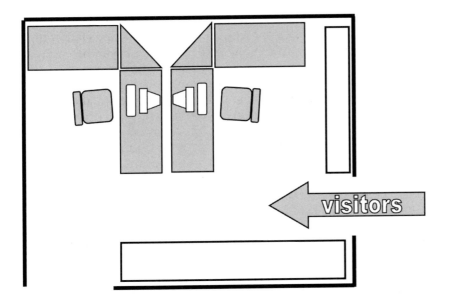

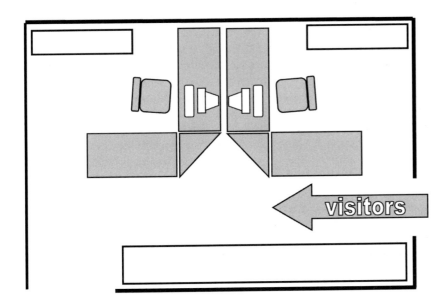

6.13 A secretarial space that did not originally provide for 'back of house'. Although taking up more room without accommodating any more people, the new arrangement was seen as far better because it marks out front and back of house in a way naturally respected by all. Such apparently small differences can make a huge difference to the people who have to occupy such spaces every day

they simply want to erect some sort of 'front' and only reveal to the customer the part of their domain that is presentable.

I was working for a large company, advising it on new central headquarters. This company rather dominated the small town it was in, and had grown up over the years to occupy many small buildings dotted around the town for offices. The company did, however, have a large central site, which had been occupied by a now defunct industrial process. The idea was to move all the office staff into this old industrial building in a large open-plan office. The company secretary had what he thought to be a rather nice idea, which was to locate the telephone operators in an area just inside the entrance to the office space. Previously they were in a windowless and airless basement in thoroughly uncomfortable surroundings. He reasoned that since they spoke daily on the telephone to all the staff it would be nice for them actually to meet and put faces to all the voices. This re-location was completed, and indeed as all the office staff arrived in the morning they would greet the telephonists as they passed and this was genuinely appreciated. However after a few weeks, and for the first time in the history of the company, these telephonists went on strike. They claimed that they wanted more pay since they were using new technology, but the new technology actually made their job easier rather than more difficult. It eventually turned out that this was a dispute about the loss of 'back of house' space. Telephone exchange operators can only work in responsive mode, and unless the telephone rings there is nothing for them to do. Being previously entirely in 'back of house' space, they had adopted the practice of bringing in magazines to read, jumpers to knit and so on. Once they were positioned 'front of house', they felt unable to continue this practice in full view of other staff. They even felt uncomfortable about having the knitting or magazines lying on their desk, giving the game away. Such a complaint is simply too difficult to express to an employer, especially one who meant so well in the first place. Consequently, through an inevitable series of misunderstandings the whole situation had escalated to a strike!

Variations

Just as with our study of distance in the previous chapter, there are many variations in proxemic behaviour. These variations can be driven by personality, status and culture.

A man comes into a colleague's office. The occupant of the office is talking on the telephone, but gestures a welcome and indication for the visitor to sit down. The visitor does not sit down, but remains standing over him. After a short while the office occupant tells the person on the other end of the line that he will call them back. In an alternative to this scenario the visitor waves his hand as a return acknowledgement and quietly leaves the office. Finally, in the third variant the visitor actually sits and waits for the call to finish. It is clear surely in each of these variants which of the participants has the higher status, if either.

The design of office workplace settings is extraordinarily rich in these issues. A study of an open-plan office, which I made some years ago, revealed a clear difference of view as to how status should be reflected in accommodation. It was decided that the vast majority of the office was to be open plan, but those senior managers who wished to could have their own private offices situated round the perimeter. In the end, most of them chose not to do this. When questioned about their decisions, they largely referred to a desire not to emphasize status as the main reason for their choice, and most admitted that deep down they would have preferred their own room. When we asked the lower ranking staff about this issue, they were almost unanimous in their wish to see the senior managers have separate offices. Once we probed further into this, three main reasons emerged: first, they felt constantly overlooked by managers who 'shared their space'; secondly, they felt embarrassed in front of their colleagues when talking to their boss, and this was especially true when they were being told off or when they were asking for promotion or some special treatment; and finally they were all striving for promotion and could see what they viewed as a perk of the higher status they hoped to attain being eroded.

My brother worked for a very well known British company who moved into a large open-office headquarters designed on very regular 'bureaulandschaft' principles. Each of the senior and middle managers were provided with potted plants as part of the office landscaping. Since my brother was an enthusiastic horticulturist, he managed to get his plant to grow larger than all the others. One morning when he came in, it had been replaced with a much smaller plant. Looking around the office, he eventually found his original plant by the desk of the most senior manager!

Some cultural observers and analysts have suggested that our whole attitude towards the environment is subject to significant cultural varia-tion (Trompenaars and Hampden-Turner 1997). This seems particu-larly true between eastern and western cultures. For example, some cultures take the very general view that the major forces driving people to good or evil come from within the individual, whereas other cultures tend to see the world as more powerful than the individual and take a more fatalistic view. In these latter cultures the environment, and most particularly the natural environment, is something that individuals should become 'in-tune' with. Trompenaars and Hampden-Turner illustrate this with a nice example in relation to the now prolific Walkman®. They claim that the chairman of Sony himself, Mr Morita, who first had the idea for the Walkman, had a particular motivation in creating it. This motivation was that he would be able to listen to classical music on his way to work without disturbing his fellow commuters. By contrast, most Westerners seem to like the Walkman because it enables them to listen to music without being disturbed by other people. The irritation that many cause on London Tube trains by the high frequency sound that escapes from the earphones is perhaps further confirmation of this.

What constitutes an infringement of privacy does seem to be subject to variation across cultures, even within continental Europe. The British seem more able to ignore the nearby presence of others than some of their European neighbours, and also than Americans. Hall describes this through the trials and tribulations of an English student sharing accommodation with an American at a university in the USA:

I'm walking around the apartment and it seems that whenever I want to be alone my roommate starts talking to me. Pretty soon he's asking 'What's the matter?' and wants to know if I'm angry. By then I am angry and say something.

Americans, it seems, expect that in such a situation you would go into another room and close the door to be private. In England we might well leave the door to an office ajar, thus indicating a preparedness to be interrupted. In such circumstances colleagues might put their head around the door, possibly knocking as they do so, and would then immediately withdraw if they saw you were already busy with someone else. In Germany, such behaviour would definitely be unacceptable; first, Germans would be less likely to leave their doors open, and secondly, any sort of crossing of a threshold without explicit invitation is considered an invasion of privacy.

The British stereotype of Germans is that they are formal, unbending and humourless. In reality, nothing could be further from the truth. I spent some time discussing these misconceptions with a German member of the British Council, who had worked for the British for many years although remaining in her native country, mainly in Hamburg. She told me that there is really no German equivalent of the English invitation to 'pull up a chair', meaning 'come and join the group'. Germans dislike the movement of furniture as this breaks the order of a space, and to move some furniture in someone else's house or office would be considered offensive. In England we expect such behaviour, and would not normally take offence at it.

Of course culture is itself not some separate and meaningless set of behavioural rules. The way in which cultures modify the global language of space to give it a local accent depends on a number of fairly obvious factors. Religion and climate seem to be the most powerful forces at work here. My research student Yusoff Abbas, whose work we have already mentioned, is one of a very few researchers to investigate this in a systematic way. He looked at the way patients in health centres chose the seats they would sit on to wait for their appointments. He compared behaviour in two very different cultures, those of the United Kingdom and of Malaysia. In general we found very similar overall patterns, as one would expect from all the research already done. For example, where there are long rows of seats people will tend to choose the end ones first, and then space themselves out fairly evenly when these are all occupied. People also tend to choose seats that are not overlooked from behind and offer good views of the activity in the space. However, Malaysians did make choices that suggested a greater sensitivity to other people already in the waiting room. They were less likely than the British to choose seats that overlooked other people. Malaysians seemed more likely to chat to each other, which certainly accords with my experience of that country. For example, if sitting drinking or eating in public, I am frequently addressed by complete strangers who seem genuinely interested in where I have come from and why I am there! Following their dominant Islamic faith, Malaysians would also choose seats so as to avoid close proximity between people of the opposite gender. In traditional Malay architecture, which is of course not air-conditioned, the distinction between indoors and outdoors is much less clear than is frequently necessary in the British climate. We also saw a tendency amongst our Malaysian subjects to choose seats near windows or with views out of windows.

Hall considers the different preferences nationalities have for organizing geometry, and makes particular reference to the French propensity for centralization and radial geometry. He describes how a French member of his team asked for a rise in pay because his desk was in the middle of the office. In England, the periphery would be more likely to be thought of as prestigious. This French liking for centrality perhaps explains why Charles de Gaulle airport is so confusingly round and thus difficult for me as an Englishman to get my bearings in. It also means extremely long taxiing times for aircraft on the ground as they rotate around the terminal. For a number of years I used to take a flight from England to Singapore, which stopped at Charles de Gaulle Airport. I once timed it, and the halfway point of the journey from England to France was just about when we touched down in Paris! A French research student of mine was astonished that I should be so critical, and remained puzzled that airports all over the world had not been redesigned on these lines, which he considered innovatory and logical. He further pointed out that an airport is seen as a 'hub', and should therefore clearly be circular!

I find that design students from Eastern cultures who study in the UK often struggle to understand their tutors, and the difficulty seems mutual. In essence, I think this often comes down to the higher degree of preference many Eastern cultures have for geometry that is symbolic, whereas their British tutors may well be concentrating on its formal properties. The plans of many buildings in the Far East often have quite symbolic significance. I remember an Indian student in my year at Oxford who was failed for designing a cricket pavilion that had a moon-like crescent-shaped plan. This outline resulted in many awkward spaces and gave him many problems in organizing the activities inside. His tutors could not understand why he persisted with this problematic geometry, but to him it was perfectly logical since it was the symbol that appeared on the shirt of his local cricket team in India. He remained puzzled and angry that his tutors had not appreciated the efforts he had made to work with this difficult but, for him, right shape.

Movable and fixed furniture

Many of the situations we have considered in this chapter involve the use of furniture to help locate people in space, thus either inhibiting or facilitating their desired relationships by creating appropriate or inappropriate behavioural settings. Before leaving this subject, it is worth noting that such furniture can be fixed or movable. We have seen that willingness to move furniture can vary with culture and setting. Sommer notes that large groups arriving in a café are likely to move a seat from an adjacent table in order to establish their whole group in one location (Sommer 1969). By comparison, he could record no instance of this happening in his much-researched library reading rooms. The social norms, it seems, tell us that behaviour that is acceptable in the café setting may not be suitable in the library setting. The nature of my work as an academic means that almost every day many people will come to see me in my office. They may range from students discussing their work to staff planning a course, visitors collaborating in a research project or my secretary updating my diary. Their willingness to move the seats around is very variable. Of course it depends on many factors. When several people come in together they are much more likely to feel able to move a chair than a single person seems to. Obviously this is influenced by the nature of the activity, but it is often related to what seems to be a perceived position in the hierarchy of the institution. Those who would be thought of as more senior or with whom I have a more personal relationship seem much more likely to adjust the furniture. Such variation does not occur in neutral spaces such as meeting and seminar rooms. Here all furniture is deemed to be movable by all the occupants.

However, the locators of movable furniture in reality often turn out not to be the normal users of a space but rather those who service it. In a series of studies of English pubs I found the furniture arrangement was repeated with extraordinary regularity. One could enter a bar at opening time and find the furniture in exactly the position it had been at opening time on the day before, and indeed as far back as

6.14 A bar in an English public house laid out as if for a chess competition! Could the arrangement be made more sympathetic to the behavioural setting needed?

could be remembered. In one bar I studied the overall geometry was rather long and narrow, which was in itself not problematic (Fig. 6.14). The bar was doing very poorly, and was dramatically less popular than another bar in the same pub. We discovered that the cleaner was responding to the linearity of the space by arranging tables on a long row with seats on either side as if laid out for a huge chess competition. The density of the arrangement was such that it was hard to move the furniture later, and clearly the setting was unsuitable for most people's needs. Those attracted to it were the solitary types who in turn gave off an air of defiant defence of their space, which discouraged others from coming in. I spent some time watching people look into the bar and then, sensing the unfriendly atmosphere, leave.

One year when discussing these ideas with my students they decided to change the seating arrangement in our departmental coffee bar. Here, seats are traditionally laid out in a very regular pattern familiar to those who attend the typical doctor's waiting room. The students came up with a much more sociopetal arrangement far better suited to groups sitting around chatting, as students do over a cup of coffee. They decided to put theory into practice and re-organized the space. However, the next morning we found that the cleaner had returned all the chairs to what she clearly regarded as their normal position. Since

6.15 A cleaner has decided exactly where each chair will go in this pub. It will in my experience be very hard to break this pattern!

cleaners rise much earlier in the mornings than students of architecture she had an absolute control over this space, and eventually the students gave up the attempt to create a better setting. I have found this phenomenon in many building types where the cleaners are able to dominate the spatial configuration. This is particularly true in spaces such as pubs that have a strong diurnal rhythm, allowing the cleaner to arrange the furniture before the main occupants arrive (Fig. 6.15).

Lipman and Sommer both made studies of patients' communal day spaces in hospitals for the elderly or mentally ill (Lipman 1968; Sommer 1969). Both these authors found that the arrangement of chairs was determined by nurses and ward managers. Patients were relatively unlikely to move the furniture, and all became used to particular arrangements. This proved to be unfortunate, since the natural tendency of the staff was to return chairs to rather rigid arrangements, often in straight lines and frequently with their backs against walls. Of course such arrangements minimized the social interaction of the patients, which might be thought to be the main function of the space. Sommer in particular reports an experiment to change the seating pattern to a more sociopetal arrangement resulting in an almost doubling of the levels of both brief interactions and sustained conversations. Interestingly, this new arrangement involved the use of tables around which the chairs were arranged. They also found an increase in the levels of magazine reading in addition to more conversation. It seems likely that this was due to the staff being more willing to leave magazines lying on tables than lying on the floor adjacent to a chair, where they looked untidy. This of course gives us the clue as to why cleaners, nurses and the like prefer such socially unsuitable arrangements. Quite simply, they look tidier and it is easier to clean around them. Quite predictably, they are not thinking about the occupants at all but about their own convenience. I often see architects' drawings of intended interior spaces with imaginative seating arrangements that I know will never be realized for this reason. However, designers can certainly influence matters greatly by the used of semi-fixed or fixed elements, which then set the pattern. Usually the space-servicing staff can be steered into a more suitable arrangement through such devices, but not always!

References

Abbas, M. Y. (2000). Proxemics in waiting areas of health centres: a cross cultural study. Ph.D., University of Sheffield.

Argyle, M. (1994). *The Psychology of Interpersonal Behaviour*, 5th edn. London, Penguin.

Davey, P. (1991). St Mary's. *Architectural Review* 189(1128): 24–33.

Dimitrius, J. E. and M. Marzzarella (1998). *Reading People: How to Understand People and Predict their Behaviour – Anytime, Anyplace*. London, Vermillion.

Fast, J. (1971). *Body Language*. London, Pan Books.

Goffman, E. (1959). *The Presentation of Self in Everyday Life*. London, Penguin.

Hall, E. T. (1959). *The Silent Language*. New York, Doubleday.

Hertzberger, H. (1991). *Lessons for Students in Architecture* (trans. Ina Rike). Rotterdam, Uitgeverij 010.

Joiner, D. (1971). Social ritual and architectural space. In Honikman, B. (eds), *AP70: Proceedings of the Architectural Psychology Conference at Kingston Polytechnic*, pp. 7–11. London, RIBA.

Lipman, A. (1968). Building design and social interaction. *Architects' Journal* 147: 23–30.

Morris, D. (1969). *The Human Zoo*. London, Jonathan Cape.

Morris, D. (2000). *The Naked Eye: Travels in Search of the Human Species*. London, Edbury Press.

Osmond, H. (1959). The relationship between architect and pyschiatrist. In Goshen, C. (ed), *Psychiatric Architecture*. Washington DC, American Psychiatric Association.

Rapoport, A. (1982). *The Meaning of the Built Environment: A Nonverbal Communication Approach*. Beverly Hills, Sage Publications.

Sommer, R. (1969). *Personal Space: The Behavioural Basis of Design*. Englewood Cliffs, Prentice Hall.

Sommer, R. (1998). Shopping at the Co-op. *Journal of Environmental Psychology* 18: 45–53.

Steinzor, B. (1950). The spatial factor in face to face discussion groups. *Journal of Abnormal and Social Psychology* 45: 552–555.

Trompenaars, F. and D. Hampden-Turner (1997). *Riding the Waves of Culture: Understanding Cultural Diversity in Business*. London, Nicholas Brealey.

7 The territory

Love your neighbour, yet don't pull down your hedge.

Benjamin Franklin

Nationalism is an infantile disease, it is the measles of mankind.

Albert Einstein

Territoriality and territorial behaviour are found all around us in the animal world. The bird building a nest and singing to announce its presence is behaving in an instinctive way common to all members of its species. The tribes of monkeys who congregate to argue so noisily with their neighbours are playing out their particular version of territoriality. The emperor penguins who huddle together to increase bodily warmth in the Antarctic to give their eggs a better chance of hatching are similarly responding to their own internal territorial drives. The beaver who builds a dam does so in order to rear a family located in their own special reserved area of forest. The tussling deer that cross antlers to establish dominance and obtain the prime site are behaving territorially. These are just a few examples of a myriad of ways of establishing territorial propriety. There are two important constituents common to all such behaviour, and they are lie behind many of the phenomena described in this book. These central and crucial ideas are that territory is essential for the survival of the species not only in terms of physical comfort but also in terms of its social well-being, and it that achieves this through the provision, organization and structuring of space.

Are we really territorial?

Some have disputed whether we humans really are territorial creatures, and yet the apparent evidence of our territorial behaviour abounds. Whether this is instinctive in the strict way it clearly is for many animals is less clear, and it is unlikely that we will ever really be able to answer this question fully. Our understanding of animal territoriality depends largely on a field known as 'ethology', which is the study of animals in their natural habitat. We saw some of the work done in this field in

Chapter 5. The human race has developed so far so that we can no longer define our natural habitat. I wrote much of the first draft of this book sitting on an isolated beach on a small island in the Atlantic Ocean, and even in this remote, wild and least urban of places I was reminded daily of our tendency to take, occupy and defend territory. People would find particular places to establish themselves; using the many volcanic rocks littering the back of the beach they would arrange walls around their patch, usually against the walls of a cliff, but occasionally out in the open. They would develop considerable attachments to such locations and return to them daily. They would show very obvious signs of displeasure if someone else tried to build another patch too close to theirs, and would become quite angry if a stranger arrived early and actually tried to occupy their patch. All this in spite of there being enough room to build a tented village large enough to accommodate a complete army of invasion and occupation should any martial mind feel so inclined!

Many have argued that some of our inner-city social problems result from pushing our urban lifestyles too far and that the inner-city problems bear a striking similarity to the breakdown of social behaviour observed in some animal species when their natural habitat is put under similar pressure.

Our attachment to particular places and our willingness and indeed enthusiasm for defending them is undoubted. Lawyers probably make more money from disputes between neighbours than from any other form of legal quarrel. Sadly in many such cases the problem is triggered by an ambiguity caused by spatial design, or lack of it. Unclear boundaries and tracts of land that cannot easily be defended can cause enormous distress to some people, and make the lives of many others quite unpleasant (Fig. 7.1). The offence that is felt when a newcomer accidentally occupies a chair traditionally belonging to a regular is very real. The propensity that children show for building dens and secret hideaways is known to us all. The sad proliferation of wars between neighbouring nations about land that seems less than essential economically or culturally is blazoned across the front of our daily newspapers. We may sympathize with Einstein when he rails against nationalism, describing it as 'an infantile disease' and as being 'the measles of mankind'. However, the nation is deep down one of the many faces of territoriality that we seem locked into. It is when the wish to identify ourselves as part of a nation oversteps the mark and becomes 'nationalism' that we show the weakness in our makeup. It is a line the human race has still not yet learned to avoid crossing from time to time, no matter how civilized other aspects of our culture may have become.

The fact is that, whether we like it or not, much of what we know about territoriality we have learned from animal studies. Some writers appear to extrapolate from animal to human behaviour with gay

7.1 This piece of land is obviously either owned or at least claimed by the residents of the adjacent houses. Each stakes their claim in their own manner, and some are clearly visually highly disruptive. A clear indication of the need to define and mark territory!

abandon. Some delight in drawing the parallels in order to shock and amuse, and some have even gone so far as to describe us as 'the naked ape' (Morris 1967). At the other extreme, some have tried to argue that none of this is relevant to human behaviour since we are civilized by having culture. Whilst the latter is certainly the case, it is difficult to argue that cultural behaviour demonstrates some taming of nature. Rather it should perhaps be seen as the inevitable outcome of our natural development. Perhaps Claude Levi-Strauss has offered the most coherent advancement of this argument:

... we should not forget that the main usefulness of these primate studies is twofold: first, they permit us to make hypotheses about early forms of incipient human cultures – that is to say, what took place about one or two million years ago. Second, they disclose facts which are so fundamental that if they hold true for primates, they also hold true for the whole of mankind.

There are numerous anthropological studies of the various primitive societies that still exist around the world today. The vast bulk of this work also shows that these tribes can almost invariably accurately describe what they consider to be their territory and where the borders with the neighbouring territories can be found. Indeed in many cases the cultures of such tribes cannot be understood without reference to their concept of territory and their sense of belonging in a special place that they regard as exclusively theirs. Other evidence of the strength of our territorial drive comes from reports of those who have tried to live without individual territories. A study of the Israeli kibbutz described the limits many members would go to contrive a way of cultivating their own plot of land. An analysis of the performance of the agricultural industry in Soviet Russia offers another form of evidence. In 1975 it was claimed that private land, which amounted to less than 1 per cent of cultivated areas, was actually responsible for generating over half the food supply of the Soviet Union! It seems that a willingness to work hard and territoriality are bound together in a kind of virtuous circle. Work by Alan Lipman on the behaviour of residents in an old peoples' home also reinforces the strong underlying need for permanently defended territory. Here the old people might reasonably be expected to have lost what territories they originally had before moving into the home. Lipman recorded that although the home had a definite policy that chairs in the communal sitting rooms were not to be exclusively reserved, this could not be enforced. So strong was the defence of territorial chairs by these elderly residents that the staff eventually had to bow to this wish and allow the practice, even though this contradicted policy (Lipman 1968).

Children seem to begin to show territorial behaviour remarkably early in life, and some claim it is fully formed by the age of 7 years. In very early life a child is not able to distinguish or understand the locality of space. At this stage the territory is that area within reach of the parent, most often the mother, in which the infant feels secure. Malmberg has suggested that it is probably from this that we get the powerful description of national territory as the 'motherland' or the 'fatherland', and the idea of 'patriotism' (Malmberg 1980). Malmberg also reports studies of war refugees, particularly children who are put in emergency accommodation. Although safe and comfortable, the children continued to exhibit a large number of psychological problems until their emergency space was divided up so that each could establish a personal territory and 'make a home'.

The extent to which our territorial behaviour is instinctive in the way exhibited by other animals will remain open to debate. Certainly simple extrapolation from animal studies is both foolish and dangerous. There are many more variations of territorial behaviour in the human species than found in any other species, and we have civilized our basic behaviour with culture. Nevertheless, our behaviour shows so many examples of the territorial drive that for the purposes of this book we shall proceed cautiously to examine territoriality in humans and use whatever animal lessons seem useful.

The nature and purpose of territory

It is important then to understand some of the essential characteristics of a territory as found in the animal world before trying to unravel our own tendencies. Territory is not purely spatial, it is also very much a social phenomenon. In fact, territoriality is about the location of societies in space. Territories help animals to structure and organize their societies. The animal territory is a defined area of land or water or air, depending on the species, which a single creature or more often group of creatures occupy. However, in general they only defend the territory from other members of their own species. Naturally any animal will take evasive or challenging action should a predator cross the boundary, but this is basic survival and not territorial behaviour at all. In fact, modern territorial theory does not so much stress the process of defence as the characteristic of exclusivity, and so a territory is now usually thought of as an area exclusively occupied by an individual or group of a particular species. In fact in the animal world few serious fights about territory ever actually take place – it seems the owner of a territory has such a strong psychological advantage that mere display is enough to deter the would-be intruder. A natural result of such a system is that territorial species spread themselves out in space rather than all congregating together. This is a natural force acting in favour of the species as a whole, although of course not necessarily in the interests of any one individual. It enhances the species' chance of survival and prosperity by maximizing the use of the food supply.

The next rather hard lesson for us squeamish humans is that animal territoriality is also about the survival of the fittest. Not all territories are equally attractive or desirable, and the general rule is that the strongest win the best territories. This can be an entirely sexist affair, where usually the males compete for territories and then females compete for the desirable males. Such an arrangement is again in favour of the species as a whole, whilst being rather hard on at least some less fortunate individuals. The strongest males reproduce with the most desirable females, and thus the lineage of the species is given its best chance of perfection. It must be remembered for completeness that not all species work this way – the hyena, for example, lives in a matriarchal society in which males find themselves in solitary isolation and at the bottom of the pecking order, bullied even by the young of high-ranking females. Whatever the territorial variation any one species has devised for itself, the fact remains that it is the territory that is at the heart of this Darwinian system. We see from this that territory is not some trivial luxury but one of the most basic components of natural law. Space and place have massive roles to play, not just in human life but also in the life of the multitude of territorial species that share the world with us.

However, the territory is a remarkable device going well beyond the provision of simple space. Ardrey first advanced the argument that territory serves as a mechanism for supplying the three great needs of stimulation, identity and security that we discussed in Chapter 2. Malmberg, in his study of human territoriality, lends his support to Ardrey's thesis. Through the competition between neighbours, whether in the street or the nation, we are kept permanently stimulated. As we shall see later, more complex forms of human territoriality as realized through sport provide substantial quantities of stimulation and entertainment. Football, perhaps the archetypal territorial game, generates the largest television revenues worldwide of any form of live broadcast. The importance of football and the supporters' allegiance to the team is now a global phenomenon. As the great Liverpool manager Bill Shankly is reported to have said, 'football is not a matter of life or death, it's far more important than that'! Through the social arrangements of the territory, whether pairs, families, tribes or nations, the occupants are given order and security in their lives. It is hard to imagine a human society without such a structure surviving and thriving, and none has ever been found. Life would simply be so confusing and the levels of anxiety so high that members of the society would be unable to devote time and energy to more progressive matters.

The national territory
The territory provides a place and symbol of identity uniquely locating us in the world both individually and socially. One of the first questions one is asked when abroad is 'where are you from?'. I find that often in the Far East the assumption is that I might be Australian, whereas in the Middle East I might be thought to be American. It is clear that foreign strangers frequently seem to find my national identity a useful tool in beginning the process of interacting with me. Indeed, when under such interrogation I have to admit my Britishness, it is often quite noticeable that the attitude and conversational style change. The extent to which we all rely upon our clothes, cars and houses as extensions of ourselves to express to others our identity is evident in daily life. To disregard the importance of territory in our lives is to miss one of the most basic elements of human existence.

Whilst there are instances of behaviour in the animal world which resemble national characteristics, the nation as we know it is a uniquely human phenomenon. However, many animal species do exhibit a form of territorial behaviour that we might recognize as having the basic qualities of nationhood. Even some very primitive creatures, such as ants and termites, defend a location and co-operate on a nationwide scale in the communal cause, but it is amongst primates that most of the nation-like forms of behaviour can be found. Some lemurs, baboons, chimpanzees and many species of ape operate in societies based on nations. In essence, these societies thrive on external animosity and have strong internal amity. Adults will show an interest in and sense of responsibility for the young of other families, for example. A recent British television series on the behaviour of primates clearly showed a young chimpanzee being passed around its apparently adoring aunts and uncles, who all took a turn in its grooming. This is remarkably like a human society with its extended families. However, in one regard the animal nation is totally unlike our own, since it does not lead them to kill each other or indeed to try permanently to deprive enemies of their territory. Disputes at territorial borders can be noisy and highly excitable affairs, especially in the case of some apes, but they rarely lead to anything other than darting minor incursions into other territories, and even these are apparently not motivated by imperialist expansionism! Whilst there may be monkey nations, there are no recorded instance of monkey empires. Indeed those species that do operate national territorial behaviour seem remarkably affable – to us the chimpanzee seems, and indeed is, a friendly, apparently fun-loving creature who cares for and helps fellow members of the nation. The level of dominance in such animal societies is very low compared with that found in non-territorial parallels, and the inward amity is thus maintained entirely without compulsion or threat by strongly dominant individuals. Whilst they are not free from violence altogether, such animals are generally peace loving. Ardrey argues that the primates have developed the nation as a natural response to their strengths and weakness.

We primates are distinguishable from the rest of nature by two main characteristics. We have generally capable, flexible bodies with hands that enable us to manipulate tools, and we have highly advanced brains that enable us to develop strategies for dealing with problems. Otherwise our bodies are generalized rather than specialized. We do not have any particularly strong attacking features like the jaws of a crocodile or the claw of a crab, and nor do we have effective defensive capabilities like the spines of the hedgehog or the camouflage of the chameleon. Under such circumstances, when we want to hunt or to defend ourselves against others we need to co-operate and win our battles through force of numbers and execution of strategic operations. Put this way, the nation looks a pretty effective device for promoting and ensuring collaboration.

Morris has argued that our deep-seated need for structures based on social dominance related to territory are reflected in our invention of religion. He argues that we evolved away from the dominance through fear that characterized our early ancestral beginnings and replaced this with leaders who commanded respect. This was necessary to develop societies that initially co-operated in hunting and later in farming, and we needed to maximize the benefit to society as a whole of the intellectual capabilities of all its members. Such leaders were thus no longer all-powerful figures to whom we gave unquestioning allegiance. Morris argues that we were unable to totally free ourselves of the basic need to submit ourselves to an all-powerful dominant member of the group, and thus invented one outside society in the form of either single or multiple gods (Morris 1969). The social cohesion generated by religious beliefs has, he argues, proved immensely valuable to human society, and he doubts whether the species could have progressed far without it.

Such an analysis will undoubtedly seem offensive to some, but it remains an intriguing fact of history that a huge variety of religious beliefs have centred on the notion of all-powerful beings. Such belief systems have often developed to be coterminous with national boundaries, and have sadly contributed to the flipside of human national territorial behaviour, which can undoubtedly have an ugly face. However, where multiple religious belief systems are found within a single national territorial boundary, confusion can arise between the political and religious leadership. Political leaders can be found in many varieties spanning the whole range of the dominance/consultation spectrum. Ultimately they are all replaceable, a lesson hard to learn for some and dramatically demonstrated in recent years. Religious leaders, however, by consensus and tradition, acquire the infallibility of the gods they represent. The two systems work differently, and our history reveals the evidence of our problem with reconciling them. Regular watchers of television news will have seen the Papal visits to foreign territories and the often-repeated gesture of kissing the ground on arrival. It seems that the Pontiff brings with him the infallibility of his god and transfers it to the territory with this gesture. Such a gesture would seem strange if made by political visitors. By contrast they are often allowed to inspect some small part of the armed forces, and such a gesture seems remarkably sophisticated in its symbolism. At once the visitor is shown the existence and strength of the army that could defend the territory, and yet is momentarily given some authority over it to show that this force is not directed towards the state of the visiting dignitary.

While, like Einstein, we may deplore nationalism, we nevertheless understand, appreciate and feel very attached to our nation, our home country, its language and cultural traditions. There is currently something of a resurgence in feelings about the nation. We have of course seen the terrible consequences of this in the Balkans, but we see it in a more acceptable form in many parts of the world. Countries that have been politically 'manufactured' in the past are beginning to come apart as people feel the need to express their national identity. The United Kingdom is now far from 'united', with Wales, Scotland and Northern Ireland all having their own particular sets of problems with the concept. Paradoxically, all this is happening just as conventional national governments are losing more power than ever before as three other types of organizations increasingly flourish and gain power and influence. The rise of multinational companies has begun to break down national boundaries in terms of some of the most important products in our lives, such as motor cars and computers, which are now largely international in their specifications. Banks and money markets have reduced the power of national governments over their own currencies, as has been made only too painfully obvious in the United Kingdom and other places. Finally, political and economic groupings such as those based on geographical location, for example the European Union, and on trade interests, such as OPEC, have further diminished the power of nations over their own economies. However, this discussion of the politics of nationality and nationalism is beginning to take us too far from our purpose here.

The borders and the heartland

In environmental terms, territories are usually defined by two important features; their borders with other territories, and their heartland. Human nations are thus recognizable through their frontiers and their capital city. Many external disputes and, sadly, wars develop over the former, but feelings can run just as high internally over the latter. The re-unification of Germany and the need to re-establish Berlin as the national capital is an example of the symbolic importance of such things. In Malaysia, the capital Kuala Lumpur was originally built on the Klang River, which indirectly gives it its name (Kuala Lumpur means muddy river). It has now become extremely congested and has had generally poor transportation infrastructure. It lies more or less in the centre of the main peninsular part of the country. At the extreme southern tip of the country we find the city of Johor Bahru, which sits just across the causeway from Singapore. As the Singaporean economy grew rapidly it spread its economic tentacles out into neighbouring countries. Land values in Johor started to rise as a consequence, and a very dramatic new development was proposed on the waterfront to allow the city to expand. Talking to Malaysians, it seemed to become a common concern that unless action was taken Johor could rival Kuala Lumpur and this would be undesirable. The capital must be the most important city and act as an icon for a nation. If the nation is defined by its borders and capital, so the capital is defined by both its own boundary and its core. In many capital cities there is a building, or perhaps a few buildings, which act as the icon of the city. The Eiffel Tower in Paris, St Paul's Cathedral in London and Hagia Sofia in Istanbul are all very obvious examples (Plate 12). So important are these icons that we lavish attention on them in quite extravagant ways. A long time ago it seems that the architect of St Paul's, Christopher Wren, knew that he was building a national symbol and not just a church. He wrote in Parentalia:

Architecture has its political use, public buildings being the ornament of the country; it establishes a nation, draws people and commerce, and makes people love their native country.

To return to Kuala Lumpur, we have seen the nation take action through its government to restore the balance. A new airport of massive proportions has been designed by the Japanese architect Kisho Kurakawa (Plate 13). This is far larger than the traffic can possibly justify, and is planned to be very much larger still. It is clear that this airport is designed to compete with Changi in Singapore and 'draw people and commerce' to Kuala Lumpur. The construction of the world's tallest building, the Petronas Towers by Cesar Pelli, is another indication of this drive. There was no particular need for such a huge building, and certainly no need to build so high. The result has put enormous added strain on the ground level infrastructure. In Australia there was a competition to design a new opera house on a very prominent site in the harbour, and this was famously won by Jorn Utzon, whose wonderful creation has become the icon of Sydney. However, it is said that he submitted drawings late, in the wrong format and broke many other rules of the competition. Initially his design seemed virtually unbuildable due to its complex geometrical form, but eventually both the structure and cladding were made to work by ingenious technical solutions. However, then huge acoustic problems emerged with the interior. So why did Utzon win this competition with such a problematic design? It seems likely that, when the assessors saw his design, they recognized what they had always known but failed to articulate. The competition brief was for an opera house, but primarily Utzon had given them an icon for the capital and a symbol for the nation. Thankfully they had the wit to recognize his genius, and made the opera house work well enough!

The city territory
These great cities seem also themselves to be the product of a rather unusual and specialized form of territorial behaviour known as the 'arena'. Ardrey's description of the arena behaviour of the Uganda Kob draws the parallel quite clearly. In territorial terms, the arena is an area of land that might be thought of as a breeding ground. It is through the mechanism of this special place that Darwinian principles of selection for breeding are enabled, and thus the arena is a territory, or more strictly a whole set of territories, over which the males of some species compete. The winners of the battles take ownership of the most central and prized territories and thus become sexually attractive to the females, so the strongest and most dominant males are selected for reproductive purposes. Ardrey's description of the behaviour of the Uganda Kob owes perhaps almost as much to his experience as a playwright as to his training as an anthropologist. It is graphic and imaginative, but sets the scene quite delightfully:

A stamping ground, the breeding arena of a single population of Kob, looks like nothing so much as a series of putting greens conveniently laid out for the benefit of idle guests behind a luxurious resort hotel ... Each little putting green with its close cropped grass is about fifty feet [18 metres] in diameter and is a territory occupied by a single male. A closely bunched cluster of a dozen or fifteen or eighteen such territories in a main arena may occupy an area of no more than two hundred yards across. Here the champion males out of a population of almost a thousand – a kind of sexual Olympic team-fight, display, and jockey for position ... Within the arena some properties have greater value than others. In a normal city, real-estate values increase block by block to the city's core; so on the stamping ground sexual values increase from the suburban market of the periphery to the flashing excitement of Times Square.

So what are the human equivalents of the arena? The prestige and consequent associated high land values of a city centre can be seen as parallels with the most desirable central places in the animal arena. An important company will require its offices to be centrally located not for convenience or necessity but for symbolic reasons. A quick tour around the central business districts of any of the world's great capital cities today tends to reveal many familiar names. These huge multinational banks, manufacturers, service providers and so on need to maintain the image of their potency and power through their location and address. There is, however, far more to it than just economics. We expect our cities to have an increasing intensity towards their core. This is where 'it all happens'. Great cities depend upon this central intensity for their very character and attraction. A respected colleague of mine who joined my university from a job in London left after only a few years without any job to go to, largely in order to return to London. He frequently told me that crossing one of the great bridges over the Thames gave him the feeling that he was 'at the centre of things'. Out in the suburbs we see much the same game played out on the domestic front. It is commonly said in the UK that there are three important factors in choosing your house; location, location and location. Nothing else, it seems, comes near in terms of social prestige; the address is all! The price of domestic property in this country is hardly related to the value of buildings at all, but almost entirely to the value of the land on which they sit. However, the price buys a social prestige that matters greatly to many people. In England your postal address is defined by a postcode, a parallel to the American zip code, and I know people who have changed their mind and decided not to buy a house once they learned that its postcode was an unfashionable one.

One can see parallels of arena behaviour inside buildings too. The competition for the best office and, even more dramatically in my experience, for the best desk in open-plan offices can be intense. The case quoted in the previous chapter by Edward Hall of the French colleague demanding a pay rise because his desk was in the middle of the office is a clear example of the arena at work in such a setting. The relationship between location and status is often clearly expressed. The higher floor levels of hotels often house the more expensive rooms, and the penthouse suite is of course right on the very top. The so-called executive floor in office blocks is rarely low down in the building. Seats near to or immediately opposite the person chairing a meeting are often highly prized. I remember causing chaos by failing to respect this in a meeting I chaired a few years ago. This meeting was the first of a sequence I was chairing, and involved senior members from all parts of my university. We were to hold these meetings in the most important room on our campus where the main University Council meets. Since this room is so symbolically important it has one very special chair with a higher back, arms and the university crest, in which the chairperson normally sits. After discussing the agenda with an assistant, I arrived just in time for the meeting to find most people were already seated at the table. However I did not, as they had obviously expected, sit in this special chair, which they had left empty for me, but rather in the chair I normally used in the centre of an adjacent side of the table. I noticed that some people immediately changed their seats. Later in the meeting, one senior member of the University complained that I was not giving him enough opportunity to speak. He was sitting immediately opposite the special chair!

The family territory

We occupy territory in many quite different ways, and traditionally none has been more important than the family. However, the family, once such a conventional and ubiquitous building block of society, does seem to be breaking down in the West. In spite of this, the family home represents one of our most enduring territorial phenomena. The typical two parents and their children may not be as universal as they once seemed, but the home with its house and garden remain powerful symbols of our aspiration. 'A home of your own' is still the ambition of most. The family represented security and stability and through the marital contract provided for this stability throughout the children's extended years of dependency.

The nature and organization of the family and how it organizes its generations have a direct bearing on the structure of spaces provided in the family home. Many species of animals are also organized on a pair-bond basis, and Robert Ardrey describes in detail the life and family of the North American beaver to illustrate the principle (Ardrey 1967). The beaver family founds a dam, which includes the family home in its heartland. The size and structure of the territory it defends, however, provides for the parents, the immediately newborn and the yearlings of the previous year. Older offspring leave the home to find their own mates and form their own territories, so spatially the organization remains stable. We humans have an extraordinarily long period of dependency for the children, and in relation to the span of our lives this is about one quarter. The traditional family home in Western Europe and North America would have therefore included the grandparents, parents and children. Today in these cultures the specialism and mobility of the parents is such that this is decreasingly likely.

No more thorough study of the organization of the family home in terms of contemporary intra-family territory can be found than in Chermayeff and Alexander's classic treatise *Community and Privacy* (Chermayeff and Alexander 1963), although it is somewhat blind to the varying cultural traditions to be found outside the USA. In the modern homes of a number of Malaysian friends I have found a common tendency to establish a space known as the 'family room'. Most British houses have only spaces for sleeping and washing on their upper levels, but this family space is indeed on the top floor and it also doubles up as the circulation space for that level – a kind of enlarged landing in which the children can play, where the parents may exercise and where television might be watched. It is not expected that guests would come here; they would be received in the main space downstairs, which is more formally laid out for discussion and conversation. This perhaps reflects the older and now largely unobserved European tradition of the 'reception room'. The receiving of guests and their entertainment represents a highly symbolic invitation into the family home or territory.

In Britain we have a phrase, 'hearth and home', referring to the space around the open fire that represents the inner sanctum, the heartland of the family territory. In other climates and cultures this is replaced by more appropriate devices. The extraordinary wind tower houses of Dubai on the Arabian Gulf certainly need no heating (Fig. 7.2); here there is a year-round need for cooling. Due to the proximity of the Gulf and the adjacency of large land and sea masses there is always a movement of air resulting from the exchange of heat between them, and these wonderful houses use the reverse of the principle of the chimney. A square tower rising up from the middle of the dwelling to a height greater than the surrounding roof has louvred openings on all four sides and whatever the direction of the breeze, whether it be onshore or offshore, this passes through the tower, sucking a column of air up and causing a circulation at the foot. This then is where the inner sanctum and social hub of this house can be found, for here one can sit cross-legged on a carpet and be cooled by the constant motion of a natural airconditioning system entirely free from CFCs. As one enters one of these houses this space is shielded from view. The passing visitor or tradesman will not be able to see from the door to this territorial heartland into which only family and close friends are invited.

(a)

(b)

7.2 The 'wind-tower' houses of Dubai in the Arabian Gulf. One is permanent (a) and one portable (b), but they share the same principles. In both cases a wonderful and simple device for using the sea breeze to cool a space has been woven into the fabric of the house to also create the most precious and inner sanctum of the family territory

In the Western world, we may be seeing the breakdown of the traditional family with dramatically increased rates of divorce and equally significant reductions in marriage rates. This pattern can be seen as an inevitable consequence of forces acting on modern life. The diminution of the influence of religion has removed taboos about childbirth outside marriage, which were constructed from those belief systems. The increased economic necessity for two incomes and improved access to education, training and job opportunities for women has led to a need for greater mobility and thus looser ties in marriage as both partners develop careers, rather than one being focused on maintaining the home. However, this trend has not affected the need for the family territory. Desmond Morris points out that this remains a constant in the spatial organization of our societies (Morris 1967):

The spatial defence of the home site of the family unit has remained with us though all our massive architectural advances. Even our largest buildings, when designed as living-quarters, are assiduously divided into repetitive units, one per family.

Trouble with the neighbours!

A territory must have its boundaries, and an inevitable consequence of this is that beyond them reside the neighbours. It seems that all territorial creatures feel some sort of animosity towards their neighbours, although it rarely amounts to anything more than a petty squabble. One of the most popular themes for situation comedy programmes is that of the friendly rivalry between neighbours. The English phrase 'keeping up with the Jones's' exactly captures the spirit of this relationship. We share much with our neighbours but somehow just want to be one step ahead, or at the very least level with them, in wider society. In the animal world Ardrey shows this antagonism to be very common. I am lucky to have a large garden in a country setting on the outskirts of a large town. On a lovely English spring morning in my garden the birds sing from their favourite trees to complement the visual scene with their sound, and on such occasions it is hard to realize that much of the pretty birdsong so romanticized by us is in fact a warning to neighbouring birds of the same species to keep out. In fact most birds only sing when inside their own territorial borders. The song is a defiant message to neighbours that dreadful things will become of them if they dare to cross the invisible borders of the avian territories. It is particularly hard for us English to realize that what we view as the most friendly and English of all birds, the robin, is in reality as territorial as they come and aggressive to the point of delinquency! If we only put aside our rose-coloured spectacles we can see with more objective eyes that the male is rarely seen in company and never in the company of another male. It certainly is just as it seems. It is indeed the same bird that perches on your fence, garden shed or spade every day. No others would dare come near! Out in the open we rarely see the violence, but Ardrey reports studies showing how robins in confined captive spaces commit murder with apparent willingness if not enthusiasm. Of course here the poor victim is trapped and prevented from fleeing, as would most often happen in the open.

Human society being so complex, the phenomenon of the neighbour is similarly rather more elaborate than that found in the robin! Nowhere is the rivalry of neighbours more obvious than in the football stadium. When the team I support runs out onto the pitch there is a huge roar of support for them from the crowd. For 90 minutes they represent not only Sheffield, but that part of Sheffield known on the football pitch as Sheffield Wednesday. Frankly this is logically absurd, since at the time of writing the team comprises two Italians, a Swede, a Norwegian, two Dutchmen, a Czech and several Scots. Yes there are also one or two Englishmen, but these do not actually come from Sheffield, and the real heroes are the Italians. Now when England plays Italy that is another matter altogether! Of course this just shows how complex human territoriality really is, and how dangerous and simplistic it is to extrapolate blindly from animal behaviour, no matter how tempting that might be.

After this initial roar of approval the crowd is likely to raise the loudest cheer for a goal scored by the home team. Sadly, on many occasions this either does not happen enough or even at all. On such depressing afternoons the loudest cheer might well accompany the announcement of the score of our nearest neighbours, but only if they are losing! A rule about territory seems to be that those who are your nearest neighbours, and especially those with whom you share some territorial boundary, are those who you most wish to beat!

In England the football stadium is organized so as to position the most fiercely loyal supporters at one end of the ground (Inglis 1983). Here traditionally they stand looking down the pitch from behind their goal as if they were a collective twelfth player. Indeed they are almost recognized as such, with managers frequently appealing to the supporters to 'get behind the team' and shout loudly for them. These most faithful supporters generally paid less than the more well-heeled citizens who are comfortably accommodated sitting down the sides of the pitch. The opposite end is reserved for supporters of the away team, thus opposing them against the home end like two great medieval armies. These often massive and originally uncovered slopes resembled natural hills, and many are still known as Kops. In fact their full name is Spion Kop after a hill in South Africa, which was somewhat pointlessly fought over during the Boer War at the turn of the century. Thousands of British soldiers were killed in taking the Spion Kop from the Boers, but the force was so weakened by the effort that they withdrew almost immediately. The Spion Kop thus came to represent the ultimate devotion to a cause, whatever the cost. Rather too often on a Saturday afternoon one realizes the absolute appropriateness of this association!

Of course the very game of football itself, like many others, is basically territorial. The teams each have their own half of the pitch with their own goal as its heartland, which must be defended at all costs. Behind this on the Kop the faithful gather patiently waiting not only for the game to begin but also for enough of the opposing fans to arrive to make it worth the effort of hurling defiance in their direction. The songs and chants which recall historic victories, celebrate individual players and denigrate the opposition form a kind of community singing, bringing together the crowd into a single shared experience. This seems so fundamental and basic that having once experienced it one cannot dismiss altogether the elemental nature of our territorial behaviour. One is also struck by the fact that it is the very antagonism of the fans for the opposing supporters that seems enjoyable to them. The so-called 'local derby', where two geographically neighbouring teams compete, is often a particularly passionate affair since the antagonism is all the greater for its neighbourliness! Ardrey makes this point about our embarrassing wish to enjoy aggressive behaviour:

Nature may abhor a vacuum, but it has even less use for boredom. In species after species, natural selection has encouraged social mechanisms that seem ultimately to exist for no reason other than to provide conditions for antagonism, conflict and excitement.

Thankfully on such occasions the home team is more likely to win than the away team, since they have 'home' advantage. Desmond Morris, in his amusing analysis of the social dimension of football, has considered the effect of this territorial advantage of the home team (Morris 1981), and his figures show that it is roughly twice as easy to win at home as away. Of course in reality there are many contributing factors here. The away team suffers a journey and may not have such good knowledge about the peculiarities of the pitch, but the effect of being on someone else's turf and in their territory also seems likely to have a significant psychological effect.

One is struck time and again by the remarkable similarity between this behaviour and what Ardrey describes as the *noyau*, a French term used by the ethologist Jean-Jacques Petter and taken to mean a society based on inward antagonism. Ardrey charmingly describes the *noyau* through the example of the callicebus monkey, a treetop animal living in family groups that occupy exclusive territories. Each day the family awakes in its sleeping tree, to be found in the heart of the territory. After only minor feeding, the family leaves the sleeping tree and moves to boundary of its territory:

The little family makes no compromise with principle, but bright and early is on duty at the border, only partly fed, hankering for action, waiting for the arrival of neighbours to be angry at. Shoulder to shoulder mother and father wait, tails intertwined, nursing their grudges, feeding on their animosities, impatient for the arrival of their beloved enemies. Not one foot will the family place on the neighbour's domain unless neighbours are present to make the intrusion worthwhile. But let the neighbours appear, having had their dew and scanty snack, and callicebus hell will break loose.

It is often the case that those who fail to understand the true nature of human spatial behaviour can make dreadful mistakes. An appalling tragedy occurred in 1989 at my own football ground, Hillsborough, when Liverpool played Nottingham Forest in the FA Cup semi-final. Many of the Liverpool supporters arrived late, a behaviour pattern which had at that time become rather common. A great crush developed outside the ground and there was real cause for concern for the safety of the crowd, so the police made what was to prove an awful mistake. They opened the large escape gates to allow the pressing crowd in. The noise of the crowd inside suggested events were afoot on the pitch, and the inevitable surging crush killed many innocent supporters, who were unable to escape due to the fencing that was then thought necessary to keep crowds off the pitch. Much has been written and said about this disaster, and this is certainly not the place to analyse the whole event. Some have wanted quite understandably to apportion blame. There were so many mistakes made that led to the tragedy that in fact no one person or group of people can be sensibly thought to be completely responsible. However, without doubt the fencing was a product of a form of thinking about human behaviour that has since been demonstrated to be wholly wrong. If people are herded and corralled by police and kept in crowded pens, it seems hardly surprising that some at least will respond by behaving as if this is really necessary. Thankfully the fences have since gone, and we now wonder why they were ever there in the first place.

However, another subtler mistake has followed. Lord Justice Taylor, who led the subsequent enquiry into the disaster, recommended that football stadia should be made entirely seated. This seemed to be argued on the basis of the better behaviour of people sitting down and the reduced likelihood of large swaying crowds resulting. This has changed quite fundamentally the nature of the human experience, and in the eyes of most has changed it for the worse. Seats are in neat and tidy rows and have numbers. They are sold individually, and one must go to the specified location. My son used to gather with friends before the match, and after a good lunch and some drinks they would walk to the ground together and stand together. Thus however many of them there were on that particular day, they all remained in a group enjoying the match together. This is no longer possible, and the social communal experience of the Kop with its groups of friends and wit and banter has been destroyed. The device of a fixed seat is more profound in its behavioural outcome than Taylor and others who fail to listen to the language of space have ever appreciated.

Defending the territory and beyond

The defence of territory is a natural tendency that designers can both promote and exploit. Equally, designers can make the defence of territory a veritable nightmare for the occupants by the careless arrangement of boundaries. I know of many heartrending tales of house-proud people who have suffered lives of protracted misery as they battle with neighbours or strangers to defend and maintain what they perceive to be their boundaries and territory. A public sector housing development I studied for quite different reasons for a number of months in Birmingham revealed several examples. The houses here were arranged on a Radburn principle – that is to say, there were a series of spaces between terraces of houses with segregation of pedestrians and vehicles. To one side of the dwellings there were garage courts for parking the residents' cars, and the pedestrian side of the dwellings created an area which was open landscaped with no fences or hedges of substance but generously planted with trees and shrubs.

A woman who described a whole history of territorial problems to me lived in a house at the end of a terrace (Fig. 7.3). She was interested

BALL GAMES PROHIBITED

7.3 A dreadful misunderstanding of territory leads to this silly notice. It has no deterrent effect on children, of course, and actually encourages them to try to hit it with their ball! The trees that it is meant to protect provide convenient goalposts for a game!

in gardening and tended the plants near to her house. The architects had quite unthinkingly used exactly the same house type for the end of terrace as they had for centre terrace situations, so there was no window in her end gable wall. The public authority had planted particularly generously at this terrace end, and this woman tried for many months to care for these plants. Of course, since she did not overlook the area she could not spot troublemakers who were either intentionally or otherwise damaging the landscape. Actually I discovered through observation that the damage was mainly done by youngsters, who naturally congregated, as they will, at a spot least likely to be supervised by adults. There was nothing malicious in their behaviour; thoughtless and mischievous maybe, but which of us can claim not to have been the same in our time? It is also sadly true that the elderly, and particularly the single elderly woman, may regard their congregation with suspicion, the teenagers in turn encourage this with a little bravado, which can easily overstep the mark. Such was the case here. They were stretching their teenage wings and she was a soft target for their rebellion. However, the situation was to deteriorate further when, after she complained to the authority, they replanted the area with some young trees.

What my poor old lady saw as two tender specimens of flowering tree, the teenagers saw as goalposts! To them they were brilliantly sited – two trees just about far enough apart to make a goal, and conveniently the wall of the house behind would stop the ball. Excellent! Her irritation at the damage caused to the trees became compounded by the incessant noise of the football kicked against the wall of her house. Again she complained, and this time the response of the authority was as stunning a misjudgement of the situation as I have ever seen. A notice was fixed to the wall announcing that ball games were banned. Of course this tin notice made a dramatic ping when hit by any ball, and now became the target for a whole series of new games invented by even younger children to exploit the phenomenon. This might seem an amusing tale, and from one perspective it is. However, the distress caused to this old lady was immense, the inconvenience and work generated for employees of the authority expensive, and the damage to the landscape ultimately unstoppable. All this came about as a result of a little thoughtlessness by an architect about territory. A window in this wall would have given the old lady a nicer house and led to the children finding a more suitable place to gather. Of course the architects should have provided that too, but we shall come to that in a later chapter!

The territory invaded

Vargas suggests that there are three types of territorial trespass, which she calls 'contamination', 'violation' and 'invasion' (Vargas 1986). Contamination is where an invasion has taken place, and either some actual or perceived contamination has occurred in the concept of the territory. Many people who have been burgled report the depth with which these feelings can be experienced. The knowledge that someone unknown has been in the territory can even result in the owner feeling the need to move house, not for reasons of lack of security but simply because the place no longer feels theirs in the way it had prior to the contamination. The neighbour's dog that comes through the fence and defecates on your lawn is another example of contamination. My experience of this is that people are less offended by the event itself than by some perceived indifference displayed by the neighbours about the event!

Violation occurs when some actual harm is done by the invasion. If the burglars actually damage property during their illegal occupation, this can seriously heighten the sense of violation people may feel. The interruption to your sleep resulting from the noise of the neighbours' children having a late night party might be an example.

Finally, invasion is the attempt by others to take over a territory on a more or less permanent basis. Coming home from a very long holiday and finding squatters in your house might be an example. The rooms in the family house previously occupied by children who have left home are particularly problematic here! I remember the sense of invasion I felt when, after having left home, I went back to stay in my parents' house and found they had redecorated and totally rearranged 'my' room. Of course any sensible analysis would have told me this would happen. It was not actually the redecoration of course that offended, it was the realization that a territory I considered mine had now been taken over, even if entirely legitimately!

In his now seminal book *Defensible Space*, Oscar Newman discusses this problem in detail, supporting his thesis with empirical data (Newman 1973). His argument, though, goes further. Neutral space non-overlooked and indefensible not only goes undefended but also becomes more susceptible to crime. In a comparison of two housing developments of otherwise equivalent characteristics, he reveals higher levels of crime in the development that has higher rise. What these data show, however, is not necessarily a relationship between high rise and crime *per se*, but a relationship between the design of communal space and crime. In the lower rise scheme studied by Newman there is much less circulation space that is both internal and not overlooked than is the case in the higher rise scheme. The recorded crime figures from the police records show this is just where the increase in crime takes place.

In my adopted home city of Sheffield we have a series of deck access housing schemes all based on the same system made famous at Park Hill. Here the architects concentrated on giving people well-designed flats and maisonettes with well-lit south-facing prospects concentrated

7.4   The so-called 'streets in the air' of the famous Sheffield housing schemes of Park Hill, Hyde Park and Kelvin. In reality they contain few of the social features of a real street in terms of the relationship of territories and defensible spaces. In practice they thus failed to offer the behavioural setting clearly in the minds of the architects

into a huge wall snaking up the hills surrounding the city centre. This left large areas of the site available for landscaping, over which the residents would be able to look from their airy living rooms. The access decks located on the opposite side of the dwellings were open to the air on one side and in many cases reached ground level as the scheme climbed the hill. The architects famously described these decks as 'streets in the air' (Fig. 7.4). This phrase and the whole design were widely published, and many architects visited the schemes and were influenced by them and the writings of their architects. English Heritage has campaigned to have the one remaining development listed as of historical interest and to be conserved.

Sadly, however, the reality of the spatial provision and the resultant social behaviour is far from the romantic image presented by the architects. Of course the decks are not 'streets in the air' at all, but more like open-air corridors. The word 'street' is of vital importance here, as it conjures up not just a spatial organization but also the social consequence that we intuitively know results by applying the language of space. First, these 'streets' are long and yet go nowhere. Although the architects argued that the scheme would operate as if it were low rise since the majority of decks meet the ground, again the reality is different. The decks do meet ground, but at the out of town end, although we might expect more journeys in a city centre scheme would be towards rather than away from the centre. At this city end and at intermediate points, lifts are provided. I observed the scheme for a day and recorded the journeys people made by leaving their homes. The vast majority of journeys were indeed made by people moving townwards along the deck and then taking a lift, rather than taking the alternative route along the deck to ground. So in reality the scheme works more as high rise.

Another way in which these decks fail to resemble streets is the relationship the actual dwellings have with them. Most importantly, no living spaces overlook the decks, and this means that in Newman's terms the street is totally undefended. What is worse is that residents are effectively isolated in their dwellings, since they do not see each other coming and going and have no garden fence over which to chat to their immediate neighbours. Unless by an extraordinary coincidence you were to arrive at your front door at exactly the same time as your neighbour, you might easily live in such a scheme without meeting for many weeks, months or even years. The architects extended their image of the decks as streets by describing the originally installed communal refuse chutes as 'the modern equivalent of the village pump' (Lynn 1962). Whilst the analogy holds in purely technical terms of a communal servicing facility, the social reality is very different. The image conjured up is of course of people casually meeting and chatting as they collect their water/empty their bins. Quite simply, the natural communal territory is not there and cannot be manufactured simply by the positioning of a refuse chute.

In any event there is unlikely to be any spatial promotion of community spirit, and the harsh reality of these schemes was far from ideal for family life. Whilst the density of the building itself leaves much open space, this is remote from parental oversight and is too dangerous for children to be left unattended. The unsupervised and undefended nature of the decks resulted in much antisocial behaviour, such as the tipping of redundant household items – old television sets, refrigerators etc. Such a place could of course work quite well for singles or couples whose life is focused not on a locality but on a professional territory, and who do not really want to communicate extensively with those who surround them. However, as a place to rear children and for more conventional families it is a disaster, since it fails to make places for families to establish territories and develop communal territories beyond the family. It is in such territories that much of the good rearing of children takes place, just as in the animal world.

We must be careful, though, not to generalize this into a critique of deck access housing systems. The same authority was to build a scheme achieving similar density several decades later, and here completely reversed the emphasis on community and privacy (Plate 14). The decks were placed on the south side of the dwellings, which had their kitchens and main living spaces overlooking the deck. In fact there was wall-to-wall and floor-to-ceiling glazing in the living rooms, which were also set back a short distance from the deck, providing a small amount of transition space from public to private. The decks were never longer than about ten dwellings. An indication of the different atmosphere here is that to take these photographs it seemed necessary to ask the permission of the residents. Indeed, several asked me who I was and what I was doing, something which has never happened in all my visits to the Park Hill, Hyde Park and Kelvin complexes. Two things had happened here of crucial importance. The residents had actually taken possession of the deck as it passed their dwelling – a small planting trough provided by the architects on the balustrade had invited this. Some had even put down outdoor carpets or Astroturf®, so as you walk along this deck you literally invade a series of territories. Secondly, the residents can see each other and soon get to know all on their deck. Regular visitors such as postmen and milkmen also know their customers and are likely to report anything strange or worrying. Strangers then are easily detected, as a community has formed and another level of territory, that of a deck as a whole, has become defensible and defended. When I returned to this development some 20 years after it was first occupied to take photographs for this book, I found a group of residents singing its praises very loudly indeed. They appreciated exactly how it worked socially, and felt safe, secure and among friends. 'We never want to leave here', one of them said to me, and they all agreed. When I asked if they were worried about any lack of privacy with such large windows opening directly onto the decks, they all dismissed this as not a problem. 'You know everybody anyway', one of them said. The community was clearly able through this architecture to care for its members. They told tales of how if anyone was ill it was soon picked up by the others. They recalled the one incident in living memory when an intruder tried to walk into one of the flats, but of course was quickly chased and caught. An apparently small design difference here has undoubtedly contributed to a huge variation in the quality of life of the residents of these two housing schemes.

Care must be taken here also to relate these behaviours to culture. The Malaysian culture is of course more eastern in its orientation, and is distinctly Asian rather than European in spite of invasions by the Portuguese, Dutch and finally British. The traditional Malay Kampong, or village, is a much more communal affair than a British one (Fig. 7.5). There are few markers of territory on the ground, with dwellings occupying space often raised off the ground for environmental reasons. However, again here we find great stability and little

7.5   In a Malay Kampong we do not see the same marking of territory as with an English housing estate, where fences and hedges mark every boundary

mobility together with the predominance of extended families. Such a community cannot be imagined in middle-class England for economic as well as social reasons. Of course in every culture there is a degree of territorial definition that is considered acceptable, but to go beyond this unwritten convention in the language of space seems not only unnecessary but may be quite offensive. Figure 7.6 shows a pretentious, almost castle-like boundary wall, and although this example may be amusing the lesson is important. What works as territory in one culture does not necessarily work in another. It is odd that writers such as Ardrey have drawn widely from the different species of animals, and yet implicitly been rather restricted in their understanding of humans to North American and Western European cultures!

Territorial behaviour can be exploited by designers to facilitate the maintenance of spaces, particularly those between dwellings. Take a walk around any social housing scheme, and you will almost invariably notice that the places where the landscape suffers most damage are in general not seen as extended territories. Recently there has been much interest taken in defensible space ideas by the police in several countries. As a result advice is now given to architects on how to design crime out of housing areas, and to the general public on how to make their homes less susceptible to burglary. However, care must be taken with all this. First, there is no real evidence that crime can be reduced

7.6 In the suburban English village where this can be found, it is known locally as the 'Great Wall of ...'. Is this the ultimate marking of territory for an English housing area? Behind this wall is simply another house, large certainly, and without doubt the occupant has more money than most – at least enough to totally ignore the neighbours' feelings!

overall, but that perhaps instead it is simply moved from one area to another. Second, there is some evidence that the perception of the police and of the public may be out of step with that of the criminals (Ham-Rowbottom, Gifford and Shaw 1999). A study has shown that the cues used by police and public are fairly similar, but that burglars may pay attention to some other features of properties when choosing where to practise their crimes. There is also a potential conflict here between the provision of physical barriers around territories and the need to provide the visibility that affords publicly defensible space. In fact, the main finding of virtually all empirical work on defensible space ideas in relation to crime and security suggests the need for openness and visibility. In particular, what is now called 'road surveillability' in the jargon is seen as extremely important in fighting crime. Actual barriers such as walls and fences, whilst increasing the difficulty of invasion and further expressing territorial identity, may often paradoxically increase the vulnerability of a dwelling to burglary. Not only does this decrease public surveillance, but it may also increase the perceived value of property, which burglars appear to use as a cue in choosing their targets!

The collapse of the territory

What happens when we are put into a situation where it is impossible to maintain territories? The central importance of the territory to the survival of animal species was demonstrated in a distressing, dramatic and now classic experiment by Calhoun as long ago as the late 1950s. As a result of this work, he coined the now much-used phrase 'the behaviour sink' (Calhoun 1962). Calhoun was studying Norwegian rats and found that, when restricted to a given area and given an unlimited supply of food, their population stabilized at a fraction of that it could grow to. In a period of over 2 years this creature is capable of growing from a population of two to 50 000, but in fact it reached a ceiling of about 200 and settled at about 150. Calhoun found groups of about a dozen rats maintaining a social order, which facilitated the protection of pregnant and newly delivered mothers and the rearing and weaning of the young. Calhoun ran many highly structured and rigorously controlled experiments. In a later experiment Calhoun introduced about the double the number of rats into the same area originally occupied by a stable number. He found the social order breaking down, fighting was common, nest-building activity was incomplete, and violence such as tail biting broke out. Females were unresponsive to courting behaviour, they became harassed, and pregnancies were aborted. Calhoun also noticed that the social structure of groups of about a dozen rats also disappeared. In short, society was not sustainable. Calhoun's and subsequent studies have suggested that there is an upper limit to density beyond which animals are unable to maintain a regulated and effective society. This seems clearly related to their inability to operate territorial behavioural rules, since the space simply does not allow it.

Does high-density living have the same effect on humans? It is tempting to draw parallels with inner-city crime and riots. It is also tempting to see the dreadful behaviour recently experienced in the Balkans as a result of territorial confusions between races. However, any detailed analysis of such events shows so many interwoven factors and so much history that to diagnose the ills as simple territorial failure is to trivialize a rich pattern of human complexity and contradiction. Clearly some nations live with much higher density than others, and some societies have quite different cultural traditions about privacy. What may be acceptable in the Borneo longhouse in terms of communal living in close quarters may drive people mad in rural England. The human city relies upon a whole series of technically achieved boundaries. The actual density of people in mass housing schemes in inner-urban western cities or very high-density cities such as Hong Kong is achieved through walls dividing horizontally, and high rise stacking families above each other vertically. In life then we can never actually see the reality of high density in the way Calhoun's rats could. In a block of flats we are kept from pestering our neighbours constantly by the technology of high-rise structures. However, some problems may remain. The family is not our only territorial unit, and high-density housing schemes may find it hard to deliver a structured hierarchy of territorial experience that may be important to us.

The territory as social reinforcement

The potential of shared territories for the development of social cohesion is now well recognized. An interesting example of this was revealed in a study in Singapore of why there seemed to be little sense of community in the otherwise remarkable public housing provided in this rapidly advancing city/state. Walter comments on this by comparing the reality of life in the HDB high-rise tower blocks in Singapore with the traditional Malay Kampong still to be found just across the causeway in Malaysia (Walter 1978). In the latter there seems to be a very highly developed sense of community, and Walter ascribes this to several causes. First, he points out that the Kampong usually has an almost total homogeneity of race and religion, whereas the Singapore tower block does not. However, probably far more importantly, he points out that the Kampong is so designed as to leave almost no space that is indefensible, and has extremely high levels of surveillance. The traditional Malay house has much less definition of indoors, with its natural cross-ventilation, compared with much architecture with which we in the West are familiar. It is bounded on at least one side and often three sides by a verandah, which overlooks the adjacent space. There are no fences and houses are within loud speaking distance of each other. This seems to operate rather like an extended social distance, and neighbours can actually hold conversations across the intervening space from within their own territories. The whole works rather like a flock system in which the detection of strangers and intruders is a communal responsibility. A high level of interdependency thus develops, where all living within the Kampong will know all their neighbours well. Paradoxically, although the Singapore tower block has higher levels of density there is little communal space and very clearly demarcated private territories. Walter suggests a number of devices to improve community in the Singapore tower block, including opening some flats out as communal facilities such as crèches and the like.

Whilst a central shared facility that becomes group territory seems to be one way of strengthening community, a shared threat seems equally effective! I learned a truth about the sociology of territorial defence as a young architect working on a very large new housing development. The people living there had come from many different locations, and in most cases found all their new neighbours to be strangers. Such an event is rather unnatural, and the newness of the place, with its lack of history, events and even mature landscape, contributes to the feeling of artificiality so often experienced in new towns. Communities simply cannot be invented. Some notable exceptions have been the attempts made to keep communities together when re-housed, as with the famous Byker scheme in Newcastle by Ralf Erskine. However, this was certainly not so in our case. Being an architect as much interested in people as in buildings I could not help but notice this failing in our work, and the social sterility with which our residents' lives was imbued. As the scheme was nearing completion a rumour spread, quite inaccurately as it turned out, that a new motorway was being planned right alongside the housing estate. In fact this was one of a number of routes under some investigation, but it was always one of the least likely and never reached what one might call the planning stage. However, the rumour caught hold. The result, although causing some temporary concern and even in some cases distress, was actually a wholly positive one. A few leaders began to identify themselves, and a residents' society was formed. Meetings were held and campaigns planned to counter the threat. The community began to pull together. Quite soon the threat of the road evaporated, but the social momentum was gained and the sense of community thrived. Initially the new society acted as a more powerful voice for the newcomers to complain about deficiencies in their homes, and the architects and builders came under fire. Soon a campaign was launched to improve the landscape, and trees were planted. Self-help facilities sprang up for childcare. They eventually raised enough cash to build community facilities.

I was reminded of how my parents had described their wartime experiences. They lived in Birmingham, which was heavily bombed during the Second World War by the German Luftwaffe. Indeed their own home was destroyed one night, and they simply set off on foot walking out of the city in a kind of collective daze, punch-drunk from the successive nights of bombardment. You might think they would recall this with horror, but decades later their recollection was of the way people helped one another and how good a time it had all been socially. In fact my parents' long walk reached its conclusion when, late at night and having no real plans, they were stopped in a small village on the outskirts of Birmingham by a family just leaving in their car to go on holiday. They gave them the keys to their house, told my parents to stay, and left! Of course my parents never forgot them, and remained friends for the rest of their lives.

Ardrey advances an argument about this effect of external threat on territorial behaviour. Not only does the animosity of neighbours help to hold families together, it seems, but the hazards of nature also give rise to equally touching examples of animal collaboration and sympathy. He describes how the Antarctic emperor penguin males stand in a huddle, each with an egg on his foot incubating it, while the females return to the sea and the food supply. The males suspend all arguments and hostilities and take it in turns to stand on the edge of the huddle where it is cold, giving their colleagues a brief respite from the winter gales! Ardrey describes this phenomenon as the 'amity enmity equation', and formulates this as $A = E + h$, where A is the level of internal amity in a society, E is the degree of enmity from others, and h is the natural hazard. An illustration contemporary with the writing of this book would be the offer by Greece to Turkey of assistance after a dreadful earthquake. Some political commentators at the time suggested this could herald a permanent and long-lasting reduction in the mutual hostility between these two nations, which often finds expression in disputes over the territory that is the island of Cyprus. Let us hope so!

This is a nice illustration of the paradoxical qualities of the territorial phenomenon. On the one hand it drives us towards such unpleasant manifestations as nationalism and football hooliganism; on the other hand it results in a love of the family, a dedication to child rearing, and acts of friendship and compassion. Perhaps this is just what Einstein was getting at in the quotation at the head of this chapter. Of course he was right, but sadly we probably have to take territoriality the way we take the rest of our psyche. We would like the good without the bad, but it seldom just works out like that. It all comes together as a package deal.

References

Ardrey, R. (1967). *The Territorial Imperative: A Personal Inquiry into the Animal Origins of Property and Nations*. London, Collins.

Calhoun, J. B. (1962). Population density and social pathology. *Scientific American* **206**: 139–146.

Chermayeff, S. and C. Alexander (1963). *Community and Privacy*. Harmondsworth, Penguin.

Ham-Rowbottom, K. A., R. Gifford, et al. (1999). Defensible space theory and the police: assessing the vulnerability of residences to burglary. *Journal of Environmental Psychology* **19**: 117–129.

Inglis, S. (1983). *The Football Grounds of England and Wales*. London, Willow Books Collins.

Lipman, A. (1968). Building design and social interaction. *Architects' Journal* **147**: 23–30.

Lynn, J. (1962). Park Hill redevelopment. *RIBA Journal* **69** (12).

Malmberg, T. (1980). *Human Territoriality*. The Hague, Mouton Publishers.

Morris, D. (1967). *The Naked Ape: A Zoologist's Study of the Human Animal*. London, Jonathan Cape.

Morris, D. (1969). *The Human Zoo*. London, Jonathan Cape.

Morris, D. (1981). *The Soccer Tribe*. London, Jonathan Cape.

Newman, O. (1973). *Defensible Space: People and Design in the Violent City*. London, Architectural Press.

Vargas, M. F. (1986). *Louder than Words*. Iowa, Iowa State University Press.

Walter, M. A. H. B. (1978). The territorial and the social: perspectives on the lack of community in high-rise/high-density living in Singapore. *Ekistics* **270**: 236–242.

8 Space and time

We shape our buildings, and afterwards our buildings shape us.
Winston Churchill, Parliamentary speech 1943

All buildings are predictions. All predictions are wrong.
Stewart Brand, *How Buildings Learn*

Predictions

Any good and useful language enables its users to communicate about what is happening now, what has happened in the past, and what will or might happen in the future. So languages usually have past, present and future tenses. We do not always know exactly what actually happened in the past, as we have uncertain and incomplete knowledge of it, and this keeps historians busy. However, our knowledge of the future is uncertain in a much more profound way. We sometimes think we know what is going to happen and turn out to be very wrong indeed. This happens perhaps more often than we care to admit. We are particularly poor at predicting the future when people are involved and, although we know a great deal about ourselves, we are also very unpredictable. This problem besets architecture, since, as Stewart Brand tells us, 'all buildings are predictions'. His claim that 'all predictions are wrong' might be a slight exaggeration, but his point is well made nonetheless.

Design strategies for uncertainty

I have suggested elsewhere that designers seem to have adopted three main ways of dealing with this uncertainty about the future in the design process (Lawson 1997). I have called these three strategies 'procrastination', 'non-committal design' and 'throw-away design', and it seems that each of these strategies has its exponents in different design fields. Procrastination is based on the idea that somehow the future may become more certain if only we wait a little. I regularly meet people who are paralysed by this approach when buying a computer. If I buy now, goes the argument, they might bring out a new machine and I will be left with an out-of-date model. I try to point out that this will also be true next week, next month and next year, so it is no reason to delay. This strategy is also popular with very long time-scale decision-makers such as politicians and town planners. Design decisions taken by governments, whether regional, national or local, that can later be criticized are potential electoral millstones around the necks of the politicians. Far better then to be detached and free of all blame! But procrastination rarely leaves a situation unaffected. Once an inner-city area has been identified as in need of some planning action, that area is likely to become 'blighted' and run down even more rapidly until decisions are taken about its future.

By contrast, some architects have tended to design bland, anonymous and neutral buildings, which are non-specific in terms of either their functions or their locations. Not surprisingly there has been a reaction against such architecture, which has been accused of failing to provide places of character. The notion of flexible and adaptable environments was popular for a while in schools of architecture. Habraken and his followers were highly influential for a time, and went so far as to suggest that architects should design support structures that would provide only shelter, support and services, leaving future users free to create their own homes and express their own identity by arranging the kits of parts that fit within these 'supports' (Habraken 1972).

The third response to uncertainty is to design for the present only. Thus obsolescence is built in, and the designed object is intended to be thrown away and replaced with a more up-to-date design. This strategy has been increasingly adopted by the designers of mass-produced goods. Everything from clothes to motorcars may be discarded in favour of new styles and images. Such an approach is particularly favoured by fashion designers, with the very word 'fashion' confirming its transient nature. However, such ideas have already begun to invade more traditionally stable fields such as interior design. We are expected not only to wear this year's clothes, but also to prepare this year's food in this year's kitchens. I recently saw an advertisement for office furniture systems that exhorted us to buy a new office, not because we needed it but simply because our existing one was old. 'You change your car every three years', went the text, 'when did you last change your office?' Unfortunately this consumerist approach is not only wasteful of resources but also leads to short-lived goods of continually reduced quality, and thus the need to replace things becomes not just an option but a necessity.

The span of time in space
Perhaps the real problem here is the way in which we have come to view time in our current age. The twentieth century will eventually be

remembered for many things, some good and many not so good. However, what in my view most distinguishes the latter half of the twentieth century is the way our perception of time changed so fundamentally. Of course Einstein was first to point out that time and space are not unrelated phenomena, and eventually Stephen Hawking was able even to write a *Brief History of Time* (Hawking 1988). Fascinating they may be, but such concepts have little impact on everyday life. What really changed for the average person was the way the western world accelerated time in relation to the span of human life. A thorough essay on this can be found in James Gleick's amusing book, *Faster: The Acceleration of Just About Everything* (Gleick 1999). In earlier centuries time had passed almost unnoticed, and we were much less conscious of it. Originally the problem was one of devising a sensible and repeatable calendar rather than the more precise span of time later to be measured by clocks. In fact even this problem was not fully resolved until the middle of the twentieth century – the Imperial Russian team travelled all the way to the London Olympics only to discover that due to an incompatibility of their calendar they were two weeks late and the event had already taken place!

It was the advent of travel that necessitated precise timekeeping – another example of the linking of time and space! Until we travelled long distances, time could simply be a local affair and entirely related to the movement of the sun in the sky. However, as soon as the great coaching era began and people travelled across England from London to Bristol in a few days, time began to matter. For one thing, we needed a table of times for the journey so that passengers could plan and know their departures and arrivals. The need for a 'carriage' clock became apparent so that London time could be kept in Bristol. England is only just about wide enough east to west for the local time difference to matter here. The real problems were to be posed by travel at sea, and in fact reliable navigation could only become a reality once clocks could be designed that would go to sea, withstand the motion of a ship, and still keep time accurately to within a few seconds over periods of weeks and months. The establishment of an international time system and the location of the base for this at Greenwich in England are no coincidence; it relates exactly to the need to keep time for naval navigation. However, the advent of the even faster air travel and its accompanying jetlag now makes an impact on millions of lives every year as we struggle to come to terms with the somewhat strange reality of spatially varying time systems.

Of course jetlag only happens because our bodies cannot adapt immediately to the rapid change in time, but there are many other ways we cannot adapt psychologically to rapid change. It is now unlikely that our school and university education will prepare us for the whole of our lives. Technical innovations come along more rapidly than society can absorb. The Internet is one of the latest; technically this is no longer the latest thing, and yet society has hardly even begun to adapt to the new ways of communicating and doing business that it enables. Buildings used to be built for a much more stable and predictable society. It is simply no longer possible to think in this kind of way. The building is probably one of the most permanent artefacts we use in our daily lives. Our cars, clothes, books, computers, televisions and most other belongings get out of date many times during a lifetime, but we still think of buildings as having longevity. The very phrase 'bricks and mortar' implies permanence and reliability. Invest in bricks and mortar and you will be safe, was the motto.

So we have a wonderful paradox here. On the one hand we have learned to be precise about time, and in fact we can manipulate it technically – we have slow-motion replays on television, and we can fly faster than the speed of sound. Marshall McLuhan's global village has arrived and, as he warned, our only certainty is change. Yet we persist with these lumbering leviathans called buildings. Architects still persist with the notion that they can be designed to work not just at the moment they are built but well beyond. We now even view historical buildings this way. Our whole concept of conservation implies some 'golden moment' to which a building should be restored, a complete and concrete freezing of time in space when the building was perfect. However, this hardly bears any serious examination. Most important buildings were adapted well before they were finished. The huge cathedrals and palaces of the cultural heritage trails of Europe were rarely planned as complete entities, and were often built by many generations who continually adapted the construction to the needs of society and development of technology. As Jeremy Till has pointed out, it was the modern movement that indulged this paradox to a level of absurdity that we still fail to recognize (Till 2000). Such buildings are monuments of functionalist dogma in which the whole structure expresses a precisely known way of living, working and playing. Of course they can never really work in the sense they were intended to. We have evidence of this every day of our lives as we struggle to use them, and yet the myth remains deeply rooted in our unconscious acceptance of functionalism. Till has suggested that we need a concept of 'thick time' to deal with this paradox. He relies on James Joyce's Ulysses as a way of explaining the idea:

Ulysses invokes a sense of time not as a series of successive slices of instants, but as an expanded present. Thick Time. It is a present that gathers the past and pregnantly holds the future.

For Till this 'thick time' is the time of everyday life, of the real experience of life as we live it. How this should be used to create a new approach to architecture is only hinted at in his essay. He argues that such a view of time 'avoids mere repetition of past times or the instant celebration of new futures'. We can see that such notions would embrace the ideas of change, decay, weathering, the forming and breaking of habits, the taking of and losing possession of space, and the many other concepts we have discussed in this book. It requires a maturity to see architecture not as a work of art that is the sole creation of the architect, but as a dynamic, almost organic, extension of the everyday lives of its inhabitants. Such an idea is in stark contrast to much modern architectural theory. It requires us to engineer some fundamental changes of attitudes not only about the theory and practice of architecture but also about how architects are educated and engaged by society. It will not come easily in a world that has come to expect mastery over the marking of time!

Identifying levels of uncertainty

There are some other ways of dealing with our uncertainty about the future. Where it comes to both buildings and human behaviour, this unpredictability is not uniform. There are ways in which human behaviour is remarkably conventional, and at other times we can hardly predict what will happen at all. So the two main problems for architects are how they can identify their varying levels of certainty about the future, and then how they can design accordingly. This first of these is hardly ever taught in schools of architecture, and the second has had periods when it has been popular, but mostly it is not.

Some readers of this book may be inclined to see the design of architectural space as largely a matter of social engineering. Nothing could be further from the truth. Our preparedness to do as others wish or as designers may imagine is always a matter of degree, and varies from almost total compliance to downright pigheaded obstruction! Designers, whether they are architects, engineers, town planners, urban designers, interior designers or landscape architects, regularly demonstrate their inability to understand the human condition in this regard. Their assumptions about our compliance with their schemes is often so naive that we may wonder if these designers have actually lived ordinary lives themselves. Of course all designers are themselves also ordinary people, but somehow they seem capable of de-coupling their experience of life in the real world from their imagined life in design worlds. It is as if when they enter the design studio they open their heads and remove that part of their brains that contains ordinary everyday experience, inserting instead a new cortical segment programmed with 'designer knowledge'!

'Designer' knowledge versus 'ordinary' knowledge

Let us then try to see if we can identify where this 'designer knowledge' departs from 'ordinary knowledge', and find some remedies. The first problem here is that design knowledge is formal and explicit. As

students of architecture, we read books, attend lectures and study existing designs. This knowledge is consciously, we might almost say artificially, implanted in our heads. In order to help us do this teachers use
theoretical arguments to bind the knowledge together into meaningful
structures, without which it would simply be a collection of disjointed
facts. Sometimes these theories belong to the teachers themselves, but
more often they come from philosophical positions taken up by other
designers. It is interesting that architects seem to theorize very much
more than other kinds of designers. You can see the effect of this by
going into the library of any university where architecture and other
design fields are taught – by comparison with the product design
section, the architectural shelves are groaning with theory-laden tomes!
I am guilty of contributing to the effect myself by writing this and all
of my previous books and articles! Over the years I have frequently
reflected on why this is, and in discussion with a leading British
product designer, Richard Seymour, I think I have at least part of the
answer. Richard points out that, in the UK at least, most students of
product design come from that part of the school educational system
that focuses on making and doing. They would have learned crafts and
skills, probably doing woodwork and metalwork, and perhaps technical drawing and possibly art. By comparison, the architectural students
will have had a much more classical education, having studied sciences
or humanities or, if they are exceptionally lucky, a combination of the
two. When I asked Richard why it is that architects and product designers, who do such similar things, hardly seem to know about each other,
he had an ingenious explanation (Lawson 1994):

Although some architecture and product designs look very close it is really the
extreme end of the bough of the architecture tree rubbing up against a leaf at
the extremity of the product design tree. We tend to think that they are very
similar, but they are not. Fundamentally their roots are completely different.

It was of course these educational roots that he was referring to.
Product designers learn more through making and craft, and thus have
a little more of what we have been calling 'ordinary knowledge' than
architects seem to.

Ordinary knowledge is that which is acquired by people through the
experience of living their lives. By contrast with 'design knowledge', it
is unstructured and entirely devoid of theory. Instead it is implicit,
practical and predictive. It enables us to recognize situations and tells
us how to behave in them. It is largely implicit rather than explicit
knowledge, since we seldom externalize it, rarely speaking of it and
hardly ever writing it down. In fact we are usually not even aware we
have this knowledge. In a way the whole of this book is about turning
implicit understanding about how we use space into explicit knowledge
and binding it together with some theoretical structures.

So students of architecture spend their time at university very removed from the buildings and behavioural settings they are designing, and doing this largely by reference to designer knowledge rather than ordinary knowledge. It is generally recognized that students' main aim at university is to work out what their tutors want them to do. It is hardly surprising that during this period they pick up a way of thinking about architecture and buildings that can be very remote from the way people actually behave in them.

We can see from this that, as a profession, modern architects tend to follow an extremely high-risk strategy when designing. Collectively they have high regard for formal material in architecture, and often view symbolic material in a different way to those for whom they design. They tend to consider space as an abstract concept and not a behavioural phenomenon, and yet paradoxically assume that behaviour will follow their predictions. Moreover, the contemporary architect has been encouraged to be iconoclastic and inventive. The new and the original are highly valued in architectural circles, and certainly far more so than in most of society. Architects are not trained to observe and evaluate buildings as social phenomena, so they are ill-equipped to gather and learn from readily available data, which would reveal the inaccuracies of their predictions. However, they tend to rely a great deal on looking at previous designs. Often this is done by using static illustrations in books and magazines that may even be devoid of people. Most architectural awards and prizes are judged by other architects, who share the same value systems, thus reinforcing rather than correcting the vicious cycle in which designer and ordinary knowledge become thrown apart.

In short, then, we can see the architect as always trying something new, but having low predictive capability and poorly equipped to learn from mistakes. Little wonder the profession has an increasingly bad press and is less and less highly regarded by the general public! This is a harsh and probably extreme criticism of a profession of which I am a member, and which I believe genuinely tries to do its best – in fact it is a profession that is, in my experience, largely caring and socially minded. Most architects care passionately about making good places for people. It seems a sorry mess that we have got into!

It does not have to be like this. It is possible for architects to get buildings nearer to people's needs than they often do. They can improve their predictive capabilities, and they can learn to connect the real and design worlds in their minds.

One-way prediction
There is a curious paradox in the way architects think about the relationship between people and spaces, which centres on that most over-used aphorism of the twentieth century 'form follows function'. The assumption here is that functions are understood and then form

is designed around them. This is fine as far as it goes. The problem is that we do not really understand functions as well as we think we do. The next problem is that functions change with time, get combined with other functions and are sometimes even replaced as society and technology change and develop. Implicit in the idea is that once a form, or more appropriately here a space, is designed, the assumption is that the function will remain exactly as was envisaged. In fact it hardly ever does, since people actually respond to space, so now function is trying to fit into form. Winston Churchill's famous remark that 'we shape our buildings and then they shape us' was made in connection with the layout of the chamber of the House of Commons of the British Parliament. He quite explicitly argued that the chamber damaged by bombing in the Second World War should be accurately reconstructed, since he believed that its shape forced members into the right kind of relationship for debate (Brand 1995). Others since may feel that such an arrangement is far too confrontational, and is at least partly responsible for some of the remarkably childish parliamentary behaviour we can see now that proceedings are televised. Whatever your view on this, the point is made that the layout of the chamber of the House of Commons now constrains some behaviours and encourages others.

The implicit assumption made in the 'form follows function' school of design is that people will recognize the intention, and then the function will be kept to that intended by the form. In traditional vernacular architecture the process is quite the other way round – people tended to put structures and forms around their behaviour and to modify them continuously until they fitted well. Increasingly I hear architects today talking of 'function following form' and this is a very good first step in changing design theories, but it is only a beginning!

Confidence of prediction and rates of change

What Stewart Brand has taught us in his wonderful book *How Buildings Learn* is that buildings are dynamic and not static things. Buildings change over time. Things are added, things are taken out, and features are modified, moved and so on. This process of occupation and modification is going on all the time all over the world, and it is generally done with 'ordinary knowledge'. However, architects are hardly taught about this and rarely study it, which is why Brand's book is so important. Brand builds on Frank Duffy's important idea about the rate of change of parts of buildings. Duffy's idea is as simple and obvious as it is important: not all parts of buildings change at the same rate. Architecture, however, is frequently practised in such a way as to assume the exact opposite. A building is intended to be complete and to stay as originally conceived throughout its life. Some architects even take considerable offence when clients and users dare to modify what they see as 'their' buildings.

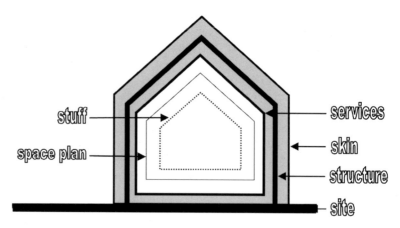

8.1   A model of a building in terms of the time cycles for typical replacement of its components. (After Stuart Brand)

Duffy suggests a simple diagram of a building as a kind of Russian doll with nested layers. This model has been extended by Brand to as many as six layers (Fig. 8.1). The 'site' is the base on which the model sits, and together with its surroundings has the longest rate of change. The 'structure' is the foundation and main load-bearing elements, and changes very infrequently. It is surrounded by the 'skin', the outer cladding, which in many buildings now changes much more frequently than in earlier times because of decay, the need for higher standards or simply visual fashion. Inside come the 'services', such as the wiring, plumbing and ducting. As technology advances and use patterns change these services may need replacing in whole or part quite frequently. Next comes the 'space plan', which we might think of as the internal walls and partitioning systems, together with floor and ceiling finishes – in other words, the surfaces that we see when using the building's interior. The contemporary office building may change some parts of this system every year, whereas in other building types this may have a slower rate of change. Finally comes what Brand calls 'stuff', which we might more accurately describe as furniture, fittings such as shelving, and equipment such as computers and television sets.

The essential feature of this analysis is that we can no longer think of the building as a single entity designed at one time, constructed and having a single lifecycle. It also suggests a form of architectural construction in which these various systems are separated and disconnected in order to facilitate the inevitable but variable changes. The structural frame as opposed to the load-bearing wall has certainly helped to separate structure from skin. In many traditional forms of building construction, much of the services systems are embedded in walls and floors and inaccessible without major surgery. There are obvious economic consequences of such strategies, which it is not the purpose of this book to explore. The issue here is how such an arrangement facilitates the changes of internal scenery and consequently of behavioural settings, as might be suggested by changes in the pattern of use of the building during its lifetime.

We have already argued that such a strategy is flawed in that it can lead to highly flexible but also sterile and featureless places that lack character and thus fail to invoke any meaningful behavioural response. We can perhaps now also see that an alternative approach can lead to some flexibility and yet have character. There seems to be a certain kind of building that is built with great confidence rather than reticence, has considerable character and is held in great affection by people, and yet proves itself to be highly adaptable. It is perhaps no coincidence that Frank Duffy's own main place of work, the headquarters of DEGW in London, is such a building – an old warehouse built solidly in brick, which has been gutted and put to an entirely new purpose. Similarly, we find the old warehouses and other canal buildings of Amsterdam live on centuries after they were originally constructed and are bent to quite new purposes. In Britain it has become popular to take old farmyard barns, country mills and other such buildings and convert them into houses.

Such buildings have their own features, which remain no matter how much they are altered. This might be in the overall form, the rhythm of window openings and the floor to ceiling heights, major structural members and so on. These features seem to give us a starting point in the design process. So it is when people take possession of and occupy a building, modifying it as they go. People generally find it easier to react to something positive than to start with a vacuum. However, let us put this argument to one side for a while and come back to it later.

Purposeful and non-purposeful behaviour (apparently!)
Some forms of human behaviour seem entirely purposeful, full of intention and directed towards one or more objectives. Others by comparison seem to have no really discernible intention and to be aimless, inconsequential and difficult to describe. Usually spaces in or around buildings are primarily intended to accommodate one of these types of behaviour. Consider two common activities in the home, cooking and relaxing. The former is directed towards a particular end, and even has a physically deliverable end product – the meal. The second is equally central and important, yet harder to describe and has no obvious outcome at all, except that perhaps we feel better afterwards. Cooking often goes on in a pretty businesslike way, and we can relatively easily identify the spatial requirements. We need good light, a clean, sheltered environment, a series of horizontal work surfaces, and easy access to food storage and to a wide range of both fixed equipment and hand

tools. Although we may all have our own personal preferences, there are fairly standard ways of providing spaces for cooking which are capable of commanding widespread approval. Relaxing is altogether another matter. We can begin to describe some of the needs, but we will soon find this becomes a very personal matter, and quite possibly capable of very wide ranges of interpretation. For example, one person may find it relaxing to look out over a panoramic landscape whereas another may prefer a more cosy small introverted space.

While all this may seem blindingly obvious, I find that architects are frequently confused about this when designing. Quite simply, it is no good assuming that our ability to predict human behaviour is uniform, since patently it is not. One way in which it varies is with this degree of purposefulness in the activity. We may be much more accurate and therefore more able to design precisely to fit form to function in the one case than the other. A common architectural mistake is to design assuming a uniform level of confidence. There are some spaces where the scenery of furniture, fittings and equipment must be left much more under the control of the user than others.

There is also a paradox here. Architects can easily make yet another mistake with this variation. In our search for meaningful ideas to use as generators of form, we often push the purposive activities even further up the scale of predictability than they deserve to be. It is also rather noticeable that highly specialized functions tend to dominate architects' thinking on these occasions. I described earlier how a lecture theatre that was thought very good by lecturers was not at all liked by students. This space was designed entirely functionally as a 'machine for learning in', to paraphrase a well-known saying! However, students do not stop living as ordinary human beings just because they are in a lecture theatre. The design was much less satisfactory as a container for the less focused and purposive behaviour of the real student, and was instead predicated on the notion that all students are simply automata for learning. This problem was probably also exacerbated by the way the architects concentrated on what was one end of a non-reciprocal transaction. In simple terms, they thought more about the space as a setting for teaching and not enough about it as a setting for learning.

Some research work we have been doing on hospital design gives an interesting clue to the way this works. We have evaluated new hospitals and compared them to the older ones they replaced. One study that is of particular interest here was of a new mental hospital replacing an old Victorian institutional building (Lawson and Phiri 2000). The patients clearly expressed their liking for the new place compared with the old (Fig. 8.2). It is not always easy to find out how people feel about places, and we shall discuss some of these methodological issues in the next chapter. However, if mental patients are asked the right questions in the right way by the right people they can be remark-

8.2 Patients in this new mental health building not only liked it more than the old Victorian institute it replaced, but they even rated the medical staff more highly and thought their treatment was better. In fact the staff, patients and treatments were very similar indeed, but patients were shown to be less aggressive and to require shorter treatment periods in the more suitable place

ably articulate about their surroundings. In this case they could tell us quite clearly that they preferred a whole series of attributes of the newer, more carefully designed, hospital to the old one. Not only did they prefer the spaces, colours and so on, but they also preferred the way the building facilitated both community and privacy. In fact they told us that they thought the environment helped them to get better more quickly. Actually this feeling of satisfaction was more generalized, and they also thought their whole medical treatment was better. They even rated the medical staff, who were largely the same as in the older hospital, more highly! In turn, the clinical staff in the newer unit thought the patients were making better progress. This was then confirmed by more objective measurements. We recorded far fewer incidents of serious verbal and physical abuse from the patients, and they required much less restraint. In fact their treatment times came down significantly. In a parallel study we completed in an acute general hospital, we found similar results leading to reduced needs for analgesic medication. What mattered most to patients seemed to be whether they were in a single bedroom or a multiple-bed bay. Neither of these quite different designs produced better results by themselves, but those patients who were in the type of accommodation of their own choice felt more satisfied with their treatment and made better progress than those who were not.

What is interesting about this study is that the improvements in the environment of the newer hospitals were really hardly at all about medical or clinical issues. Quite simply, they were more pleasant places to be in. In particular, they gave the patients better options about how to manage privacy and community than the older buildings did. In a parallel with, our lecture theatre, architects should perhaps concentrate more on the patients feeling better than on the doctors and nurses treating them.

In studies of this kind we repeatedly find that it is the ordinary everyday things in buildings that make an impact on people's lives. These might include having a pleasant view rather than being in an internal room or looking onto a brick wall. Simply being warm enough and not too hot, having a reasonable degree of quiet and good lighting, are all significant factors. Beyond these, we find that people want to be able to control such things – the frustration of being in a hospital room where you cannot open the windows yourself to get a little fresh air, or turn off the light yourself when you want to rest, were described to us by quite infuriated patients. However, not only did the architects fail to see the need to provide such controls, we also found that the medics thought the patients would be incapable of operating them satisfactorily. Somehow both these professional groups had come to view patients not as ordinary human beings but as some special sub-human species with reduced capabilities and rights. In more recent work I have done on hospitals, I have also found that generally patients and the nurses who treat them every day recognize the value of good settings and good places. They fully expect that a well-designed hospital may help patients to recover more quickly. Sadly, those who are responsible for commissioning and briefing the architects are not so convinced and prefer to concentrate on the technicalities of buildings and medical facilities. Thus they concentrate on treatment rather than recovery. They concentrate on the special conditions, again tending to forget the general needs of living people.

The paradox of this, I find, is that when architects come to design specialized buildings, such as a psychiatric unit, they tend to focus on the special factors rather than the ordinary ones. This is of course entirely understandable. I have shown in my studies of the design process that all designers have an almost desperate need to identify some special factors around which they can generate design ideas in what is often a hugely complex and confusing situation (Lawson 1997). This leads designers, it seems to me, to concentrate on the identifiably purposeful activities in spaces, and neglect the less purposeful but no less important aspects of daily life. Thus we design lecture theatres with no windows as perfectly ergonomic machines for teaching, and then forget how unpleasant such a place might be for the student who is there for many hours, day after day. Similarly, we make hospitals convenient for the doctors and sterile in order to avoid transmission of disease, but end up with places that isolate patients from their normal world, depress the spirit and sap the will to recover!

Learning from children

Children's play has already been mentioned several times in this book, and I make no apology for turning to it again, since the failure to appreciate its true nature seems endemic amongst architects, planners and landscape designers. Such designers must, during their careers, design for all sorts of highly specialized situations of which they may have no direct experience of their own, and yet I find somewhat ironically that architects and planners can be at their most naive when designing for children. It almost seems that many of them somehow totally avoided childhood and were born as adults, such is their lack of understanding of the child's mind and behaviour!

In Chapter 7 we saw how putting up a sign in a housing estate actually encouraged the football games it sought to ban. In fact the mistake had begun much earlier in the very basis of the whole layout of the estate. The Radburn principle of segregating vehicles from pedestrians in housing areas is intended to increase comfort and safety, and is predicated on the assumption that all will comply. Those most likely to benefit, children, are in fact least likely to do so in my experience. Children are essentially trying to learn about the world through their play. Often they are trying to find the limits of acceptable behaviour, so in this sense they are intended to be naughty! Without naughtiness there can be no discovery of the limits. Children are therefore not naturally compliant and disciplined, but rather they are creative and potentially disruptive. I am sorry to say that the failure to understand this is fostered in schools of design everywhere I have been. The Radburn layout creates 'safe' areas of grassy spaces overlooked by the living room windows of all the surrounding houses, and it creates hidden garage courts of concrete where there will be parked cars, garages left open, cans of oil, tools and many more exciting objects. To me it is obvious where the children will want to play! The writing on a plan of the words 'children's play area' seems to be enough to seduce both the student and tutors alike into believing that this will in fact happen. The intentions behind Radburn were laudable, but the assumptions embedded in it were that people, and particularly children, would behave logically. Well actually of course they do, but it is the logic of the child not the logic of the designer that prevails here!

In fact, even as parents we seem to have put our own memories of childhood behind us. How often does one hear a parent say to the bored and fractious child 'why don't you go out and play?' The assumption behind such a remark is that play is an identifiable, discrete and purposeful activity. We have 'playtime' at school, which suggests very much the same. In fact, play is really not a separate activity at all. There are of course times when it is formalized into a game or carried out with a very particular kind of toy, but in fact children play more or less all the time. It is better thought of as the child's way of interacting with others and with the world. Most importantly, it is also the way children learn about the world. It is through imitating adults, acting out our situations and through pretence that children come to understand how the world works. Even the simple laws of nature, such as gravity, are explored through the bouncing of a ball or bumping down the stairs on your bottom! The institutionalization of play into formal times and places is thus an imposition on the child by adults, and is mainly done for the convenience of those adults. It is much easier to design environments that work well for children if you just bear these simple ideas in mind.

Jane Jacobs' essay on the 'The uses of sidewalks: assimilating children' beautifully explored these ideas (Jacobs, 1961). She showed that in older parts of the city children played mainly on the streets and sidewalks (pavements in British parlance), whereas in the newer cities such structures had been swept away and the children given purpose-designed playgrounds. At first sight such a change seems an improvement – the newer playgrounds could be safe and supervised places after all. However, in reality such an analysis is far too simple, and is again based on the misconception of play as a discrete and purposeful activity in its own right.

Jacobs goes further, and argues that children who play on the street are incidentally also likely to learn that any adult will look out for them and care for their safety. The shopkeeper who tells them not to run across the road does not just increase safety, but also helps to socialize the child. By contrast, the playground supervisor is paid to do this and has a totally different relationship with children. We can go even further, of course, and see that play on the streets does not separate out children from other adult life. Such play is far more likely to create useful learning than the more sterile activity of the playground.

Of course children know all this, even if planners and architects do not, and this is because they are using 'ordinary knowledge', not 'designer knowledge'. For a number of years I used to shop every week at a supermarket in a suburban shopping centre in Birmingham. In effect this was designed as a podium on top of which were the car parks for the shoppers, and rising out above were housing blocks (Fig. 8.3). One part of the roof of the shopping centre had been 'designed' as a children's playground for the residents of the high-rise housing. I never once saw children play there; it was too bleak, sterile and dull, and the

(a)

(b)

8.3 A purpose-designed 'children's play area' in a housing scheme over a shopping centre (a). On this nice sunny day in the school holidays, children are not convinced of its merits! In fact they can be found playing hide and seek behind the ventilating ducts in the shopping centre (b)!

whole space was overlooked by potentially several hundred mums or dads from the windows of their flats. How could a child possibly be naughty in such a place? Indeed, how could a child learn anything here? However, every week I did see children playing in the car park, where you could hide behind all the cars and play 'chicken' with the drivers. Another favourite place for play was down in the shopping centre itself, where you could hide behind street furniture and then threaten the elderly, bag-laden shopper with your water pistol! I have since observed many parallels to this. This is really quite predictable.

Individuals, groups and crowds

Yet another way in which our ability to predict behaviour varies is in terms of the numbers of people involved. At one extreme we might be designing for a known individual with very clearly expressed preferences and well-defined repeated patterns of behaviour, and at the other extreme we might be designing for a very large group in the form of an audience, assembly, meeting, congregation or crowd. Curiously, both these extremes are where our predictions are most likely to be accurate and reliable. Designing the house for a known client has given us some famous and memorable architecture. Sir Edwin Lutyens designed many such houses, each different and yet mostly sharing some attributes of his own particular style. The owners were generally highly delighted with the way he had interpreted their needs and managed to fit the house to them almost like a glove. The landscape architect Gertrude Jekyll had one such house built at Munstead Wood, and she marvelled at how Lutyens had seemed to understand her wishes. Interestingly, such great houses usually survive the changes that time brings to their ownership well. They seem to have the strength of character to attract other sufficiently like-minded residents. However, we simply cannot design large-scale social housing on this basis. The residents of such dwellings will inevitably show huge variations in lifestyles and tastes, and will be pressed fairly close together and need to express their identity at least partly through the house. This is going to be a much less precise business. Le Corbusier tried to do this at Pessac, where he built a series of houses that, in conventional architectural terms are spatially iconoclastic and exciting. However, they enshrined a particular set of values and lifestyles that the eventual residents were largely unable to adjust to, and inevitably they adjusted the buildings instead. Le Corbusier's vision was soon lost, and Pierre Boudon has documented and commented on this in a cautionary tale for architects (Boudon 1972).

Spaces that are for large crowds accommodate behaviour that is often highly predictable, since what really matters here is not what each individual does but what the mass does as a whole. The foyers and entrance areas of large public buildings such as theatres and galleries or railway stations and airports show almost military precision in the regularity of their overall use patterns.

It is sometimes said that the two most frequently told lies are, 'the cheque is in the post' and 'of course I love you', but in the case of architects' drawings it seems that the lettering 'play area' and 'sitting area' should be regarded with equal levels of distrust! People will sit where they want to sit, and not where architects put seats. A student of mine carried out an extensive study of how patients attending health centres chose the seat they would sit on. Of course, as we have seen, this is heavily influenced by who else is there already, but two important principles emerge repeatedly from this and other similar studies we have conducted. On the whole, people seek to maximize their view and minimize the extent to which they are themselves overlooked. There are exceptions, and the extrovert who wants to be the centre of attention is one such, but in general people prefer to protect their back and open out their front. Beautifully designed seats in the middle of an open space may look very sculptural, but will remain just that – sculpture. By comparison people will sit on any object which is well located. Herman Hertzberger's sequence of studies shows the bases of columns and the steps of fountains as obvious examples (Hertzberger 1991). The classical column is particularly good, as it always provides shade somewhere around its base and usually also a sunny side, something to lean your back on and a view of passing crowds.

Hertzberger laments the passing of such detail in the rather minimalist forms of the modern movement. I have a large collection of photographs of seats that have been provided for people by architects and designers. A few are shown here, and they are all empty (Fig. 8.4). These are not carefully arranged photographs, but typical shots of seats that simply do not provide the conditions that encourage people to sit. They are mostly in public places such as shopping centres and the like. By contrast, you will see the second collection of images show people sitting on steps, parapets and all sorts of other features because these happen to offer good places to sit (Fig. 8.5). In the third collection you can see how authorities have tried to prevent people from sitting in places that are thought to be either untidy or dangerous (Fig. 8.6). These notices sometimes work and sometimes do not, depending on the culture and context. However, they are all indications that we collectively know what makes a good place to sit. If only architects could learn this lesson too!

This wish to be located rather than simply lost in a space is symbolized by the sentry box. The sentry box shown in Figure 8.7 for a soldier guarding the Ameliebourg Palace in Copenhagen is entirely vestigial – the soldier could not actually get inside the box even if he wanted to and was allowed to. Certainly rain does not drive him in! The poor man has few other comforts in what must be the most unnatural of all

8.4   Seats that are carefully designed, but for one reason or another are simply not in the right place to sit

8.5   Good places to sit that are not designed as seats are still well occupied

8.6   Good places to sit will attract people even if they are dangerous, or inconvenient to the authorities!

8.7 This sentry box is entirely symbolic in order to locate the soldier in space. It is not large enough to shelter him, and in any case he is not allowed to stand in it

8.8   The idea that people will walk where the hard landscape goes is so silly that one wonders how designers can become so detached from reality!

jobs. He must behave in public as though no other people were on the planet, or at least in his vicinity! He cannot acknowledge them or move, except when he periodically performs a token march up and down the territory he guards. The sentry box, however, symbolizes his personal place in the space for the duration of his duty, and it protects his back so that he may remain confidently and unblinkingly looking straight ahead in the sure and certain knowledge that no one is behind him. It is his temporary territorial heartland.

Movement

Much of the space we have to design in and around buildings provides primarily for people to move from place to place. If we simply observe this movement as a whole it looks terribly complex and confusing, and this is because we cannot tell exactly where each person is going to come from or want to go. However, once we examine the movement itself more closely we find that people are quite predictable in some aspects of their movement.

The footpath seems to give designers no end of trouble (Fig. 8.8). The tyranny of the set-square and tee-square and of the formal geometrical systems designers have become enslaved to will so often dictate where footpaths are drawn. Do these same designers always follow footpaths themselves and never take short cuts? I doubt it. Somehow they have managed to divorce the two aspects of their lives. People simply will tend to want to minimize the distance they travel to where

8.9   A car park that did not give its users any clues as to how to use it. The result was that we got in a terrible mess every day. Although rather unimaginative the subsequently landscaping scheme provided the behavioural cues we needed, and we never found our cars blocked in again!

ever they are going. This is really not very difficult to understand! I find that the more purposeful the journey, the less likely is the traveller to be deflected from this. Simply wandering in a garden is a different business to going to the corner shop for some much needed food or drink, perhaps in the interval between two television programmes. The short cut here is virtually a certainty, and unless the designer provides hard landscape for it the soft landscape will suffer. This is as sure as night follows day, and yet examples need not be sought out, they come into sight everywhere you look. This of course does not necessarily mean that designers must use straight-edged paths with kerbstones like some miniature interstate highway. The edge of the hard landscape is another matter, but hard it must be where the desire line is, or damaged the landscape will surely become!

Another rule that seems to offer good guidance in general is that people seem to seek to overcome perceived obstacles in their journeys as early as possible. So, all things being equal, if you want to visit a shop that is at the other end of the street but also on the other side, you are likely to cross the street first or at the first sensible opportunity. Similarly, we have found people using the first staircase they come to in journeys inside buildings that involve a change of floor. Naturally other influences can change these simple rules – walking on the sunny side of the street or where there is shelter from the wind in a cold climate, for example. By contrast, you soon learn to walk on the shady side of the street in the more aggressively hot sun of tropical countries. Interesting shop windows might also cause changes of behaviour from the simple rule.

Some years ago I worked at a city centre university where we were given the exclusive use of a car park (Fig. 8.9). This was in reality no more than an uncared for space between the buildings and the nearby major road. The plot was roughly triangular, and gave few clues as to how we should park. We proved totally incapable of managing ourselves in an organized way. Being a naturally early bird, I was usually one of the first to arrive and park. If I came to leave before the normal end of the working day, I frequently found my car blocked in. It seemed that as people arrived they always somehow managed to find just one more parking space. Since people so often take their cues from the behaviour of others, no one person was ever to blame for the mess. It just seemed when you arrived that others had already parked haphazardly so you followed suit, as it were. The whole thing became such a nuisance that we appealed to the university to do something about it. Eventually they did, employing a rather unimaginative landscaping arrangement, but this gave just enough clues as to how to park that we never had the problem of blocked vehicles again. Of course the car park now had a much smaller capacity, and this would always have been an answer, but people are often unable to help themselves in such a situation. They need the environment to spell out some rules to which they will quite happily conform.

The tyranny of functionalist space

There is a form of tyranny of space planning which seems to have become prevalent during the second half of the twentieth century. Perhaps it has its roots in the functionalism of the modern movement. If so, it has long outlived its welcome and usefulness, but still it persists. The underlying idea here is that functions must be located in space and have space that is somehow precisely adjusted to their needs. Needless to say, this idea prevails amongst professional designers such as architects and town planners rather than in the minds and actions of ordinary people. We find examples at the level of interior design, at the level of architecture and the layout of complete buildings, and in town planning at the scale of the organization of urban space.

An interesting experiment was conducted by Edwards, who looked at a large public-sector housing development of 360 houses (Edwards 1974). At this time in the UK it was normal to require architects to draw basic furniture on the 1 : 50 plans they did of the house types when seeking public funding. This followed the great Parker Morris report on the needs and requirements of such housing, which was to be partially enshrined in the 'Mandatory Minimum Standards' for public sector housing in the United Kingdom. Architects were therefore well used to laying out furniture on house plans at the time. In this experiment, some 28 architects were shown the plans of the main spaces of the standard house type, including the kitchens, living rooms and so on. Edwards' students also visited the actual development itself, and recorded how over 200 real residents actually arranged their furniture. There were several remarkable findings from this study. The architects showed themselves to be generally less creative and imaginative than the residents, and more conventional in the way they laid out the furniture. There were two features worthy of note here: there was much more of a consensus between the architects than the residents; and the architects seemed to be more likely to be bound by the orthogonal discipline of the dwelling plans and by their own tee-squares and set-squares. In short, this can be summarized as the architects showing general agreement about, for example, where to put the television set, and that arrangement was likely to be aligned with the walls. By contrast, the residents showed much greater variety of locations for the various items of furniture, and they were more likely to be at skewed angles in relation to the walls. A student of mine replicated this study and confirmed another of the original findings. The underlying principles behind the architects' arrangements were of zonal functional planning, and when asked to talk about their layout the architects would frequently describe it in terms of zones of activity – 'This is the relaxing zone, and this the dining zone', for example. This almost exactly matches one of Edwards' original architect's remarks: 'One tends to group around the television set in the relaxing zone rather than in the eating zone'. In reality, the residents were more likely to sit in easy chairs while eating their meals and watching television. Life for them was simply not functionally compartmentalized, and therefore not spatially zoned or planned. When asked where they got the information from which they used to predict how the furniture would be arranged, nearly all the architects said they based it on their own experience or preference. Since architects have a highly developed sense of space in its formal sense, this does perhaps lead them to make what other people might regard as odd predictions.

We have seen the same principles at work in a great deal of city centre town planning in the second half of the twentieth century. We have business quarters, residential areas, cultural zones and many more such artificial inventions in our cities. A planner in my own city described to me with obvious pride how they encouraged applications for building types that neatly fitted their own zoning of the city and discouraged those that did not. He even went on to describe a preferred colour scheme for delineating commercial, educational and cultural buildings. Such policies have successively led to the downfall of life in the western city centre that Jane Jacobs was to warn of many years ago. Thankfully, today many authorities are moving away from such regimentation and are trying to reintroduce residential accommodation into their city centres and to mix together activities in such a way that each part of the city lives for 24 hours a day, and not just for a few hours of the day or night.

It is certainly true that in many great cities areas have grown up that are known for particular activities – for example, the West End of London with its theatres and restaurants, or the jewellery quarter of Birmingham, or the central business and banking quarter of Singapore. However, in most cases these zones were not pure, and were never subjected to the planning equivalent of ethnic cleansing we have seen in conscious planning policy. Such policies led planners to restrict areas not only to a limited range of building types and activities, but also to colours, materials and scales. In fact, what makes most great cities fascinating is their very quirkiness in this regard. It is the contrast in purpose and scale that gives them their life, for these things speak of people and activities, not abstract building forms. It is, for example, the extraordinary juxtaposition of Covent Garden vegetable and flower market with its great opera house immortalized in George Bernard Shaw's *Pygmalion*, later to become *My Fair Lady*. It is the way the massive and formal church of Sacre-Coeur sits right next to the tiny and chaotic streets of artists'

8.10   A wonderful jumble of scales and purposes that makes Montmartre the special place we all love

houses in Montmartre (Fig. 8.10). Perhaps we should ban the whole-sale redevelopment of large city areas and only permit relatively piece-meal interventions. Will the massive and highly symbolic reconstruction of Pottsdammer Platz in Berlin prove to be a noble exception to this rule? So far it rather looks as if not. There is a sameness of scale and purpose that speaks of large corporations more concerned with their international positions than the spaces of Pottsdammerplatz. Curiously, the little temporary building erected to allow us to view the construction was the most alive building on the site when I visited it, but sadly that will probably have gone before this book is even published!

Invitational space

The parking bays in our university car park were in a sense an invita-tion to behave in a particular way. Some architects have developed a very subtle ability to create rather more open-ended or even ambigu-ous invitations. In his Glasgow School of Art, Charles Rennie Mackintosh ran a corridor at a high level along the rear of the build-ing. From this position there are spectacular views down from the relative heights of Sauchiehall Street, where the main façade is located, over the city centre. A series of small windows each set out into a bay invites the passer-by to sit and read or to meet with another colleague just off the main route for a chat. The function does not need to be specified, since the spatial invitation to sit on the windowsills is quite enough to trigger the behaviour.

Herman Hertzberger, perhaps the arch-exponent of such ideas, frequently developed such spatial invitations (Hertzberger 1971). In a housing scheme, he placed a small concrete block outside each dwelling. It carried the number and had a light that illuminated the area in front of the entrance at night, so it helped to generate some identity for each dwelling. However, it could also be used for a myriad of other purposes; residents could sit on it and chat, or even hold picnics around it, delivery boys and postmen could leave parcels by it and so on. I remember some few years ago visiting Hertzberger's office to discuss his work for another book I was writing on the design process. Since it was a rather pleasant autum-nal day, he suggested we sat in the garden. What I took to be a prototype of these ingeniously designed concrete blocks was found out there, and he clearly intended us to sit around it. However, to his evident slight irritation and my amusement it had suggested yet another function to his staff, who had propped a mass of bicycles up against it!

Of course Hertzberger went much further than this in his theory of 'structuralism' in design. He advocated a way of thinking about designed objects and spaces as 'instruments' rather than 'tools'. His distinction is a lovely one for our purposes here. To Hertzberger, space should be like a musical instrument that suggests how it is to be played but does not predict all the wonderful music that can be made by its owner. Contrast this with space that is a tool, tightly designed for a single highly specific task or purpose.

The trick of designing, then, seems to be a more intelligent and mature view of time, change and human behaviour in space. The designer needs to know above all else when to make a move in space that frames or invites behaviour, and when to leave the space more ambiguous. This is extremely hard to get right, and perhaps we can never expect fully to do so. There is probably no substitute for experience and observation in teaching us how this all works, and the problem for architects and such designers is that they get so little experience. Even in the most active and successful of careers most architects will only construct a handful of major buildings, and it is hard to learn from such limited experience spread out over such a long period of time. Many other professions, such as medicine, for example, allow for greater degrees of specialization and operate repetitively on such a rapid time scale that it is much easier to see what works well and what does not. Of course, the older ways of working that relied on vernacular processes solved this problem by relying on the accumulated experience of successive generations. In such a rapidly changing world as ours, this seems unlikely to be successful again.

Patterns of settings

An alternative approach has been suggested by Christopher Alexander in his now classic treatise on *A Pattern Language* (Alexander 1977). He believes that this can lead to a 'timeless way of building' (Alexander 1979), and he has many enthusiastic followers. What Alexander means by 'patterns' seems similar to what in this book we have been calling behavioural settings. Alexander argues that we experience remarkably few frequently and regularly repeated patterns of behaviour in our lives. He describes his own:

Being in bed, having a shower, having breakfast in the kitchen, sitting in my study writing, walking in the garden, cooking and eating our common lunch at my office with my friends, going to the movies, taking my family to eat at a restaurant, having a drink at a friend's house, driving on the freeway, going to bed again. There are a few more.

We can all write our own personal and individual list of these patterns. Whilst they will undoubtedly vary from one to another, Alexander argues there are only about a dozen such patterns. If they work well then our life can seem to go well, and *vice versa*. Alexander does not support such arguments with any empirical data, but his idea feels about right at least for the sort of lives many of us will lead. Of course the next step in the argument is to explore how well the spaces that accommodate these patterns are suited to their task. Alexander argues as we have done that this success is a matter of space and events. We have already relied on Aldo van Eyck's description of place to indicate a similar idea. Alexander next argues that many patterns are so common that they can be recorded as basic spatial configurations. Alexander also comes close to Hertzberger's notion of space that gently invites rather than officiously commands patterns of behaviour.

Alexander writes almost poetically in this series of books, which at times have a quasi-religious quality. They seem largely based on belief rather than evidence, but are nonetheless persuasive for that. In fact they seem to contain very good common sense by making explicit and formalizing knowledge, which we otherwise normally hold implicitly and unselfconsciously. This is entirely in the spirit of this book, and thus it seems appropriate to dwell on the ideas for a little while.

I find that often when one describes some of Alexander's patterns to people they nod their heads in agreement rather more than they contest them. The ideas behind the patterns also often chime with rather more theoretically advanced ideas about design or even empirically gathered data. As an example we shall consider just one of Alexander's patterns, that which he calls 'work community'. This is headed by a simple and sensible general suggestion:

If you spend eight hours a day at work, and eight hours at home, there is no reason why your workplace should be any less of a community than your home.

No one could seriously argue with this simply taken at face value. However, it goes a little further by drawing something else to our attention. In considering the design of the workplace, it puts the emphasis not on work but on human relationships. We have seen from our work on hospitals that if patients can choose whether to have community or privacy, and are able to control these, they feel better. Hertzberger's whole argument in the design of his famous office building for Centraal Beheer was not to create efficient workplaces, but to give the occupants opportunities to form and express the identity of their close groups as well as expressing their individuality.

Alexander explores this idea in much more detail and makes some quite specific recommendations. He suggests that 'workplaces should not be too scattered not too agglomerated, but clustered in groups of about 15'. Again this makes sense in terms of what we learned about territoriality. Such a number at least offers the opportunity for a sense of community through acquaintance. Alexander goes on to suggest some 'common piece of land within the work community, which ties the individual workshops and offices together'. This of course enhances the opportunity for community by enabling a sharing of some physical space and resource, a sort of territorial heartland.

Finally Alexander points out that the communal facility may need 'to exist at two distinct and separate levels'. Here he suggests that perhaps half a dozen workgroups would naturally and easily share a games area for, say, table tennis or volleyball. On the contrary, 20 or 30 would be needed to support a lunch counter. Again all this makes sense, and certainly accords with Aldo van Eych's famous exhortation to 'make of each space a bunch of spaces'. However this is also where Alexander's rather prescriptive approach begins to run into trouble. The scale at which any group can support communal services is not of course fixed, but varies considerably with time and economics. Bill Mitchell, in his books *The City of Bits* (Mitchell 1995) and *E-topia* (Mitchell 1999) describes this changing process very well. There was a time when we would have gathered around water wells, then along came the mains supply. The well might have been replaced as a communal structuring device by the café, but what happens now we have the Internet? So we can certainly see that Alexander's ideas in principle are very sound, but by concentrating on solutions rather than problems he may be guilty of simply describing the past and not envisioning the future, which after all is just what design needs to be about! It is in the end probably far easier to write a book like this than it is to design a really good building!

However, there are also some other problems with Alexander's ideas. There is a description of Venice as a collection of patterns. We are told that it has islands and canals with houses opening on to them, and hump-backed bridges and so on. 'Venice is the special place it is, only because it has those patterns of events in it, which happen to be congruent with all these patterns in the space'. Well of course no one can deny Venice is special and that many of its patterns are highly unusual and some entirely specific to Venice alone; however, Venice is also special to me because it has a great deal of very fine architecture and beautiful art. It is not just the organizational patterns but also the very appearance and beauty of its buildings, whatever purposes they serve now or were originally constructed for. Venice is also largely untouched by modern times, and thus gives us that special contact with the past only available in a handful of great cities.

It seems likely that special patterns are also important to us. One of the best things about being away from home is the way you have to construct new and temporary ones. In recent years I have been working at the National University of Singapore and staying in hotels along the famous Orchard Road in the city centre. I have come to adopt the practice of sitting at a table outside a café on the pavement at one end of this busy and bustling street. As a feeble westerner I find the climate hard work, and this café serves the most delicious and refreshing iced coffee, which revives me after exploring the city. But the café is raised up above the normal street level and I can sit at a table under an umbrella, read and write a little, and watch the world go by below with a slight detachment. In Alexander's terms this has become a frequently repeated pattern on each occasion I visit, and I associate it strongly with Singapore. There are of course many more such experiences. The point here, however, is that I strongly dislike the rather nasty aluminium garden furniture used by the café, and I hate the loud noise and pollution of the traffic. There is in fact much that could be improved in this setting, and I doubt I would tolerate it as an everyday event at home.

Thus knowing what is good and bad about a setting, and for who, is not so easy to establish, and Alexander and his followers are somewhat mute on such matters. Their work can thus be seen not as a theory but as a collection of practices that might be useful to know about. In effect, this is a sort of distilled vernacular process. Whether architecture that would be seen to have lasting value can really be constructed as a collection of such patterns is even less certain. Venice works as a whole, not just as a collection of parts. There is a meta-language used in Venice of form, shape, proportion and material beyond the organizational features of the place. In fact, to reprise an earlier chapter of this book, it is highly redundant, just as Amsterdam is in a different way. Of course what is repeated is worth repeating, and there is enough variation on the theme, with a few major exceptions thrown in, to keep us interested.

Where Alexander's work comes close to our argument here is by laying emphasis on the qualities of space that come from the repetition of similar patterns of behaviour. After all, in my little café in Singapore I tolerate the inelegant tables, chairs and umbrellas that actually form the space mainly because of the coffee and the views of passers-by and the possibility of detaching oneself from them for a short while. It is perhaps a sobering thought for architects that even for me the desirable dimensions of human relationships and food overcome the rather undesirable fixed architectural features!

References

Alexander, C. (1977). *A Pattern Language*. New York, Oxford University Press.

Alexander, C. (1979). *The Timeless Way of Building*. New York, Oxford University Press.

Boudon, P. (1972). *Lived-in Architecture*. London, Lund Humphries.

Brand, S. (1995). *How Buildings Learn: What Happens after They're Built*. Harmondsworth, Penguin.

Edwards, M. (1974). Comparison of some expectations of a sample of housing architects with known data. In Canter, D. and T. Lee (eds), *Psychology and the Built Environment*. London, The Architectural Press.

Gleick, J. (1999). *Faster: The Acceleration of Just About Everything*. London, Little, Brown and Company.

Habraken, N. J. (1972). *Supports: An Alternative to Mass Housing*. London, The Architectural Press.

Hawking, S. W. (1988). *A Brief History of Time*. London, Bantam Press.

Hertzberger, H. (1971). Looking for the beach under the pavement. *RIBA Journal* **78**(8).

Hertzberger, H. (1991). *Lessons for Students in Architecture* (trans. Ina Rike). Rotterdam, Uitgeverij 010.

Jacobs, J. (1961). *The Death and Life of Great American Cities: The Failure of Town Planning*. Harmondsworth, Penguin.

Lawson, B. R. (1994). Architects are losing out in the professional divide. *The Architects' Journal* **199**(16): 13–14.

Lawson, B. R. (1997). *How Designers Think* (3rd edn). Oxford, Architectural Press.

Lawson, B. R. and M. Phiri (2000). Room for improvement. *Health Service Journal* **110**(5688): 24–27.

Mitchell, W. J. (1995). *City of Bits*. Cambridge, Mass., MIT Press.

Mitchell, W. J. (1999). *E-topia*. Cambridge, Mass., MIT Press.

Till, J. (2000). Thick time. In Borden, I. and J. Rendell (eds), *Intersections*. London, Routledge.

9 Recording space

There is a central quality which is the root criterion of life and spirit in a man, a town a building or a wilderness. This quality is objective and precise, but it cannot be named.

Christopher Alexander, *The Timeless Way of Building*

There's no such thing as a bad Picasso, but some are less good than others.

Pablo Picasso, *Come to Judgement*

Measuring place

We have repeatedly seen throughout this book that space is not abstract but is governed by a complex meaningful language. This language is implicit rather than explicit. It is understood by all except, it seems to many, the designers of modern architecture. This cannot be better summed up than by Aldo van Eyck in 1962, in a quotation I make no apology for repeating:

Whatever space and time mean, place and occasion mean more. For space in the image of man is place, and time in the image of man is occasion.

His distinction between space and place is a nice one, and in reality this book is probably best understood as how to make places out of spaces. As Aldo Van Eyck tells us, though, this is done not so much by architects as by the people who inhabit space with their activities and thus turn them into places. However, architects can of course develop spaces that seem to celebrate those activities and rituals. This is very similar to the argument of Alexander that we saw in the last chapter.

People often seem rather inarticulate when asked for a brief by a designer about place, and this is probably largely due to the way the language of space is understood by them implicitly rather than explicitly – they are not used to translating the language into words. For this reason, many people not associated professionally with design may be quite definite about their likes and dislikes but comparatively hazy about what underpins these preferences. Consequently, when pressed to articulate these preferences they may resort to referring to styles or periods of history. Sometimes they can refer you to another place they would like the new one to resemble, but they cannot describe it in the abstract. I was asked to help deal with this problem by two of the large national brewery combines in England, who were refurbishing a large number of the public houses which they either owned or licensed. In many cases the refurbishment was not successful in attracting additional or even the same amount of custom. Frequently, however, the tenants or managers of these pubs knew very well what sort of places their customers wanted, but they were not trained to express this. Consequently they would, if asked at all by the designers, explain their answer by referring to what they had before, or in terms of other pubs they knew. The designers took exception to being told what they saw as the answer instead of the problem – as an architect, to be told the customer wants horse brasses on the wall, nicotine-stained ceilings and oak beams is not encouraging!

From this, though, we know some important things. We know that some spaces seem to work well for a particular setting whereas others do not, and we know that people can often judge the likely success of spaces by looking at them, even though they may find it hard to describe a successful space without referring to one already built. We therefore now need to find out two more things. First, what are the aspects of a space that people commonly use to judge its overall quality – in other words, what are the dimensions along which people assess spaces? Secondly, for the particular setting in mind, how do they rate spaces they judge as successful along these dimensions?

Obviously we can simply ask a lot of people to describe how they feel about a particular space. Simply put in that way the question rarely elicits useful information, but if it is more specifically constructed, even this simple tool can often be revealing. I often use a question inviting respondents to list the first three adjectives that come into their mind about a space. Whilst this may yield interesting and rich data, it is not likely that many people will use exactly the same words, which makes it difficult to compare how people feel and thus get a generic assessment. To make more useful tools, we need to rely on a little simple psychological theory.

In fact, a remarkably large number of psychological measurement tools have now been created to elicit people's feelings about a place in a formal way, and some other tools have been developed to analyse place in terms of its physical characteristics. A popular form of research in recent years has been to try to link these two. In other words, can we find ways of linking people's reactions, feelings, emotions, and even behaviours to physical and perceivable attributes of places, spaces or forms? We shall now spend some time exploring this question.

Semantic differentials

One of the most popular and yet simple of all of the ways of eliciting reactions, feelings and emotions is that of the semantic differential. In its most basic form this technique depends upon asking people to respond to a stimulus by placing it along a series of dimensions, which are created by opposing adjectives such as 'friendly' and 'unfriendly' or 'ordered' and 'chaotic'. This sort of investigation ultimately depends upon the idea of constructs first developed by Kelly (Kelly 1955). Kelly showed that people use a limited number of constructs to judge things, and that many of these constructs overlap. For example, when assessing people you meet and know, you may notice that they vary in a number of characteristics. You may think that some are extremely trustworthy, while some may seem to be more creative, others may be very optimistic, some clever, humorous, punctual, and so on. There may well be many more dimensions along which you could, if asked, judge people. However, you may find that in general if people are trustworthy you also find them punctual, and if they are creative they usually also have a good sense of humour. Overall you will also undoubtedly like some people more than others, and we may well find that this liking depends much more on some dimensions than others.

If you are very open minded, you might like a wide variety of people for quite different reasons. However, some people have rather narrowly defined sets of critical constructs. Kelly, for example, reported a subject who seemed to judge people more or less on whether or not they had been in the army. If they had, he thought them to be reliable, good, polite and so on. From such ideas Kelly was to go on to build a complete theory of personality as defined by the constructs we employ (Kelly 1963). I certainly know some people who tend to judge buildings in similarly simplistic ways – I know quite a few people who seem to dislike all modern buildings and to like all old ones! Now it seems likely that architects will have more elaborate constructs to judge architecture than the average person in the street, and it also seems likely that they value some of these constructs differently to the ordinary users of their buildings. We can use construct theory and its applications to establish such things and to measure them in some way.

Relying on such ideas makes tools available to render ordinary people quite articulate and lucid about the qualities of places. The semantic differential is a simplification of the original notion of constructs and enables us to obtain useful comparative data. Psychologists are just like architects in their liking for long and grand-sounding names for simple ideas! The semantic differential as used in investigating place has to rely upon appropriate bipolar adjectives. Examples might include a scale from 'hard' to 'soft', one from 'open' to 'closed' and so on. Usually these scales are either five or seven points long; an odd number of points allow a respondent to choose a middle point and two or three degrees of emphasis in either direction. As with our short-term memory span discussed earlier, research has shown that we can generally make consistent judgements of scales of up to about seven points long – much shorter than this and we are unable to express all the differences we might wish, much longer and we become inconsistent in our judgements. Experience with research of this kind has enabled us to determine those adjectival scales that are appropriate to the situation being assessed.

Whilst the semantic differential is relatively unlikely to yield any fundamental theoretical and conceptual truths about place, it can serve several very useful purposes. It can provide a simple method of comparing how an individual or group feels about two or more places. Alternatively, it can reveal how different groups of people view the same place. Finally, it offers a way of externalizing feelings for briefing and criticism.

I used semantic differentials to enable the pub landlords and tenants to express the quality of place that they wanted to the interior designers, who then tried to recreate this atmosphere but using their own interpretation rather than copying previous schemes. I was also asked by one of the brewery combines to determine the optimal commercial difference of place between the two traditional bars of the English pub (Plate 15). In the traditional pub there were usually two bars, known by various names around the country, but always with one slightly more plush and upmarket than the other. In many parts of the country they were known as the 'saloon' and 'lounge' bars. By creating two slightly different atmospheres and encouraging different behavioural norms in each, a wider range of clientele could be attracted to one pub. We used semantic differentials to measure the psychological distance between successful examples, and then used this to promote discussion between the architects and interior designers responsible for refitting existing pubs and the managers or landlords (Plate 16). In fact we were able to have very detailed conversations about which dimensions seemed important and in what direction it would be desirable to change a design, and then we could discuss which design features seemed most likely to effect such a change. Customers, publicans, managers and designers could all take part in the discussion without any of them feeling shut out by jargon or made to feel ignorant by the assumed expertise of another group.

Basil Honikman used the same idea to show how students, staff, cleaning and portering staff all viewed images of the same spaces (Honikman 1971). I have used a similar technique to illustrate the views that patients and various staff groups have of hospital interiors. A student of mine has used semantic differentials to enable students of architecture to describe their feelings about the studios they work in and would ideally like. The intention was again to use these data as part of the briefing process for other students trying to design a new school of architecture.

This technique has been used to distinguish the image of competitors in a marketplace. For example, we might ask people to compare several supermarket shops. Such data could be used to help define a niche in the market, enabling one company to make its shops different to the others. Alternatively they might show the aspects of the corporate design image may need attention, and so on. Of course not all people might view a place in the same way. It might be that a particular chain of shops is trying to attract a particular group of customers, perhaps teenagers for example, and therefore need to know how they judge spaces compared with other groups (Fig. 9.1).

I have also used this technique to make the crit session in design schools more focused. Here we asked the students of interior design to fill in a semantic differential about the kind of space they were trying to create, and they were asked to hand this in before actually doing their design work. Their drawings and models were then exhibited, and all the other students completed semantic differentials of the design as they saw it. The crit then focused on whether the intentions had been realized or not, and if not why. Not surprisingly, it sometimes proved rather difficult for students to accept that that their design was not seen by others as they had intended! However, such students could no longer dismiss this as purely the product of a vicious and cruel tutor with eccentric tastes and no understanding of their intentions.

Problems with the semantic differential
This tool is so simple to use and potentially so valuable that it has become very popular, and is now commonly used by people with insufficient psychological training to appreciate its limitations and dangers. Some of these might seem obvious, and yet can so easily be missed by the uncritical enthusiast. Some of the more frequent limitations are worth briefly recognizing here.

The tool is really only suitable if it can be assumed that a single response is being made by all respondents to all scales. If complex objects like whole buildings are being assessed, this becomes increasingly unlikely – one respondent may be more responsive to shape and form while another may be more focused on colour or materials, for example. The method of representation also creates dangers. Frequently studies rely not on actual places but on photographs as the stimulus. Other studies have clearly shown that the drawing or photograph is a surprisingly poor representation of space, and respondents may react quite differently to the photograph as opposed to the real space. A way of appreciating this is to look at photographs you have taken while on holiday. Frequently you notice people or objects in the photographs of which you were not aware at the time you took them. This effect may be considerably enhanced

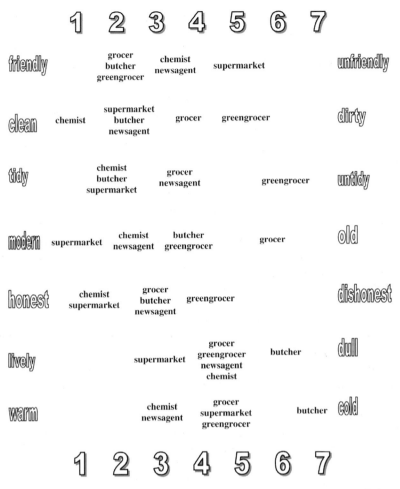

9.1 The semantic differential used to discover how different types of shops are seen. People were asked to place each type of shop on a seven-point scale running between bi-polar adjectives. Such a tool was used to help to brief designers and to discuss with a well-known chain store how they should redesign their interior spaces to create an identifiable niche in the market with which they were happy

when subjects are asked to respond to an academic researcher who might obviously be an architect or a psychologist, thus unwittingly directing the subjects' attention to some features of the scene.

Another set of problems can arise with the actual adjectival scales themselves. Often words can be interpreted in a variety of ways, and the choice of adjectives needs very careful consideration to avoid this. In a recent study proposed by some of my students, we suddenly became aware that the word 'cool' might have several quite different meanings. Often different groups of people are prone to common and yet distinct definitions of words.

The special attention of differently experienced subjects is also a major limitation of this technique, although this can also be used to advantage. For this reason, homogeneous groups of subjects should be used when aggregating results. It would, for example, be very dangerous to have architects and non-architects in the same sample, but the technique may be useful for demonstrating their differential perception of space.

But what does it mean?

So the semantic differential and other similar techniques can tell us how someone or a group of people feel about a space. However, we have still no idea which attributes of the space are causing which aspects of the emotions. We may guess at this, but if we want more objective measurements then some further investigations are going to be required. An obvious way of tackling this problem is to do some parametric studies. Here we might systematically vary some attributes of a scene and compare the score achieved on the semantic differential scales. One of our students has recently used this device for examining Iranian streetscapes. She compared streetscapes that had very varied skylines, for example, with ones that had more regular skylines, and compared streets where the predominant shapes gave horizontal proportions with those that gave vertical ones. She was able to show that this factor changed the way people saw these streets significantly, but the effect was different for Iranian and British subjects (Rezazadeh 1999).

Such studies are difficult to complete in the real world, since it does not nicely come in parametric variations. Usually many characteristics are changed as we move from place to place. For this reason some researchers have resorted to analytical measurement of the scene itself and tried to correlate this with semantic differential scores. Some have taken up the information theory ideas, which we looked at in Chapter 4, and which enable us in theory to measure the uncertainty or levels of information in a scene. Again, however, such studies are usually confounded by the various items of a façade or building that could be analysed. Is it the overall proportion, the variation of colour or texture, variations in sizes of features, or their proportions or frequencies of occurrence? In reality, we known so little about such matters that it is extremely difficult to do such research.

For this reason, effort has been expended on determining the features of buildings that most influence our perception of them. One line of investigation has focused on building façades, and has developed into what is known as the 'type/token' ratio. This simple measurement relates the variety of a feature to its frequency of occurrence. For example, a type/token ratio (TTR) for building façades might be arrived at by dividing the number of different types of openings, such as windows and doors, by the total number of openings in the façade. Although simple and crude, this measurement has shown some results. In one of the most thorough early studies, Krampen showed a whole series of relationships between TTR measurements and subjective assessments (Krampen 1980). For example, higher TTRs were associated with façades evaluated by subjects as friendly than those evaluated as unfriendly. It is also interesting to note that generally older buildings in this study had higher TTRs than more modern buildings. Such work still leaves us with another problem; are the subjects responding to the pattern of windows and doors, or to the perceived age of the building? Do they like old buildings because they have more variation in the fenestration, or do they like variation in fenestration because they like old buildings?

Attention and focus

All these studies lead us to a question to which we paid some attention in a very early chapter of this book – what are the features of an environment that are most attended to by people as they move around in it? What are the features that most determine how people feel about and react to places? An early and now classic attempt to address this question on the urban scale was published by Kevin Lynch. Lynch studied three American cities, Boston, Jersey and Los Angeles (Lynch 1960). In a fairly well structured interview, he asked residents to describe the city they lived and worked in. Amongst other things they were in fact asked to describe their journey to work, to sketch a map, and how they would recognize and describe places. From these studies Lynch discovered that, although there was much variation, there was also some form of collective public image of the city.

Lynch makes a distinction that is useful to us here between three components of an environmental image, and he called these identity, structure and meaning. What Lynch meant by 'structure' and 'meaning' seems very close to the 'formal' and 'symbolic' modes of perception that we discussed in Chapter 4 – that is to say, structure here refers to the order and pattern that connects and relates the various parts of a place, and consists of the rules we perceive as reducing visual uncertainty. The meaning is that which the place stands for or represents. However, Lynch's work centred more on his first component of identity. By 'identity' Lynch refers to all those special attributes of a place that make it both recognizable and ultimately unique. For Lynch, the 'image' of the city is a combination of identity and structure.

So can these be articulated and even measured? Lynch suggested a common language of five major elements, which has now passed into common currency. He suggested that we build our image of city places through a combination of knowledge about paths, edges, nodes, districts and landmarks. Lynch was able from his empirical work to draw maps of his studied cities that described their commonly held public image using these five elements. It is therefore worth studying Lynch's elements to see what generic value they have. In fact, two of them, nodes and landmarks, are effectively points. Two more, paths and edges, are linear in nature. Finally, the district is an areal or two-dimensional concept. Paths are simply the routes along which people move or think they could move. Edges are the boundaries between places or the barriers that prevent movement. Nodes are points where routes intersect or where one might naturally pause, perhaps to change methods of transport. Districts are the regions that can be identified as in some way homogeneous and distinctly different from other regions. Landmarks are objects of special uniqueness or of high contrast to their surroundings.

In both his original and later texts on site planning (Lynch and Hack 1984), Lynch argues persuasively that careful design of each of these elements can improve the quality of the urban environment. For example, making paths have direction rather than simply being routes is, he argues, desirable. This would perhaps include having meaningful visual termini at either end of routes and vistas towards them. Giving clues as to which way you are travelling by means of gradients or distinctly different sides would be another.

We are increasingly making indoor cities in the world. Airports and some larger shopping centres are now so large and complex that they begin to take on many of the characteristics of the traditional town centre. One of my students recently studied a major airport, Changi in Singapore, and the huge out of town shopping centre at Meadowhall near Sheffield using Lynch's techniques. She compared the results to a similar study of the centre of Glasgow to see what we could learn about such places. In general we found that the airport lacked landmarks, probably largely because of the lack of verticality within the spaces. This made route finding much more difficult for passengers, who became almost entirely reliant on signage to get around. Our shopping centre had used a number of features in its design clearly intended to create urban-like qualities. The linear malls were given a slight slope, which was intended to create a sense of direction. We found that this had virtually no effect, and people were frequently confused as to which direction they were travelling in. The malls were themed and zoned by grouping together certain types of shops and by means of the interior decoration, and were then given names such as 'Market Street' and 'Park Lane', but again our shoppers were largely oblivious to such devices (Fig. 9.2). It seems that the designers were simply tinkering at the margins and not really manipulating the features that people see as foreground.

9.2 A shopping centre that tries to create zones, nodes and directional routes but, according to our study, largely fails to communicate this to the shoppers

Donald Appleyard looked in much more detail at what makes some buildings well known and others less so (Appleyard 1980). Appleyard interviewed several hundred residents of a city in Venezuela. He was testing four ideas, that buildings would be well known first because of their imageability or distinctiveness of form in Lynch's terms; secondly, because of their visibility as people move around the city; thirdly because of their role as a setting for activity; and finally because of the significance of the role of the building in society. To test the first idea of geometrical distinctiveness, Appleyard analysed the reported buildings in terms of a wide variety of properties, including their contour, size, shape, colours and the presence of signs and movement of people in and out. In terms of visibility, he measured whether buildings were visible from main routes or spaces. In terms of the role of the building, he distinguished between small personal or group spaces such as bars compared with major communal facilities such as hospitals, schools or churches. He also rated buildings for the perceived cultural importance of their function, so radio stations and police stations, for example, would rate highly.

This work strongly supported Lynch's taxonomy and showed that all his elements, whether point, linear or areal, could be well known for a combination of reasons, including form, visibility, use and significance. However, what Appleyard also argued was that the traditional site plan used by urban designers is poor at indicating the variation of many of these important attributes. In essence, plan-based information focuses attention far too much on plan layout, location and plan size, missing all the richness of information about visibility, use and significance. Appleyard argued that designers thus tend to manipulate a limited vocabulary of features in their design process, and come to view cities in a different manner to the way their inhabitants do.

Lynch's work has of course become a classic, and his ideas have influenced many designers and his methods many researchers. What, however, is rather neglected in his work is the extent to which his subjects were oriented towards the human and social rather than the physical in their use of these elements. The descriptions Lynch published quite clearly show references to the human meanings of things rather than their geometric properties. We see references to the nature of businesses, such as what is made or sold in different premises, and whether places are empty or well occupied. The names of streets or squares are used more often than descriptions of their size and orientation. Similarly, districts tend often to be defined by the social class, ethnic character or occupations of their occupants. Even landmarks are not exempt from strong human dimensions. We are all familiar with the descriptions and commentary offered by tour guides in overseas cities. These often feature stories that associate these places with their builders, people who lived there or momentous events that happened there. All this supports the theme and message of this book. Architecture and place are human and social concepts at least as much as they are physical ones.

Measuring geometry

This approach contrasts strongly with another highly influential method of measuring place, that of space syntax (Hillier and Hanson 1984). These ideas have developed into what might almost be described as an industry, so influential have they been on a wide constituency of researchers. Hillier himself has worked on these ideas and refined them over many years (Hillier 1996). Space syntax is at heart a measure of the geometric physicality of place. Hillier and his followers have advocated a number of measures which record the relationships between spaces within buildings or in urban areas. At their most basic these ideas are an application of the mathematics of topology to the domain of enclosed space. The measures can thus usefully distinguish between different topological relationships of spaces. For example, this allows us to see that many traditional urban forms are based on quite different topologies to those invented in modern times.

At the centre of this argument lies an analysis of the way spaces are connected and how one progresses through them from one space to another. Hillier uses mathematical notations throughout his work, which has the added benefit of enabling logical transformations and manipulations. However, such notation is not necessary to understand the principles and, because of its abstraction, may deter the mathematically fainthearted. To understand this principle we might consider several basic types of spatial relationships. Our first example might be the normal corridor in an office building. Here each office opens directly off the single central connecting space, the corridor. Essentially this is also the principle of the street at the urban scale. However, those familiar with the great country houses and palaces of the past will be aware that this is not the only way of organizing a series of cells inside a building. An alternative is that each cell is simply connected to the previous cell, like links in a chain or beads on a string. A third alternative might be for cells to sit inside other cells in the manner of Russian dolls. Of course combinations of these and other basic topologies are also common (Fig. 9.3).

Why should we be interested in such mathematical measures of the physicality of space here? There would seem to be at least two good reasons for such an interest. The first and most obvious argument would be that the particular aspects of physicality that are being described are those that most impact on social relationships and human activity in creating settings for behaviour, and therefore designers should try to create appropriate spatial relationships by basing their

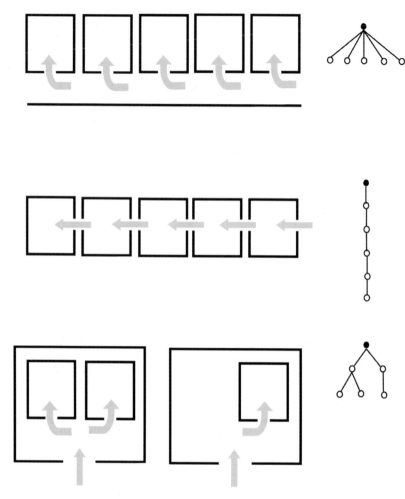

9.3 Three typologically different ways of connecting five simple spaces together with simple graphs showing their connectivity. Such differences are likely to change the levels of interaction between people using the spaces. The extent to which it is possible to maintain privacy, develop community, operate surveillance and develop ritual are all to some extent dependent on such arrangements

geometry on the abstract principle outlined. A second and perhaps even more interesting argument is that over the lengthy time periods of vernacular architecture societies have evolved spatial configurations that reflect their social structures, and by studying them we might better understand those societies. We shall return to an example of this a little later.

Tom Markus, in his masterful study of the way buildings relate to systems of power and domination, has used this form of analysis most persuasively (Markus 1993). When we consider the question of surveillance and supervision, such geometry is likely to be quite critical in determining the success or otherwise of a spatial organization. Markus shows that prisons and hospitals have mostly been designed with a topology that centralizes control and facilitates supervision. In fact, the so-called Nightingale hospital ward was first suggested by Florence Nightingale entirely from the nurse's perspective (Nightingale 1860) – such layouts make it easy to see all the patients from the single nurse's station, thus minimizing effort. Only recently have we started to regard privacy and its benefits to the patient leading to an enhanced sense of well-being as an alternative generative idea. During the course of this book we have repeatedly discussed the notion of a behavioural setting and how in Barker's terms a setting may have synomorphy – that is, how the physical and social structures are in harmony. We have at various points discussed many ways in which people may choose to relate to each other in space, and in particular we have raised such key ideas as privacy, community, surveillance and ritual. It does seem quite likely that this very simple idea of the topology of space has a strong impact on the synomorphy of spaces in which such social arrangements are of prime importance.

Hillier and his followers have however moved on from such simple measures to rather more sophisticated ideas concerning axial geometry. This enables them to study not just simple cell-like buildings but more amorphous and complex urban situations. Urban spaces are so called by convention, but are in fact most usually simply indentations in the surface of the global sky. That is to say, an urban space is not normally a fully enclosed and easily defined cell. This is almost by definition, since as soon as space is enclosed so precisely we normally think of this as a building! Rather urban spaces are most often open to the sky, flow one into another and are relatively seldom separated by opening devices such as doors and gates. How then can we define where one space begins and another ends in such a spatial organization? Typically space syntax has developed a form of analysis that depends upon drawing the longest straight line of sight available in all the urban spaces. These lines can then be studied in plan, and their intersections and interconnections studied in a similar way to that already seen for cells. This enables an interesting range of statistics to be compiled that again enable spatial topologies to be distinguished.

Such statistics can be used to compare places that seem to us to be quite different – old towns and new towns, or various forms of housing estates, for example. Hillier and others have argued that these geometric measures have a strong influence on the way people become aware of each other. A careful and important distinction is made in this argument between this concept and the more normal sociological one of community. This is an interesting idea that certainly deserves further study. What is of most importance here is the way routes in a complex urban area are organized in such a way as to increase or decrease the likelihood of the inhabitants coming into contact with each other. We know, for example, that many forms of high-rise housing design minimize such contact and can lead to lonely and anonymous lives. However, there is also another step in the argument here. It seems reasonable to suppose that occupants of an area come to understand implicitly how the geometry works in terms of the contact they have with their neighbours, and this in turn may lead to them having more or less certainty about whether they know all their neighbours or not. The final step in the argument would suggest that this leads to a greater or lesser ability to detect strangers in their neighbourhood. Such analysis has led Hillier to conclude that some forms are more likely to be associated with street crime than others (Hillier 1983).

This seems reasonable on the face of it for another reason. Such statistics may also reveal the number of alternative routes that can be taken to travel from one point to a place outside the system. In her study of American cities, Jane Jacobs long ago suggested that children expressed high levels of safety in the older parts of cities with their myriad of interconnecting streets and alleys (Jacobs 1961). Jane Jacobs describes how Charles Guggenheim, who was making a documentary film in a St Louis children's day-care centre, stumbled upon this understanding. He noticed that the children who lived in the newer housing projects were reluctant to leave at the end of the day, whereas the children who came from the old so-called 'slum' streets left happily. Investigation showed the children returning to the newer housing had fewer routes to use and were often passing through parks, playgrounds and lawns that were unsupervised by adults, and consequently were frequently bullied by older or more aggressive children. By contrast, the children returning home through the older streets could use many alternative routes, each of which were overseen by adults in the houses, standing in the doorways of corner shops or simply walking along the streets themselves:

The children going back to the old streets were safe from extortion ... They had many streets to select from, and they astutely chose the safest. 'If anybody picked on them, there was always a storekeeper they could run to or somebody to come to their aid,' says Guggenheim. 'They also had any number of ways of escaping along different routes if anybody was lying in wait for them. These little kids felt safe and cocky and they enjoyed their trip home too.'

Jacobs pointed out that planners frequently underestimate the high ratio of adults needed to rear children safely and satisfactorily. Designing places where these adults are unlikely to be by segregating out play areas is thus likely to lead to disaster and not improvement, as we saw in Chapter 8.

By such measuring of the geometry of urban routes, space syntax has enabled its followers to argue that we may unwittingly be creating quite different places when we design self-consciously, as in the new town or new housing estate. Traditional urban forms were not created at one single time through a grand plan, but rather grew over time, and their geometry is thus a function of what was possible:

The problem with the modern urban surface lies, we would suggest, in its complete reversal of virtually every aspect of the spatial logic of urban forms as they evolved (Hillier 1996).

This argument can be interestingly extended to study the way geometry is used in vernacular design to embody a social order. One of the most dramatic and yet simple demonstrations of this can be seen in a study of two neighbouring villages in East Africa (Fig. 9.4). Here we find totally different geometry employed, and yet the climate, topography and available natural building materials remain identical. In the first village we see largely circular forms, each standing alone, and all linked to one central space. In the second we see separate spaces, which have their own independent entrances but are attached to each other in clumps and use rectangular geometry. The fundamental difference that seems to have caused this geometrical variation

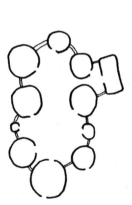
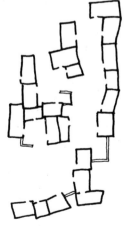

9.4 Two settlements very close to each other in the African continent. They share a common climate and available materials, and their builders had similar technology. They look so different because the two groups use their own sets of social rules to determine how the elder son of the family must relate to his father

is the culture of the two tribes that inhabited the villages. In one the cultural rules determine that on reaching the age of maturity the son of the family leaves to set up his own house, whilst in the other the rule is quite contrary. Here the son is expected to build a room onto his father's house and to continue to look after him in his old age. With the technology available to these primitive societies, the simplest form of construction is in fact a circular hut with its radius set to the longest frequently found wooden pole. However, in the village where there was a cultural need to add one space to another this has suggested rectilinear geometry, which facilities addition and extension.

Of course, geometrical analysis such as space syntax enables a simple method for coding these physical differences and thus draws our attention to some possible classification systems for what might otherwise appear infinite spatial variety. However, space syntax by itself cannot predict human perception. It cannot demonstrate that we perceive these differences when in and around space, and it cannot show that such geometrical differences are at the root of any behavioural variations. It is thus not in itself a theory of social organization, but merely one of spatial organization. Here lies a difficulty with some of the ways it has come to be used by its more enthusiastic proponents. Whereas Lynch modestly describes his work as *The Image of The City*, Hillier much more ambitiously entitles the original text outlining space syntax *The Social Logic of Space*. This is ironic in the sense that Lynch's work was based on human perception whereas Hillier's is based on physical geometry. No doubt both provide useful tools for measuring places and helping us to identify their different qualities and to study their effects on perception and behaviour. At its most basic, a measure of the organization of spaces would seem useful as a starting point in understanding not only our experience of those spaces but also of our experience of our relationships with each other. Space syntax has unfortunately been used in recent years to develop ever more intricate measurements in pieces of research that show little understanding of the essentially human nature of the language of space. To paraphrase a common saying, measuring each tree in precise detail does not necessarily increase our understanding of the forest!

Divide and conquer

There are some quite deep philosophical problems with the whole approach of measurement and quantification that we have discussed in this chapter. These problems are neither new nor undiscovered, and Janet Daley somewhat notoriously and comprehensively identified them many years ago (Daley 1969). In very practical terms, such a measurement-based approach to our experience of the world is almost certainly doomed to failure in any general theoretical sense. Quite simply, we do not ourselves experience the world around us as a series of discrete and independent dimensions. Our perceptual system is integrative and our experience is holistic. Even the very structuring of this book is an absurd artificiality imposed on this experience; we do not experience and behave as a collection of phenomena suggested by the titles of the chapters used here. The only defence that this author can muster is that over the years he has taught design students and research workers such a structure, and it seems to have helped them to get further into the subject. This book does not set out to present a comprehensive theory of human language of space, but rather to sensitize the reader to a more conscious observation of it in practice. Such an observation seems more likely to lead to the design of spaces both inside and outside buildings that might be more harmonious as behavioural settings. Sometimes it is useful to atomize our reaction to the world in order to begin to investigate what is otherwise an inaccessible mire of phenomenological existence. Sadly this will inevitably introduce distortions and bias in our analysis.

However, this book is dedicated to giving practical help to designers as much as to developing a theoretical advance for scientists. We must remember that design is a quite different matter to scientific experiment or philosophical thought. I have studied the design process for many years without coming to what I consider anything like a full understanding of it, but some things are relatively clear. Design is prescriptive rather than descriptive. It requires action in the form of decision, even in the face of inadequate time and knowledge. For these reasons sometimes it is useful to oversimplify in order to structure thought enough to make design decisions slightly less arbitrary. We cannot hope to make them perfect. I hope that we can move to reduce the arbitrariness of architecture in a more rather than less human way. We all understand and use the language of space in our daily lives, and architects, planners, interior designers, urban designers and their ilk need to reconnect with this ordinary knowledge by whatever means they can. So often they seem not to do this but to detach themselves from their own implicit knowledge of the language of space when they design and rely on more self-conscious notions about space. Indeed, so detached from the everyday human use of space can architecture become that sometimes architects seem either stupid or wilful to the public they serve. In my experience they are very rarely stupid and seldom wilful. It must of course be remembered that their job is tremendously complex. In addition to the issues we have considered here, architects are usually also trying to design sustainable and beautiful buildings that satisfy a whole series of technical and legislative demands on complex sites with architecturally problematic neighbours, for clients who change their minds, have inadequate budgets and need their building yesterday! Perhaps we should not be surprised that sometimes the fundamental but unspoken and even unconscious human language of space fails to be a significant voice in such crowded design processes. Yet if we only look around us we can see that it is silently structuring much of the human use of space. Good architecture can do so much to facilitate this, and bad architecture can make lives a misery by obstructing it. It is said that lawyers earn a high proportion of their fees from disputes between neighbours. So often the origins of such disputes can be found in the work of architects and planners!

References

Appleyard, D. (1980). Why buildings are known: a predictive tool for architects and planners. In Broadbent, G., R. Bunt, et al. (eds), *Meaning and Behaviour in the Built Environment*. Chichester, John Wiley and Sons.

Daley, J. (1969). A philosophical critique of behaviourism in architectural design. In Broadbent, G. and A. Ward (eds.), *Design Method in Architecture*. London, Lund Humphries.

Hillier, B. (1983). Space syntax: a different urban perspective. *Architects' Journal* **178**(48): 47–63.

Hillier, B. (1996). *The Space is the Machine*. Cambridge, Cambridge University Press.

Hillier, B. and J. Hanson (1984). *The Social Logic of Space*. Cambridge, Cambridge University Press.

Honikman, B. (1971). An investigation of a method for studying personal evaluation and requirement of the built environment. In Honikman, B. (ed), AP70 : *Proceedings of the Architectural Psychology Conference at Kingston Polytechnic*. London, RIBA.

Jacobs, J. (1961). *The Death and Life of Great American Cities: The Failure of Town Planning*. Harmondsworth, Penguin.

Kelly, G. A. (1955). *The Psychology of Personal Constructs*. New York, Norton.

Kelly, G. A. (1963). *A Theory of Personality*. New York, W.W. Norton and Co.

Krampen, M. (1980). The correlation of 'objective' facade measurements with subjective facade ratings. In Broadbent, G., R. Bunt, et al. (eds), *Meaning and Behaviour in the Built Environment*. Chichester, John Wiley and Sons.

Lynch, K. (1960). *The Image of the City*. Cambridge, Mass., MIT Press.

Lynch, K. and G. Hack (1984). *Site Planning* (3rd edn). Cambridge, Mass., MIT Press.

Markus, T. (1993). *Buildings and Power : Freedom and Control in the Origin of Modern Building*. London, Routledge.

Nightingale, F. (1860). *Notes on Nursing*. London, Harrison and Sons.

Rezazadeh, R. (1999) Developing principles for the design of streetscape in Tehran. PhD, University of Sheffield.

Bibliography

Abbas, M. Y. (2000). Proxemics in waiting areas of health centres: a cross-cultural study. Ph.D., University of Sheffield.

Aiello, J. R. and Jones, T. D. C. (1971). Field study of proxemic behaviour of young schoolchildren in three subcultural groups. *Journal of Personality and Social Psychology*, **19**: 351–356.

Alexander, C. (1979). *The Timeless Way of Building*. New York: Oxford University Press.

Alexander, C. et al. (1977). *A Pattern Language*. New York: Oxford University Press.

Appleyard, D. (1980). Why buildings are known: a predictive tool for architects and planners. In Broadbent, G., Bunt, R. and Llorens, T. (eds), *Meaning and Behaviour in the Built Environment*. Chichester: John Wiley and Sons.

Ardrey, R. (1967). *The Territorial Imperative: A Personal Inquiry into the Animal Origins of Property and Nations*. London: Collins.

Argyle, M. (1969). *Social Interaction*. London: Methuen.

Argyle, M. (1994). *The Psychology of Interpersonal Behaviour* (5th edn). London: Penguin.

Barker, R. G. (1968). *Ecological Psychology: Concepts and Methods for Studying the Environment of Human Behaviour*. Oxford: Oxford University Press.

Bartlett, F. C. (1932). *Remembering*. Cambridge: Cambridge University Press.

Boudon, P. (1972). *Lived-in Architecture*. London: Lund Humphries.

Brand, S. (1995). *How Buildings Learn: What Happens after They're Built*. Harmondsworth: Penguin.

Burgoon, J. K. and Saine, T. (1978). *The Unspoken Dialogue*. Boston: Houghton Mifflin.

Cherry, C. (1957). *On Human Communication: A Review, a Survey and a Criticism* (2nd edn). Cambridge, Mass.: MIT Press.

Calhoun, J. B. (1962). Population density and social pathology. *Scientific American*, **206**: 139–146.

Canter, D. and Lee, T. (eds) (1974). *Psychology and the Built Environment*. London: The Architectural Press.

Chermayeff, S. and Alexander, C. (1963). *Community and Privacy*. Harmondsworth: Penguin.

Chomsky, N. (1957). *Syntactic Structures*. The Hague: Mouton.

Daley, J. (1969). A philosophical critique of behaviourism in architectural design. In Broadbent, G. and Ward, A. (eds), *Design Method in Architecture*. London: Lund Humphries.

Darke, J., Lawson, B. R. and Spencer, C. (1979). Grumblers and complainers about the environment. In Canter, D., Lee, T. and Stringer, P. (eds), *Environmental Psychology Conference*. University of Surrey: John Wiley.

Davey, P. (1991). St Mary's. *Architectural Review*, **189**(1128): 24–33.

Dimitrius, J. E. and Marzzarella, M. (1998*). Reading People : How to Understand People and Predict their Behaviour – Anytime, Anyplace*. London: Vermillion.

Edwards, M. (1974). Comparison of some expectations of a sample of housing architects with known data. In Canter, D. and Lee, T. (eds), *Psychology and the Built Environment*. London: The Architectural Press.

Evans, G. W. and McCoy, J. M. (1998). When buildings don't work: the role of architecture in human health. *Journal of Environmental Psychology*, **18**: 85–94.

Fast, J. (1971). *Body Language*. London: Pan Books.

Garner, W. R. (1962). *Uncertainty and Structure as Psychological Concepts*. New York: John Wiley.

Gleick, J. (1999). *Faster: The Acceleration of Just About Everything*. London: Little, Brown and Company.

Goffman, E. (1959). *The Presentation of Self in Everyday Life*. London: Penguin.

Goffman, E. (1963). *Behaviour in Public Places*. New York: Glencoe Free Press.

Goodman, N. and Elgin, C. J. (1988). *Reconceptions in Philosophy and other Arts and Sciences*. London: Routledge.

Gregory, R. L. (1966). *Eye and Brain*. London: World University Library.

Gregory, R., Harris, J., Heard, P. and Rose, D. (eds) (1995). *The Artful Eye*. Oxford: Oxford University Press.

Gropius, W. (1935). *The New Architecture and the Bauhaus*. London: Faber and Faber.

Habraken, N. J. (1972). *Supports: An Alternative to Mass Housing*. London: The Architectural Press.

Ham-Rowbottom, K. A., Gifford, R. and Shaw, K. T. (1999). Defensible space theory and the police: assessing the vulnerability of residences to burglary. *Journal of Environmental Psychology*, **19**: 117–129.

Hawking, S. W. (1988). *A Brief History of Time*. London: Bantam Press.

Hall, E. T. (1959). *The Silent Language*. New York: Doubleday.

Hall, E. T. (1966). *The Hidden Dimension*. London: Bodley Head.

Hediger, H. (1955). *Studies of the Psychology and Behaviour of Captive Animals in Zoos and Circuses*. London: Butterworth.

Hertzberger, H. (1971). Looking for the beach under the pavement. *RIBA Journal*, **78**(8).

Hertzberger, H. (1991). *Lessons for Students in Architecture* (trans. Ina Rike). Rotterdam: Uitgeverij 010.

Herzog, G. R. and Barnes, G. J. (1999). Tranquillity and preference revisited. *Journal of Environmental Psychology*, **19**: 171–181.

Hildreth, A. M., Derogatis, L. R. and McCusker, K. (1971). Body-buffer zones and violence: a reassessment and confirmation. *American Journal of Psychiatry*, **127**: 1641–1645.

Hillier, B. (1983). Space syntax: a different urban perspective. *Architects' Journal*, **178**(48): 47–63.

Hillier, B. (1996). *The Space is the Machine*. Cambridge: Cambridge University Press.

Hillier, B. and Hanson, J. (1984). *The Social Logic of Space*. Cambridge: Cambridge University Press.

Honikman, B. (ed) (1971). *AP70: Proceedings of the Architectural Psychology Conference at Kingston Polytechnic*. London: RIBA Publications.

Honikman, B. (1971). An investigation of a method for studying personal evaluation and requirement of the built environment. In Honikman, B. (ed.),). *AP70: Proceedings of the Architectural Psychology Conference at Kingston Polytechnic*. London: RIBA.

Hubbard, P. (1996). Conflicting interpretations of architecture: an empirical investigation. *Journal of Environmental Psychology*, **16**: 75–92.

Inglis, S. (1983). *The Football Grounds of England and Wales*. London: Willow Books Collins.

Itten, J. (1970). *The Elements of Colour*. New York: Van Nostrand.

Jacobs, J. (1961). *The Death and Life of Great American Cities: The Failure of Town Planning*. Harmondsworth: Penguin.

Jenks, C. (1977). *The Language of Post Modern Architecture*. London: Academy Editions.

Joiner, D. (1971). Social ritual and architectural space. In Honikman, B. (eds),). *AP70: Proceedings of the Architectural Psychology Conference at Kingston Polytechnic*, pp. 7–11. London: RIBA.

Kelly, G. A. (1955). *The Psychology of Personal Constructs*. New York: Norton.

Kelly, G. A. (1963). *A Theory of Personality*. New York: W.W. Norton and Co.

Krampen, M. (1980). The correlation of 'objective' facade measurements with subjective facade ratings. In Broadbent, G., Bunt, R. and Llorens, T. (eds), *Meaning and Behaviour in the Built Environment*. Chichester: John Wiley and Sons.

Kulleer, R. and Lindstren, C. (1992). Health and behaviour of children in classrooms with and without windows. *Journal of Environmental Psychology*, **12**: 305–318.

Kwallek, N. and Lewis, C. M. (1990). Effects of environmental colour on males and females: a red or white or green office. *Applied Ergonomics*, **21**: 275–278.

Latto, R. (1995). The brain of the beholder. In Gregory, R., Harris, J., Heard, P. and Rose, D. (eds), *The Artful Eye*, pp. 66–94. Oxford: Oxford University Press.

Lawson, B. R. (1994). Architects are losing out in the professional divide. *Architects' Journal*, **199**(16): 13–14.

Lawson, B. R. (1994). *Design in Mind*. Oxford: Butterworth Architecture.

Lawson, B. R. (1997). *How Designers Think* (3rd edn). Oxford: Architectural Press.

Lawson, B. R. and Phiri, M. (2000). Room for improvement. *Health Service Journal*, **110**(5688): 24–27.

Lawson, B. R. and Spencer, C. P. (1978). Architectural intentions and user responses: the psychology building at Sheffield. *Architects' Journal*, **167**(18).

Lawson, B. R. and Walters, D. (1974). The effects of a new motorway on an established residential area. In Canter, D. and Lee, T. (eds), *Psychology and the Built Environment*, pp. 132–138. London: The Architectural Press.

Le Corbusier (1951). *The Modulor*. London: Faber and Faber.

Lipman, A. (1968). Building design and social interaction. *Architects' Journal* **147**: 23–30.

Lynch, K. (1960). *The Image of the City*. Cambridge, Mass.: MIT Press.

Lynch, K. and Hack, G. (1984). *Site Planning* (3rd edn). Cambridge, Mass.: MIT Press.

Lynn, J. (1962). Park Hill redevelopment. *RIBA Journal*, **69**(12).

Malinowski, J. C. and Thurber, C. A. (1996). Developmental shifts in the place preferences of boys aged 8–16 years. *Journal of Environmental Psychology*, **16**: 45–54.

Malmberg, T. (1980). *Human Territoriality*. The Hague: Mouton Publishers.

Markus, T. (1993). *Buildings and Power: Freedom and Control in the Origin of Modern Building*. London: Routledge.

Mitchell, W. J. (1995). *City of Bits*. Cambridge, Mass.: MIT Press.

Mitchell, W. J. (1999). *E-topia*. Cambridge, Mass.: MIT Press.

Morris, D. (1967). *The Naked Ape*. London: Jonathan Cape.

Morris, D. (1969). *The Human Zoo*. London: Jonathan Cape.

Morris, D. (1981). *The Soccer Tribe*. London: Jonathan Cape.

Morris, D. (2000). *The Naked Eye: Travels in Search of the Human Species*. London: Edbury Press.

Negroponte, N. (1995). *Being Digital*. London: Hodder and Stoughton.

Newman, O. (1973). *Defensible Space: People and Design in the Violent City*. London: Architectural Press.

Nightingale, F. (1860). *Notes on Nursing*. London: Harrison and Sons.

Orwell, G. (1940). *Down and Out in Paris and London*. Harmondsworth: Penguin.

Osmond, H. (1959). The relationship between architect and pyschiatrist. In Goshen, C. (ed), *Psychiatric Architecture*. Washington DC: American Psychiatric Association.

Proshansky, H. M., Ittleson, W. H. and Rivlin, L. G. (eds) (1970). *Environmental Psychology*. Holt Rinehart Winston.

Pugin, A. W. N. (1841). *The True Principles of Pointed or Christian Architecture*. London: J. Weale.

Rand, G. (1980). Children's images of houses: a polegomena to the study of why people want pitched roofs. In Broadbent, G., Bunt, R. and Llorens, T. (eds), *Meaning and Behaviour in the Built Environment*. Chichester: John Wiley and Sons.

Rapoport, A. (1982). *The Meaning of the Built Environment: A Nonverbal Communication Approach*. Beverly Hills: Sage Publications.

Rezazadeh, R. (1999). Developing principles for the design of streetscape in Tehran. PhD, University of Sheffield.

Rose, D. (1995). A portrait of the brain. In Gregory, R., Harris, J., Heard, P. and Rose, D. (eds), *The Artful Eye*, pp. 28–51. Oxford: Oxford University Press.

Shannon, C. E. and Weaver, W. (1949). *The Mathematical Theory of Communication*. Urbana: The University of Illinois Press.

Stirling, J. (1965). An architect's approach to architecture. *RIBA Journal*, **72**(5).

Sommer, R. (1969). *Personal Space: The Behavioural Basis of Design*. Englewood Cliffs: Prentice Hall.

Sommer, R. (1998). Shopping at the Co-op. *Journal of Environmental Psychology*, **18**: 45–53.

Steinzor, B. (1950). The spatial factor in face to face discussion groups. *Journal of Abnormal and Social Psychology*, **45**: 552–555.

Till, J. (2000). Thick time. In Borden, I. and Rendell, J. (eds), *Intersections*. London: Routledge.

Trompenaars, F. and Hampden-Turner, D. (1997). *Riding the Waves of Culture: Understanding Cultural Diversity in Business*. London: Nicholas Brealey.

Ulrich, R. S. (1984). View through a window may influence recovery from surgery. *Science*, **224**: 420–421.

Vargas, M. F. (1986). *Louder than Words*. Iowa: Iowa State University Press.

Venturi, R. (1977). *Complexity and Contradiction in Architecture*. New York: The Museum of Modern Art.

Venturi, R., Scott Brown, D. and Izenour, S. (1977). *Learning from Las Vegas: The Forgotten Symbolism of Architectural Form*. Cambridge, Mass.: MIT Press.

Walter, M. A. H. B. (1978). The territorial and the social: perspectives on the lack of community in high-rise/high-ensity living in Singapore. *Ekistics*, **270**: 236–242.

Watson, O. M. and Graves, T. D. (1966). Quantitative research in proxemic behaviour. *Anerican Anthropologist*, **68**: 971–985.

Williams, W. M. (1956). *The Sociology of an English Village*. London: Routledge and Kegan Paul.

Wilson, M. A. (1996). The socialization of architectural preference. *Journal of Environmental Psychology*, **16**: 33–44.

Wohlwill, J. F. (1974). Human response to levels of environmental stimulation. *Human Ecology*, **2**: 127–147.

Index